Classical Continuum Series 1

WITHOUT WITHIN

PARENTHETIC INTERFERENCES IN RECEPTION HISTORY

WITHOUT WITHIN

PARENTHETIC INTERFERENCES IN RECEPTION HISTORY

John T. Hamilton

New Alexandria Foundation
2025

Without Within: Parenthetic Interferences in Reception History by John T. Hamilton

Published by New Alexandria Foundation, Boston, MA in partnership with the Department of Comparative Literature, Harvard University

Distributed by Harvard University Press, Cambridge, Massachusetts and London, England
Printed by INFORM, member of AUSTRIACARD HOLDINGS, 5th km Vari-Koropi Avenue, Koropi, 194 00, Greece, info@austriacard.com

The printing of this work was a gift of EPOPS publishing.

Cover Design: Joni Godlove
Layout and typesetting: Kristin Murphy Romano

Editorial: Leonard Muellner, Gregory Nagy, Laura Slatkin
Production: Noel Spencer

The publication of this work was assisted by a grant from the Michael Marks Charitable Trust.

ISBN: 9780674301276

Library of Congress Control Number: 2025933782

EU GPSR Authorised Representative
LOGOS EUROPE, 9 rue Nicolas Poussin, 17000, La Rochelle, France
E-mail: Contact@logoseurope.eu

All close thinkers, you know, are apt to be parenthetic.

—Samuel Taylor Coleridge,
Historie and Gests of Maxilian

Parergon

When Evanthia Sistakou and Martin Vöhler invited me to propose a theme for the 2023 "Trends in Classics" conference in Thessaloniki, I did not hesitate to choose "Parentheses of Reception." I had recently been reflecting on specifically parenthetic forms of reception, whereby antiquity and modernity can be said to be a part of and apart from each other. I remain infinitely grateful for this unique opportunity, for the spectacular gathering of engaged participants, most of whom stand at the forefront of Reception Theory: Stella Alekou, Richard Armstrong, Felix Christen, Michalis Chrysanthopoulos, Mark-Georg Dehrmann, Therese Fuhrer, Eckart Goebel, Constanze Güthenke, Stephen Harrison, Brooke Holmes, Christoph Horn, Richard Hunter, Miriam Leonard, Alexandra Lianeri, Michael Lüthy, David Orrells, James Porter, Karin Schlapbach, Richard Thomas, Thomas Tsartsidis, Antje Wessels, Martin Winkler, and Christopher Wood. Their thoughtful and probing contributions have significantly provoked me into thinking further on the topic.[1] *Danken möcht' ich, und ich weiß wofür.*

I would also like to thank Cornelia Zumbusch for the invitation to spend my sabbatical year at the Hamburg Institute for Advanced Studies, which provided me the perfect parenthesis to complete this project. I am especially grateful to my co-fellows—to Marwa Arsanios, Nathan Brown, Elizabeth Bronfen, Reinaldo Funes Monzote, Rüdiger Görner, Davide Guiriato, Marc-Thorsten Hütt, Emily Jones, Christian Thorau, Viktoria Tkacyzk, and Athanassios Vergados—as well as to the Director, Dorothea Rüland, and her excellent administration and staff: Astrid Bothmann-Lucko, Ulrike Dorfmüller, Sonia Gräber-Magocsi, Kristina Hahn, Angelina Isaak, Tanja Kruse Brandão, Lola Mense, and Daniela Schröder. Heartfelt thanks also to Carlston and Petra at the nearby Windschirm pub, where I was permitted to smoke my pipe while writing.

Finally, a special note of thanks to Greg Nagy for his unflagging support from start to finish, to Jules Buchholtz, Daniel Carranza, Jonas Grethlein, Alberto Parisi, Thomas Schestag, and Christian Struck for the fruitful conversations, to Richard Sieburth for his ever-inspiring assistance and indispensable encouragement, and to Lisa Parkes, without whom there would be no words within.

1 The collection has recently been published as *Parentheses of Reception*, John Hamilton, Evanthia Sistakou, and Martin Vöhler, ed. (Berlin: de Gruyter, 2025).

Portions of the material that appear below have been published in earlier articles: "Aspects of reception: reading Goethe's Iphigenie auf Tauris with Adorno, Fassbinder, and Jauss" (*Classical Receptions Journal* 12 [2020]), 129–148; "Heidegger in Klammern, oder Wozu Philologen in dürftiger Zeit" (*Hölderlin-Jahrbuch* 42 [2020–2021]), 21–39; and "Florilegia: Influence and Cross-Pollination between Celan and Hölderlin, Pindar and Horace," *Modern Language Notes* 135 (2020), 600–619.

Contents

CHAPTER 3. IN THE WAKE OF CATASTROPHE

CHAPTER 4. IPHIGENIA AMONG THE GERMANS

CHAPTER 5. FLORILEGIA

Chapter 1
Ithaca, Interrupted

Night Thoughts

The penultimate chapter of James Joyce's *Ulysses* (1922), conventionally known as "Ithaca," was the last to be written. In concluding an eight-year project punctuated by life in exile and a world at war, the occasion furnished the wearied author an opportunity to review the episodes of his novel, tidily summarized through the consciousness of his protagonist and fellow-traveler, Leopold Bloom, as he is about to climb into bed.

> The preparation of breakfast (burnt offering): intestinal congestion and premeditative defecation (holy of holies): the bath (rite of John): the funeral (rite of Samuel): the advertisement of Alexander Keyes (Urim and Thummim): the unsubstantial lunch (rite of Melchisedek): [...][1]

Bloom's silent recapitulation drowsily goes on to itemize fifteen entries in total, each supplemented by a Biblical gloss set in parentheses.

The passage is both reaffirming and perplexing. From one perspective, in addition to providing a helpful synopsis for readers who must navigate an especially long and complex novel, nocturnal rehearsals of this kind are in themselves perfectly traditional. Since antiquity, particularly among Roman philosophers and other literati, a full appraisal of what one did and said during the waking hours was recommended as a sure path towards achieving that coveted tranquility of the soul. Hence, Seneca, in his treatise *On Anger*, praises Quintus Sextius who every night, before falling asleep, habitually examined his "whole day" (*totum diem, On Anger* 3, 36.2).[2] Indeed, the Stoic subject ought to take advantage of the quiet darkness when tasks, obligations and appeals from others no longer interfere, a time of welcome solitude without distraction when one

1 James Joyce, *Ulysses*. Hans Walter Gabler, ed. (2022), 17, 599. Subsequent quotations of the novel are from this edition and marked by *U* with chapter and page number.

2 For a comprehensive discussion, see Ker 2004.

is free to reflect on every turn, to adjudicate every word and deed, either in praise or admonishment, and thus assume personal responsibility. As Seneca attests, with nightly hindsight, he can serve as "examiner and secret censor of himself" (*speculator sui censorque secretus*) and thereby integrate the discrete moments that made up his day, bring each occurrence into accord with his established sense of identity, while also plotting a corrective course for the future, away from the tumult of self-reproach and towards the harbor of self-vindication. Appropriation is indispensable for becoming and remaining someone, for acquiring and maintaining rational and autonomous subjecthood. As for Leopold Bloom, in telling the story of his day to himself, however ordinary that story may be—from breakfast to an unremarkable lunch and onward—he is clearly inscribed in this tradition of self-possession, where meaning is ascribable only to that which can be owned and governed as private property from within, and correlatively, where everything else should be dismissed as a matter of indifference.

From another perspective, however, the parenthesized references to Judaic lore disrupt the diaristic inventory and raise a series of unsettling questions. Ranging from sound erudition ("Urim and Thummim") to schoolboy pun ("holy of holies"), the bracketed asides can be regarded either as appropriative gestures or merely as constant distractions, with either integrative or disintegrative force. The allusions from without either strengthen or undermine Bloom's subjective autonomy from within. Is the protagonist *someone* or rather *no-one*? Does he retain supervisory rights in the active voice or does he live rather in the passive voice, as if steered by supernal forces beyond his control?

Having retired after a long and exhausting day, Bloom thinks back on the ground covered and retraces every step, precisely like a self-possessed Stoic subject, and yet he is also reduced to a hapless pawn whose only hope is to discern an overarching pattern that may or may not convert what appears to have been but a contingent jaunt into a meaningful itinerary. Similar to a storm-tossed wanderer who chances to arrive home after an unforeseeably protracted and difficult journey, Bloom in "Ithaca" may well be an essential non-entity, one who must cope by gathering the pieces, shoring the fragments against his ruin, and calling out by name the powers that brought him to this point. The fractal moments may or may not amount to an integrated whole, the discrete particles may or may not constitute a "total day"—comprehended, say, by a masterful subject with a single cyclopean eye—yet nonetheless, some sort of mastery seems to be at work, perhaps a mastery that is not reliant on firm identity, not legitimized by some unimpeachable property or possession held within, a mastery that is resourceful precisely by not being committed to a set store of resources and other sophistries, the kind of mastery, for example, that obtains with the duplicitous cunning (μῆτις) implicit in being no-one (μή τις).[3]

[3] Cf. Detienne and Vernant1974.

The narrative outline in "Ithaca" trips over the insertions set in rounded brackets. Specifically, the recounting suffers from a parallactic effect whereby each scene is regarded from two distinct viewpoints, first from the ground then from above, immanently then transcendentally, in both its quotidian and occult aspects. In Bloom's bedtime recollection, the near and the remote collide. Physical reality and metaphysical ideality confront and affect each other, with each station of his day transposed *sub specie aeternitatis* and each theologeme regarded *sub specie temporis nostri*. Accordingly, his breakfast of pork kidneys conjures the matutinal sacrifices once held in the ancient Temple at Jerusalem while his consequent visit to the outhouse summons the Tabernacle's inner sanctum; his sally into the Turkish baths evokes the sacrament of baptism just as his attendance at Paddy Dignam's funeral in soggy Glasnevin Cemetery calls forth the ancient rituals of burial and mourning mentioned in the *First Book of Samuel* (1 Samuel 25:1).[4]

With Hebraic tags in brackets, the catalogue exposes the fundamental mechanics of Joyce's relentlessly allusive novel, a work in which a single day in the life of Dublin is constantly doubled. Quite schematically, the passage provides a compositional paradigm, disclosing the kind of interferences that form the literary texture of *Ulysses*. As a blueprint or recipe, it puts on display the manner by which the narrative is constructed, how the story is persistently stalled by associative digressions that break in on the descriptive observations, how an ordinary plot is disrupted and irradiated by an extraordinary dimension, informed and deformed by it. The day, experienced as a whole, turns out not to have been whole. Supplements are adduced within without integration. Rather, in showing the cuts of the montage, the brackets stage a juxtaposition that prevents seamless incorporation. With iconic legibility, the punctuation marks form a visual vessel for containing designations from afar, like a cartouche that cordons off majestic names, like a receptacle that holds foreign goods stored within the city limits.

By presenting the intersection of two parallel planes, the parentheses accomplish precisely what one expects: the positing (*thesis*) within (*en*) of information that also remains without (*para*). In general, a bracketed statement belongs by not entirely belonging, an outside that nonetheless resides inside. The parenthesis is both a part of and apart from the sentence in which it appears. Although an inserted aside may be removed without affecting the main discourse at hand, it has for some reason not been removed. It is dismissible yet not dismissed, too marginal to incorporate yet somehow too important to delete. In terms of analytic philosophy, the bracketed words are *mentioned* but not necessarily *used*. Hence, a parenthesis is said to have a disruptive nature, to be a figure of discontinuity, as in Quintilian's definition, where it is described explicitly as that which "interrupts midway the sense of some continuous utterance" (*continuationi sermonis medius aliqui sensus intervenit*, *Institutes of Oratory* 9, 3.23).

4 These and other allusions are duly identified in Gifford and Seidman 1989:601.

The stoppage is produced through the importation of supernumerary material that is grammatically or stylistically independent of what precedes and what follows. Modern linguists therefore construe the parenthesis as an interpolation that fractures the dominant idea, a circumscribed digression or hemmed-in excursus, a framed tangent or "disjunctive constituent."[5] By including within "an alternative syntactic space," the figure presents a discourse somehow divided against itself.[6]

The parenthesized incursions in Bloom's nocturnal review communicate by breaking the communication at hand. The bracketed glosses halt the story's progress, the arcane references sever the syntactic coherence of the primary diegesis.[7] Each insertion functions as a brief entr'acte, momentarily suspending the chronological account that otherwise moves from one scene to the next, from the breakfast kitchen to the privy, from the baths to the graveyard. Moreover, by postponing the delivery of the realist storyline, the imposed pauses indicate that the hero's diurnal activities are to a large degree in thrall to a liturgical pattern beyond his subjective control. Each syncope, each intrusive hiatus, constitutes an outside (*para*) that resides on the inside (*en*), a persistent, unassimilated exteriority that appears internally, like an inaccessible yet effective crypt. Still, these parenthetic additions remain ambivalent. For it is Bloom—or Joyce through Bloom—who evokes the tradition, even if the tradition eludes the protagonist's grasp and possibly the author's as well. The fragments of a transpersonal, transcultural order represent a parallel realm that is at once alongside *and* enclosed in Bloom's lifeworld, both entopic and ectopic, enthetic and parathetic.

Joyce's technique furnishes an important example of the kinds of literary reception that lie at the focus of the present study—namely, approaches that bring to the fore, in various ways and with various ramifications, the parenthetic nature of reception itself.

All reception, one could say, is parenthetic since whatever is received is, by virtue of being received, situated at once in and to the side of the receiving end. In order to identify any act specifically as an act of reception, it is necessary to discern the discrete qualities of what has been obtained from the past. A text or image or musical phrase derived from a prior source is said to reoccur in a new work precisely because it has been recognized as an inherited or adopted component, as occupying a fresh frame while still belonging to former frames. In regarding the later text as a *receptacle*, imported content retains some essential difference and therefore remains potentially separable from its present textual container.

In a classicizing mode, the encounter of a source and a receptive text is generally appreciated as a fruitful negotiation that strives toward reconciliation, assimilation,

5 For a concise overview from a modern linguistics position, see Schneider 2015, as well as Schwyzer 1939.

6 Williams1993:64.

7 Cf. Plett 2001.

or synthesis. Despite being no longer here, antiquity is felt to be present. Hence, the predominance of metaphors of dialogue, conversation, and mutual development, including the ideal "fusion of horizons" (*Horizontverschmelzung*)—all adapted from hermeneutics and reception aesthetics (*Rezeptionsästhetik*) and all continuing to inform a good deal of classical reception studies.[8] In contrast, parentextual endeavors are more blatantly confrontational. By allowing non-integrated insertions, a consideration of the parenthetic form of reception challenges attempts at fusion; it exacerbates disjunctions and discontinuities, staging collisions and schisms which a strict classicism or an exceedingly charitable hermeneutics would rather ignore or suppress.[9]

Although parenthetic treatments defy classicizing ambitions, they do not simply revert to a rigorous historicism where the past remains utterly out of reach. Joyce's method respects the radical alterity of antiquity, while still forcing a present encounter. Opposed to historicist asceticism, in Joyce's work, the There, however remote, is very much Here, albeit in brackets. Bloom's nighttime overview conjugates the preparation of breakfast in his Dublin home with the ancient burnt offerings in the Temple at Jerusalem, yet without fusing the two aspects into one transhistorical moment. As a parenthetic gesture, as that which leaves in what could just as well have been left out, the collocation of modernity and antiquity resists, while also to a point permitting, the establishment of what Martindale terms "human communalities across history, communalities that emerge only in the processes we may term 'reception.'"[10] The result is a simultaneous permission and resistance insofar as the brackets install a fencelike barrier that contains a text while obstructing its integration. In *Ulysses*, the past and other parallel sources are neither relegated to some distant domain nor available for untroubled engagement. Rather, as though in non-Euclidean space, the parallels intersect and jostle against each other to produce a modernist shock. Instead of coinciding in a symbolic totality, the two poles clash together as contiguous components, profanely illuminating each other and baffling assimilation.

The simultaneous participation and apartness that the parenthesis affords interrogates aestheticist as well as historicist positions, which both presuppose the stable and stabilizing interiority of the receiving subject. For aesthetically-driven programs, tradition tends to be understood as a property that can be acquired and held by an individual mind or soul or as a national treasure, something that has been appropriated or colonized for the sake of cultural enhancement, legitimization, or hegemonic power—that is, a possession imported and hoarded inside, assimilated into present being, style or

8 See especially Charles Martindale's seminal work, which explicitly builds upon the main tenets of Hans-Georg Gadamer's hermeneutic theory and its elaboration into reception aesthetics in the Constance School by Hans Robert Jauß (Martindale 1993:6–18, 29–34).

9 David Hopkins thus stresses the difference that constitutes continuity in transhistorical, cross-cultural conversations (Hopkins 2010:13–14).

10 Martindale 2013:173.

status. Here, inherited materials and forms appear to inform present thought and expression, which is precisely what is implied by notions of self-cultivation or acculturation. From a historicist perspective, in contrast, tradition stands as a remote object that can be neutrally observed, studied, and measured, something that is ontologically different from the observer who alone is endowed with cognitive interiority. For the stringent historicist, the past can never be internalized but rather must be resolutely sidelined, kept strictly outside. Parenthetic forms of reception, however, question whether a tradition can ever comprise a property, be it one stored aesthetically within or one located historically without. Viewed parenthetically, reception challenges efforts to establish a center at the expense of the margin, it protests criteria that discriminate between presumed insiders and outsiders while also refusing to relegate the past to the dustbin of what has been and will never return. To the extent that the past and the present are at once a part of and apart from each other, the without most certainly occurs within yet does so only in that it subsists without a within.

Friedrich Nietzsche's conception of untimeliness is especially pertinent here insofar as it challenges aestheticist and historicist positions in a modality that is ostensibly parenthetic.

> I do not know what meaning classical studies could have for our time if they were not untimely [*unzeitgemäß*]—that is to say, acting counter to our time and thereby acting on our time and, let us hope, for the benefit of a time to come.[11]

For Nietzsche, engagement with the past exhibits its critical usefulness through a negation of current norms and conventions. In other words, the positivity of the present, its notorious *it-is-what-it-isness*, is disrupted by the negativity inherent to the *no-longer* and the *not-yet*—an interference somewhat reminiscent of the Pauline Kairos. Like a parenthesis, the intrusion punctures the expected flow of chronological time. A disturbance in the order of things, antiquity thus functions as an inserted aside that interferes with the continuity of what positively lies before us in the here and now, a part of the times by remaining apart from the times. Untimeliness, in brief, causes a mess or a critical untidiness. The word *tidy*, in fact, derives from Old Saxon *tid*, "time, season," a term cognate with the German *Zeit* that is interrupted by Nietzsche's *Unzeitgemäßheit*. In English, to be tidy initially denoted to be on time, to accord with the seasons, to be opportune, to be as orderly and predictable as the ocean's tides. Accordingly, in Nietzsche's view, classics can be of service to current life only when it triggers an unpredictable collision, only when it breaks free of the aesthetic trap of being entirely

[11] Friedrich Nietzsche, *Vom Nutzen und Nachteil der Historie für das Leben* [1874] (Nietzsche 1999: vol. 1, 247); "On the Uses and Disadvantages of History for Life" (Nietzsche 1997:60).

in and the historicist trap of being utterly out, that is, only when it operates, parenthetically, as that which is simultaneously in and out, like a precocious child who upsets those who presume to know what-is-what with inopportune or importunate questions, or like an *avant-gardiste* who rattles conventional expectations by importing a vision before its time. Although of an entirely different disposition, Nietzsche is here corroborated by Karl Marx, likewise a student of ancient Greek thought, who equally observed that the French Revolution performed what the times demanded by draping itself in Roman dress.[12] Either as tragedy or farce, untimeliness forces a bracketing of present narratives that baffles expectations and can for that reason be viewed as very well-timed. After all, the importunate is often most opportune, if not for the present, then perhaps for the future.

Parallax

In *Ulysses*, the bracketed glosses in the "Ithaca" passage unsettle Bloom's cognitive control. As instances of pure typography, readable but not pronounceable, the parentheses signal the impingement of meaning from a location outside the protagonist's receptive consciousness. The practice exploits the editorial function historically assigned to rounded brackets. These *virgulae convexae*, which Erasmus, following the fourteenth-century grammarian Gasparino Barizza, called *lunulae*, were introduced by Renaissance publishers to assist readers in distinguishing inserted asides from the primary discourse.[13] Initially at least, the lunulae or tiny crescents served as a written convention to identify apartness within a received text and therefore as an intervention performed after the writing had been finished. It is understandable, then, why Joyce made only sparse use of lunulae in the realist style of the novel's first half, for punctuation marks are not articulated in interior monologues.[14] The most blatant example is the final chapter, "Penelope," which presents Molly Bloom's sweeping display of free association, a steady flow of consciousness that stretches over dozens of pages, recorded without any punctuation, a single stream unimpeded by commas, full stops or paragraph indentation, and of course, unbroken by brackets. That is not to say that the other silent monologues in the novel are non-parenthetic. On the contrary, *Ulysses* is thoroughly composed of asides, allusions, associations, and digressions that depart

12 Karl Marx, *The Eighteenth Brumaire of Louis Bonaparte* [1852] (Marx/Engels 1975–2004: vol. 11, 103).

13 The reference is to Gasparino Barriza (Gasparinus de Bergamo [ca. 1360–1431] and the treatise *De arte punctuandi* from his major work *Orthographia*. For a full discussion of this history, see Parkes 2008:48–49.

14 Cf. Senn 2022:118–119.

from the moment and resist integration; they are simply unmarked as such, parenthetic even if not graphically parenthetical.

As already suggested, the constant digressive meanderings are mainly driven by a *parallactic* imagination, a capacity that allows the protagonists to revisualize the ordinary from the perspective of extra-ordinary parallels, to "see otherwise" or "alter the viewpoint" (παραλλάσσειν), that is, to let what lies *para* in. Throughout the day, Bloom struggles to comprehend the optical phenomenon of the parallax, which enables astronomers to determine the distance of stars. He came across the concept in *The Story of the Heavens* (1886), a popular science book written by fellow-Dubliner Sir Robert Ball which, as we learn in "Ithaca," is bound in "blue cloth" and sits on Bloom's bookshelf at home (*U* 17, 582). Just before lunchtime, while passing by the Aston Quay "timeball," which the longshoremen on the Liffey consult to set their clocks, Bloom lets his thoughts stray towards the planets that wander above his wandering head, just as seamen like Odysseus once charted the heavens to find their way home. The sight of the timeball fittingly broaches a parenthesis: "Fascinating little book that is of sir Robert Ball's. Parallax. I never exactly understood. There's a priest. Could ask him. Par it's Greek: parallel, parallax" (*U* 7, 126). For Hugh Kenner, this episode demonstrates Joyce's "aesthetic of delay," which over time provides two aspects of a single phenomenon and is therefore programmatic for the novel as a whole in that it presents the same object from multiple viewpoints.[15] Thus, the timeball is first regarded as a practical device for the dockworkers and then as an illustration of a parallax—here, specifically how Dublin time is discrepant from the Greenwich Mean. Analogously, the story on the streets is disrupted by the story of the heavens, an interruption, however unadorned by lunular demarcation.

Indeed, it is Joyce's routine practice to refrain from parenthetical marking, allowing instead the stray thoughts and associations to seep in, almost inconspicuously, for example, as Bloom rereads the note he received from Martha Clifford, a clandestine paramour, an intimacy on the side, who addresses him as Henry Flower:

[15] "Joyce's aesthetic of delay, producing the simplest facts by parallax, one element now, one later, and leaving large orders of fact to be assembled late or another time or never, in solving the problem of novels that go flat after we know "how it comes out" also provides what fiction has never before really provided, an experience comparable to that of experiencing the haphazardly evidential quality of life; and, moreover, what art is supposed to offer that life cannot, a permanence to be revisited at will but not exhausted" (Kenner 1980:81). Not irrelevantly, the concept of parallax emerges again in the fourteenth episode ("Oxen of the Sun"), where the boisterous scene at the maternity hospital leads Bloom's imagination back to Agendath Netaim, the "planter's company" that he previously read about in a Zionist pamphlet. Envisioning the landscape of Palestine and the "ghosts of beasts" that roam there, he reflects: "Parallax stalks behind and goads them, the lancinating lightnings of whose brow are scorpions" (*U* 14, 338). The pamphlet reporting on Agendath Netaim is mentioned in *U* 8, 150.

> Then walking slowly forward he read the letter again, murmuring here and there a word. Angry tulips with you darling manflower punish your cactus if you don't please poor forgetmenot how I long violets to dear roses when we soon anemone meet all naughty nightstalk wife Martha's perfume. (*U* 5, 64)[16]

Only when returning to the text of the missive printed beforehand, can the reader discern the primary discourse from Bloom's murmured flowery inserts.

> Dear Henry
>
> I got your last letter to me and thank you very much for it. I am sorry you did not like my last letter. Why did you enclose the stamps? I am awfully angry with you. I do wish I could punish you for that. I called you naughty boy because I do not like that other world. Please tell me what is the real meaning of that word? Are you not happy in your home you poor little naughty boy? I do wish I could do something for you. Please tell me what you think of poor me. I often think of the beautiful name you have. Dear Henry, when will we meet? I think of you so often you have no idea. I have never felt myself so much drawn to a man as you. I feel so bad about. Please write me a long letter and tell me more. Remember if you do not I will punish you. So now you know what I will do to you, you naughty boy, if you do not wrote. O how I long to meet you. Henry dear, do not deny my request before my patience are exhausted. Then I will tell you all. Goodbye now, naughty darling, I have such a bad headache. today. and write *by return* to your longing
>
> Martha
>
> P. S. Do tell me what kind of perfume does your wife use. I want to know. (*U* 5, 63–64)

In a more moderately experimental fashion, Joyce could have offered typographic assistance, for example: *Angry (tulips) with you darling (manflower) ... I do wish I could punish you (cactus)*, etc. But instead, through Bloom, the author plants the parallactic florilegium into the letter and allows it to scatter across the text without editorial hedging.

Since unmarked parentheses are the norm for *Ulysses*, the "Ithaca" chapter comes across as a glaring exception, with well over three-hundred parentheses marks in some

16 This example is adduced by Fritz Senn (2014:24–25).

sixty pages.[17] Structured in the form of a catechism, the omniscient narrator makes his presence palpable by posing questions to an unnamed catechumen. For example, the passage we have been discussing—Bloom's bedtime précis together with the Biblical correspondences—responds to the question: "What past consecutive causes, before rising preapprehended, of accumulated fatigue did Bloom, before rising, silently recapitulate?" (*U* 17, 599) On the one hand, the reply from the internal yet unidentified examinee perpetuates the parallactic effect evident across the novel: juxtaposing a trip to the baths with the "rite of John," or a funeral for a friend to the "rite of Samuel." On the other hand, the prominent employment of parenthetical brackets now implies the author's direct involvement: The omniscient narrator has relaxed his usual detachment and intercedes by supplying the brackets, like an editor emends a draft.

The suspected work of the author's hand is further evinced by the fact that Bloom's glossed diaristic list mimics the well-known schemes that Joyce prepared around the same time he was writing the "Ithaca" chapter and bringing the whole project to completion.[18] The synopses, which Joyce confidentially shared to selected critics to serve as an interpretive guide, divulge the themes, symbols, motifs, and narrative techniques assigned to each episode. The author's own outlines, however, broach a fresh problem. For here, the episodes are clearly identified by Homeric, not Hebraic titles. According to the Joyce's private plans, the chapters that cover his protagonist's morning hours, from fry-up to funeral, are identified as "Calypso," "Lotus-Eaters," and "Hades," not "burnt offering," "holy of holies," "rite of John," and "rite of Samuel." Likewise, the novel's seventh episode, set at the printshop of the *Freeman's Journal* where Bloom submits an advert for his client Alexander Keyes, appears in Joyce's schemes as "Aeolus." The title refers to the keeper of the winds in *Odyssey* 10, 1–79 and therefore may apply to several instances in the chapter: the newspaper's windbag foreman; the popular press which drives public opinion with gale-force diatribes in a Gaelic mode; or the illicit lover of Bloom's wife Molly, Blazes Boylan, an intimidating blowhard whose sudden appearance on the street drives Bloom mercilessly off-course. In his own late-night reflections, however, Bloom seems to have missed the Homeric subtext. For him or through him, the meeting at the newspaper office evokes the "Urim and Thummim," the black and white stones mentioned in Exodus 28:30, the gems of "Light and Truth" that once adorned the breastplate of the Hebrew High Priest and endowed him with the power to reveal the will of God. Traditionally, the *Urim* and *Thummim* represent the two keys of knowledge, revelation and doctrine, which ought to guide people's thought and behavior, perhaps through cleromancy, where the stones were cast as lots to determine the right course of action—not necessarily a more sanguine assessment

17 Cf. Senn 2014:23.

18 Joyce sent the first extant scheme to Carlo Linati in September 1921, a month before finishing the "Ithaca" chapter. See Joyce's letter to Robert McAlmon, October 29, 1921 (Joyce 1957: vol. 1, 175).

of the newspaper industry but rather a jocular reference to Bloom's advert for Keyes, "two crossed keys" in a circular frame (*U* 7, 99). By inserting the *Urim* and *Thummim* in brackets, the catalogue broaches trajectories that are even more distinct from the conventional Homeric-Aeolian repertoire: allusions to Roman Catholicism via the crossed keys in the Vatican's Coat of Arms or to Yale University whose motto includes the Hebrew terms along with the Latin translation, *Lux et Veritas*, and consequently to the Yale Lock Manufacturing Company, founded in 1868 in Stamford, Connecticut, where keys, of course, would be crucial.

Joyce's schemes exclusively address the Homeric hypotext and omit all mention of the scriptural correspondences which he placed in the "Ithaca" inventory. This authorial and authorized clarity has served as a steady basis for his legion of interpreters. And to be sure, the Homeric outlines better accord with readers' expectations. As the title already forthrightly suggests, *Ulysses* should invite comparison with the *Odyssey*, not the Bible. In letters to friends and relatives, associates and publishers, Joyce consistently refers to individual episodes by Homeric titles and advises reading or re-reading the ancient epic. For example, to his frustrated aunt, Josephine Murray, he insists: "I told you to read the *Odyssey* first."[19] Accordingly, in the opening pages of the novel, Stephen Dedalus's housemate, Buck Mulligan, sounds the oboe pitch to tune the orchestra: "Ah, Dedalus, the Greeks! I must teach you. You must read them in the original" (*U* 1, 4–5). Buck's official forename, Malachi, may point to the last book of the Hebrew Prophets, yet the Semitic moniker has been suppressed, if not altogether bucked, by his sylvan nickname. Besides, as Buck himself notes, *Malachi Mulligan* forms two dactyls (*U* 1, 4), which suggests that the Hebraic source has already been sufficiently channeled through Greek poetics, however much it retains a non-Greek trace, akin to the Semitic vestiges that Victor Bérard pursued in *Les Phéniciens et l'Odysée* (1902), the two-volume study that is known to have contributed much to Joyce's literary venture.[20]

In "Ithaca," therefore, asides to Judaic lore interfere with the customary Homeric interferences. Parentheses complicate parentheses, perhaps in an effort to complicate a plan that had become too routine or obvious, too tightly woven into the novel's text and therefore no longer parenthetical enough to produce a dynamic collision, too "in" (*en*) and no longer effectively "apart" (*para*). Perhaps the bracketed Hebraic list aims to expose the parenthetic nature of all the allusions and subtexts at work in *Ulysses*; or perhaps the passage is but a gesture of authorial irony whereby Joyce undercuts his own encyclopedic, parallactically driven ambitions, a self-division or *dédoublement* that correlates to the diremption that haunts and disconcerts the minds of his protagonists. Whatever the case may be, at the end of his eight-year project, the author positions Bloom to reveal a different thematic path. An alternative pattern emerges for organizing

19 Joyce 1957: vol. 1, 193.
20 For a representative example, with bibliography, see Childress1989.

the protagonist's own disparate ephemeral activities, a different roadmap through the novel in which he figures, as if the hero or anti-hero, right before his exit, proffers a new design that may sabotage his creator's master plan and turn the *Odyssey* into theodicy.

Truancy

With its excessive use of brackets, "Ithaca" explores the relationship between Bloom, a bereaved father of Jewish descent, and Stephen Dedalus, a motherless son who sports an "absurd ... ancient Greek" name (*U* 1, 3). Up until they meet in the shady recesses of a Nighttown brothel, the two men have mirrored each other's movements along independent paths. And after removing a dangerously inebriated Stephen to a cabman's shelter, Bloom invites the young man to his home. The one who wandered apart will now be received as a guest in the other wanderer's dwelling. As though to illustrate the parenthetic structure, "Ithaca" opens with the union of the two men's "parallel courses."

> What parallel courses did Bloom and Stephen follow returning?
>
> Starting united both at normal walking pace from Beresford place they followed in the order named Lower and Middle Gardiner streets and Mountjoy square, west [...] (*U* 17, 544)

The parallel lives are finally "united," arm in arm, still separate yet also, as the remainder of the passage suggests, converging and diverging as though traversing a non-Euclidean, Riemannian plane.[21]

Upon arriving at 7 Eccles Street, through catechistic disputation, the paths of Bloom and Stephen gradually become clearer, yet despite the older man's charitable demeanor, every attempt at sympathetic merger fails, culminating with Stephen singing a rudely anti-Semitic ballad (*U* 17, 565–567). As one critic remarks, "Instead of offering the long awaited convergence of Stephen and Bloom at the end of the novel, the text confounds and confuses any satisfactory resolution to the relationship."[22] In "Ithaca," the conversation devolves into a confrontation as Stephen withdraws behind brackets of arrogance. Yet before Bloom bids his young guest farewell—before he goes up to bed and assigns Hebraic references to his diurnal itinerary—he waxes astronomically over a cup of sobering cocoa:

21 See McMorran 2020:55–57.

22 Norris 2010:74. For a comprehensive overview of early scholarship regarding the failure, see Kain 1972.

> [He spoke] of the parallax or parallactic drift of socalled fixed stars, in reality evermoving wanderers from immeasurably remote eons to infinitely remote futures in comparison with which the years, threescore and ten, of allotted human life formed a parenthesis of infinitesimal brevity" (*U* 17, 573).

The meditation represents a stark contrast. Whereas Bloom's final catalogue will place transcendent, scriptural significances within brackets—treating the parentheses as protective zones, as if to guard the sacred from profane incursion, indeed, like the Holy of Holies was once shielded by an embroidered curtain—here, it is the mundane reality of a human lifespan, the "threescore and ten," that forms the parenthesis, a negligible interval, barely a blip in the great cosmic scheme. The viewpoint accords with Christian doctrine, where human history is said to unfold within a finite zone created by God, an enclosed domain where human life meanders until it returns to its heavenly home. For John Donne, human time relates to eternity "as a short parenthesis in a long period."[23] Søren Kierkegaard follows suit:

> God's memory stretches far enough to encompass all parentheses. Men, however, have long, long, long ago totally forgotten that it is a parenthesis into which we have entered, that Christianity was introduced precisely as the divine *claudatur*. No, we live pleasantly within the parenthesis, propagate the race, and organize world history—and it is all a parenthesis.[24]

All the same, now from the perspective of the novel's realist storyline—breakfast then defecation, visits to the public baths, a funeral, a newspaper office, and so on—it is the divine plane that is parenthesized and therefore deemed subsidiary. As Jeff Scheible comments, in functioning as both a literal-typographic punctuation and a figurative scheme or trope, the parenthesis is "an inscription that separates insides and outsides and that calls into the question the boundaries between them."[25] In other words, parenthesizing is always both reversible and ambiguous. *Reversible*, insofar as the distinction between primary and parenthetical discourse, between what is useful and what is useless, is based on an evaluative judgment, which could turn either way. As we have seen, within a single hour, Bloom changes his assessment, first parenthesizing quotidian life within a theological context, then bracketing theology within an everyday frame. And *ambiguous*, insofar as the brackets can be regarded either as safeguarding the contents from the context without or shielding the context from the contents within. As Robert Williams asks, "Are the marks bastions which create a sanctuary for a

23 John Donne, *Devotions Upon Emergent Occasions* [1624] (Donne 1959:89).

24 Søren Kierkegaard, "The Human Race" [1818] (Kierkegaard 1967: vol. 2, 301–02).

25 Scheible 2013:693.

parenthesized comment under siege, or are they bars which imprison linguistic criminals, textual rogues?"[26]

For the majority of the classical rhetorical tradition, the question is settled: Parentheses are regarded as adding supplementary, potentially distracting, and therefore dismissible information. Henry Peacham, in *The Garden of Eloquence* (1577), concedes that although a parenthesis may reinforce a sentence, "being taken away, it leaves the same speech perfect enough."[27] Granted, the figure can "give light" or "resolve a doubt" (199), that is, a parenthesis works by means of privation, possibly removing obscurity but also possibly removing light. Hence Peacham's concluding word of caution, which describes the parenthesis as "a needless interposition," "like unprofitable household stuff that fills room but does no service: or like to the Mistletoe, which albeit it stands in the tree, and lives by his juice, yet is neither of the like nature, nor bears the like fruit" (199).[28] Like clutter, or even worse, like mistletoe, a *parasitic* plant that sucks energy from its host, parentheses may be more trouble than they are worth. Similarly, George Puttenham, in *The Arte of English Poesie* (1589), recognizes that a surprise intervention may arouse the audience's or reader's attention yet risks causing the recipients to lose sight of or forget the primary argument. Attraction can readily slip into distraction. Puttenham therefore urges the writer to resist the temptation "to piece or graft in the middle of your tale an unnecessary parcel of speech, which nevertheless may be thence without any detriment to the rest"; and when in fact employed, "you must not use such insertions often nor to thick, nor those that be very long [...] for it will breed great confusion to have the tale so much interrupted."[29] Like an unwelcome insemination, the thick and long asides that penetrate the sentence threaten to "breed" illegitimate perplexities.

The fear plagues pedagogically-minded writers across the centuries and elicits prophylactic measures that only confirm the figure's seductiveness. For William Cornwallis (1600), extended asides are nothing more than displays of vanity, for which he has no patience: "How shall a man hope to come to an end of their works, when he cannot with two breaths sail through a Period, and is sometimes graveled in a Parenthesis?"[30] Writing in the mid-seventeenth century, Thomas Burton (1659) despairs of the effects: "You see the inconveniency of a long parenthesis; we have forgot the sense that went before."[31] And yet, reverting to parenthetical remarks appears

26 Williams 1993:64–65.

27 Henry Peacham, *The Garden of Eloquence* [1577] (2nd ed., London, 1593), 198 (orthography modernized).

28 Cf. Jonathan Lamb's chapter "Hamlet's Parenthesis" in Lamb 2017:140–174; here, p. 145.

29 George Puttenham, *The Arte of English Poesie* (1589:III.xii, 140–141 (orthography modernized).

30 William Cornwallis, "On Vanity," in *Essays* (1600); cited in Lamb 2017:148.

31 From *The Diary of Thomas Burton* (1659), cited in the *Oxford English Dictionary*, s.v. "parenthesis."

to be too alluring. Rather curiously, in his *Grammatical Institutes* (1761), John Ash illustrates the risk by disrupting his straightforward definition of a parenthesis with a piece of advice against it in the form of a parenthesis: "A Parenthesis, to be avoided as much as possible, is used to include some Sentence in another."[32] The problematic status of the figure persists into the nineteenth century. Pierre Fontanier, for example, is compelled to urge writers to remain alert and not allow parenthetical interruptions to cause "encumbrance [*l'embarras*], obscurity, confusion."[33] On this basis, Mark Twain disparages the style of German journalists who are particularly prone to suffer from what he calls "the Parenthesis distemper," a malady that he describes with typical mimetic humor:

> An average sentence, in a German newspaper is a sublime and impressive curiosity. [...] it treats of fourteen or fifteen different subjects, each enclosed in a parenthesis of its own, with here and there extra parentheses, making pens within pens: finally, all the parentheses and reparentheses are massed together between a couple of king-parentheses, one of which is placed in the first line of the majestic sentence and the other in the middle of the last line of it—AFTER WHICH COMES THE VERB, and you find out for the first time what the man has been talking about.[34]

Needless to say, Joyce confirms these fears. The multitude of parallels in *Ulysses*, present or imported, suspend the teleological drive of the realist narrative, its propulsion from beginning to end, from morning to night. As parenthetic insertions, they encumber the novel, sowing the seeds of obscurity and confusion, injecting a deleterious dose of distemper, or even losing the reception to noisy "static"—in French, *la parasite*—noxiously interfering with the communicative signal. Even here, one is reminded that the distinction between noise and signal rests entirely on the observer. As Michel Serres stresses in the case of a telephone call during a meal: either the call is viewed as disturbing the meal or the meal is felt to disturb the call.[35] That said, what may be most fearful is for hasty readers to pass over the novel's parenthetic density, to opt for one discursive plane at the expense of others—to skate through the esoteric allusions and attend solely to the realist plot or conversely, to ignore the meticulous

32 John Ash, *Grammatical Institutes: or, An Easy Introduction to Dr. Lowth's English Grammar* [1761] (1810:xviii).

33 "Mais par cela même qu'elle interrompt le discours, et qu'elle détourne pour un moment l'attention de son objet principal, elle [la Parenthèse] tend nécessairement à produire l'embarras, l'obscurité, la confusion" Pierre Fonatnier, *Les figures du discours* [1821–1830] (1977:385).

34 Mark Twain, "The Awful German Language" in *A Tramp Abroad* (1880:603).

35 Michel Serres, *The Parasite* [1980] (2007:66–67).

fictional rendering of a June's day in turn-of-the-century Dublin and focus instead on reductive archetypes or universal truths which discount the all-too-human "parenthesis of infinitesimal brevity."

In his study on literary digression, Ross Chambers emphasizes how departing from a single chosen line is both inherently pleasurable and urgently critical, a mode that challenges a hyper-mechanized era "committed to directness, speed, and immediacy."[36] Through wandering, Leopold Bloom, the outsider on the inside, becomes the conduit for the dilatory effects and paradigm shifts that comprise *Ulysses*. By broaching contained digressions, the asides fragment the protagonist's own cohesiveness. What is demonstrated is the parenthetic nature of the flâneur, who merges with the urban crowd in order to stand apart and observe it, a figure who may be relegated to secondary status, yet precisely through relegation ends up being distinguished, like a parenthesized phrase, "specially marked as secondary" and therefore "specially marked."[37]

The simple and obvious point is that, with parenthetic force, both parallels—the trivial and the grand—remain in play. It matters little which component is deemed subsidiary or dangerously supplemental: As a parenthesis, both aspects are dismissible yet not in fact dismissed. Both persist in dynamic confrontation, colliding without merging. Each is potentially designated as secondary yet not obliterated, just like bracketed clauses persist in a text, too insignificant to incorporate yet too significant to eliminate, neither worked into the main syntax nor by the same token eradicated. What, one may ask, would the novel be, should all the parenthetic asides be removed? How would it appear, this "usylessly unreadable Blue Book of Eccles,"[38] without its unnecessary parcels of speech, without the parallactic drift described in Sir Robert Ball's study, bound in the same blue cloth as the first edition of *Ulysses*, or without the hoard of truant rogues or present absences recorded in the schoolmaster's blue ledger?[39] Through conflict, the parentheses invite the past to enliven the present and thereby allow modernity to animate antiquity. Failing that, one is left either with a series of detached allusions and vague correspondences, or with a skillet of urine-scented kidneys, fecal odor, an aromatic bath and a dismal burial.

Purely for Home Use

Ulysses may well function as a platform for the reception of boundless sources, yet without fail the Odyssean tags provide the rubrics under which everything is gathered.

36 Chambers 1999:11.

37 Chambers 1999:87.

38 James Joyce, *Finnegans Wake* [1939], 179.

39 In idiomatic German, the compound verb *blaumachen* denotes "to play hooky," a reference to the color of the standard truancy register.

There are of course good reasons not to supplant Joyce's Homeric scheme with Bloom's list of Hebraic headings. To start, it would be impractical to adopt the Biblical outline, which only applies to the episodes that directly involved Bloom. As a diegetic character, Bloom's perspective is necessarily limited. Lacking his author's omniscience, his inventory cannot be but incomplete; it must omit the opening three chapters which feature Stephen Dedalus as well the present and subsequent chapters, "Ithaca" and "Penelope." Furthermore, Bloom's fifteen entries do not perfectly line up with the thirteen corresponding episodes in the book. As already noted, the first three headings in his synopsis pertain to material that the novel covers in two chapters.

Be that as it may, in employing the Homeric chapter titles, scholarship at once accepts and rejects what Joyce wrote. Critics employ one key while neglecting the other and may therefore find themselves in a similar situation to Bloom's in "Ithaca," where, having forgotten his housekey in his other pair of trousers, he needed to break into his own home. Thus, credence is granted to what Joyce the writer provided in the form of separate schemes (the Hellenic parallels) yet dismiss what Joyce the author wrote in the novel itself (the Hebraic parallels). The *anecdotal*—that is, unpublished—evidence is taken to be decisive, while the published text is ignored. The convention is odd, especially among the first generations of literary interpreters who were schooled in New Criticism, where caution must be exercised against the intentional fallacy, where material intrinsic to the text should outweigh any extrinsic information. Why discount the Judaic parallels which are present in the text, while promulgating the Homeric parallels which are absent? Why prefer what Joyce furnished only anecdotally over that which is given in the authoritative editions? Is it because the Biblical scheme in "Ithaca" is conveyed not only intradiegetically, through a character in the novel, but also parenthetically? Is it not logical, some may argue, to bracket out whatever has been set in brackets?

The privileged Homeric scheme, however, is equally parenthetic. In the major *Critical and Synoptic Edition of Ulysses* (1984), edited by Hans Walter Gabler, the Table of Contents lists the traditional Odyssean chapter headings yet cautiously sets them in rounded brackets: "EPISODE 1 (Telemachus), EPISODE 2 (Nestor), EPISODE 3 (Proteus)," etc. The typographic gesture not only closely resembles the inventory from "Ithaca," but also recalls the fact that, although Joyce employed the Odyssean titles in his drafts, he ultimately deleted them in all the published versions, first for the serialized installments in *The Egoist* and *The Little Review*, beginning in March 1918, and then for the first edition of the book, published by Sylvia Beach in Paris in February 1922. Throughout, the episodes are simply numbered without titles. And while it is true that Joyce kept the Homeric markers for his tabulated schemes, the first outline materialized only late in the compositional process, in the autumn of 1921, soon after Joyce and his family moved from Trieste to Paris, where he set to work on the third and final part of the novel, while correcting and expanding proofs of earlier chapters.

Hardly having functioned as an original template, the first scheme coincides with a decisive shift, a departure from the realist "initial style" of the novel's first half towards the encyclopedic fervor and formal experiments that characterize the latter half. Hence, a good deal of the additions which Joyce made during this late stage betray a desire to bring the earlier episodes into greater accord with his updated vision.[40]

However much Joyce came to rely on the Homeric schemes in the final stage of writing, they were specifically prepared for a few select readers and never for the general public. So much is clear in the letter that accompanied the first outline in September 1921, sent to the Italian writer and translator, Carlo Linati, who had been commissioned to submit an article on Joyce's current work-in-progress for the journal *Poesia* based in Milan. Eager to maintain contact with the Italian literary scene, Joyce did not hesitate to respond to Linati's request:

> Vista l'enorme mole e la più enorme complessità del mio maledettissimo romanzaccione credo sia meglio mandargliene una specie di sunto-chiave-scheletro-schema (per uso puramente domestico).[41]

> In view of the enormous bulk and the most enormous complexity of my most-cursed monster-novel I believe it would be better to send you a kind of summary-key-skeleton-schema (purely for in-house use).[42]

Joyce's *captatio benevolentiae* aims to secure the goodwill of his recipient through self-deprecation and self-inflation. The adjective *enorme*, repeated in the superlative, indicates his weariness regarding the heft and complexity of his work, with the term *mole* ("bulk") not only suggesting laboriousness but also, perhaps, permitting a fond nod to his heroine Molly whose immense monologue he had just completed. The litany or complaint culminates, again superlatively, with his "most-cursed *romanzaccione*." The inventive formulation distends the "novel" (*romanza*) by melding two distinct suffixes: *-accio*, which conveys wickedness or ugliness, as in *ragazzaccio*, a "bad boy" or "tough guy," a "rebel," "ruffian," or "troublemaker"; and *-one*, which applies to someone exceedingly big, large, or tall, as in *ragazzone*, a "big boy." Posing like a worried father, Joyce the author nearly apologizes for spawning a novel that is both very long and troubling, morally or aesthetically or both, with allusion to the Callimachean quip, μέγα βιβλίον μέγα κακόν ("a big book is a big evil").

Hence, the need for a *sunto-chiave-scheletro-schema*, an unwieldy compound for an unwieldy *romanzaccione*—a "summation" (*sunto*) that offers a synoptic, bird's-eye

40 For a comprehensive overview of the compositional and prepublication history, including a discussion of the "initial style," see Groden 1977.

41 Joyce to Carlo Linati, September 21, 1920, in Joyce 1974:366.

42 Unless otherwise noted, all translations throughout are mine.

view of the work, a "key" (*chiave*) to unlock its many mysteries or open onto otherwise inaccessible passageways, a "skeleton" (*scheletro*) that forms the novel's subcutaneous structure, and a "scheme" (*schema*) that reveals the overall pattern or plan—all contained on a single page, similar to the informative tables found in most modern editions of Dante's *Divina Commedia* which certainly inspired Joyce's encyclopedic pursuits.[43] A powerful document, to be sure, yet one donated "purely for home use" (*per uso puramente domestico*), or more idiomatically, with bureaucratic overtones, "purely for in-house use." In either case, the letter's bracketed stipulation aims to ensure that the outline be handled confidentially, like a well-guarded secret or *Geheimnis*, something to be kept strictly in the home (*Heim*), held in the domestic, non-public zone, analogous, one could say, to the secret Hebraic tags that Bloom mutters in the dark silence of his own home. Yet what the parenthesized clause most suggestively communicates is that Linati should employ the "summary-key-skeleton-scheme" parenthetically: The critic is invited to let the outlines assist his interpretation, yet only as a reference kept to the side, as a pattern discernible in the work, *enthetically*, though only as long as it remained apart, *parathetically*.

Continuing, Joyce presents the scope of his frightening *romanzaccione*:

> È l'epopea di due razze (Israele-Irlanda) e nel medesimo tempo il ciclo del corpo umano ed anche la storiella di una giornata (vita). [...] È una specie di enciclopedia, anche. La mia intenzione è di rendere il mito *sub specie temporis nostri*; no soltanto ma permettendo che ogni avventura (cioè, ogni ora, ogni organo, ogni arte connessi e immedesimati nello schema somatico del tutto) condizionasse anzi creasse la propria tecnica. (366)

> It is the epic of two races (Israel-Ireland) and at the same time the cycle of the human body and also a tale of one day (life). It is a kind of encyclopedia, also. My intention is to render the myth *sub specie temporis nostri*; not only by allowing each adventure (that is, every hour, every organ, every art connected and related in the somatic scheme of the whole) to condition but rather to create its own technique.

Joyce declined to include the Hebraic parallels in his Homeric schemes, yet here, in contrast, he not only names "Israel," but omits any explicit mention of the *Odyssey*, apart from the generic markers "epic" and "myth." "Israel-Ireland"—not Israel-Greece—represent the ethnic-cultural histories that constitute the theme, dramatically juxtaposed in parenthesis, a theme moreover that is simultaneously doubled by a "tale" or "little story" (*storiella*) of a single day also parenthetically glossed as "life." The first

[43] Cf. Melchiori 2004–2005:179–180.

pair of bracketed terms (*Israel-Ireland*) clearly have an explicative, specifying function, yet also articulate the two planes that, by intersecting, generate the novel's content, while the third and final parentheses (*life; every hour, every organ*, etc.) motivate the technical form. Joyce's intention, then, is to create a *Gesamtkunstwerk*, a total work of art (*tutto*) replete with profound interconnections and interrelations. A "Work-as-Cosmos," as Umberto Eco describes it, where the "reference point is not the poet in his ivory tower but the human community and, ultimately, all history and culture."[44] An all-inclusive encyclopedia organized around a whole day, like Seneca's *totus dies*, though not to reinforce the autonomous subject as much as to create a universe from which the classical subject is exiled, where a human life is relegated to a little story yet irradiated by transpersonal, transhistorical forces, each a part of and apart from the other.

By simultaneously sharing the outline with Linati and restricting its usage, Joyce started a game of give-and-take that would persistently govern the circulation of subsequent schemes. Less than two months later, in December 1921, he prepared a similar but not identical plan to Valery Larbaud to help with his upcoming public lecture on the novel at Adrienne Monnier's bookshop, La Maison des Amis des Livres, in Paris. It was at this time that Joyce famously explained the technique of the "interior monologue," which, together with the Homeric parallels, Larbaud was asked to present as part of his own, not Joyce's, views. But even then, in a letter to his devoted patron, Harriet Shaw Weaver, the author admitted both deviousness and regret: He had furnished Larbaud "in order to help him to confuse the audience a little more. I ought not to have done so."[45] All the same, despite second thoughts, Joyce apparently could not resist continuing to manage his reception, albeit cautiously. Soon after Larbaud's lecture, to assist Jacques Benoist-Méchin in translating the "Penelope" episode, Joyce at first shared only a few portions of the scheme before reluctantly supplanting the entire plan: "If I gave it all up immediately," Joyce asserted, "I'd lose my immortality."[46]

After *Ulysses* had appeared in print, Joyce kept apace, turning a blind eye as his publisher, Sylvia Beach, shared Benoist-Méchin's copy with several interested readers, with Auguste Morel, Herbert Gorman, and Edmund Wilson, and always with the insistence that the outlines remain confidential, purely for use at home. As Joyce's secretary Paul Léon maintained: the Homeric chart "had an absolutely private character and was not meant for publication, least of all as an addition or interpretation of the text."[47] Likewise, nearly a decade after the novel was published, Joyce furnished an even larger, more elaborate scheme to Stuart Gilbert, who was working on the first book-length study devoted to the novel, again with the proviso that the Homeric

44 Eco 1989:33.

45 Unpublished Letter to Harriet Weaver, Nov. 25, 1921, cited in Richard Ellmann's 1959 biography (1982:519).

46 Cited in Ellmann 1982:521.

47 Cited in Croessman 1959:10–11.

parallels be presented as part of Gilbert's own hermeneutic labor rather than as instructions directly from the author's hand.[48] In his own Table of Contents, Gilbert organized his interpretation by listing the Odyssean titles, which henceforth secured their place in the scholarship. Joyce's approbation, however, did not spell full license. When Bernard Cerf at Random House requested permission to print the outline at the front of the first American edition, Joyce flatly refused.[49] Finally, in 1937, over a dinner with Vladimir Nabokov in the apartment of Paul Léon, Joyce reportedly disparaged the use of mythology in modern literature.

> Nabokov replied in amazement, "But you employed Homer!" "A whim," was Joyce's comment. "But you collaborated with Gilbert," Nabokov persisted. "A terrible mistake," said Joyce, "an advertisement for the book. I regret it very much."[50]

When it comes to how one's work may be received, even the most resolutely aloof author may occasionally see it fit to intervene, however regrettably. Joyce might have once likened himself to "the god of creation" who "remains within or behind or beyond or above his handiwork," he might have once preferred to stay "invisible, refined out of existence, indifferent, paring his fingernails,"[51] championing the ideals of impersonality and impassiveness associated with the pure Aestheticism of Gustave Flaubert and Stéphane Mallarmé, Walter Pater and Oscar Wilde. Yet this allegiance to high art did not prevent him from sometimes revealing his will to common mortals, especially those who may feel lost, wandering through a dense and verbose wilderness that is often difficult to traverse.

As Kevin Dettmar notes, by limiting the distribution of the Homeric schemes to a few handpicked critics, Joyce "could maintain the vaunted modernist air of impersonality, while subtly influencing the reception and interpretation of his texts."[52] In fact, such displays of what Dettmar aptly characterizes as "critical ventriloquism" are not restricted to the delivery of outlines but rather include a range of efforts on Joyce's part to steer the course in which his work was read, informing Larbaud, for example, of the interior monologue technique, or less successfully, proposing a "two plane" theory to T. S. Eliot.[53] Such efforts aimed to provide authoritative keys that should

48 Stuart Gilbert, *James Joyce's* Ulysses*: A Study* [1930] (1955). See Ellmann's note, (Ellmann 1972:187).

49 For excerpts from the exchange, see Dettmar1993:803.

50 Ellmann 1982:616.

51 James Joyce, *A Portrait of the Artist as a Young Man* [1916] (1973:215).

52 Dettmar 1993:798.

53 See Joyce's letter to Harriet Shaw Weaver, November 1923 (Joyce 1957: vol. 3, 83), cited in Dettmar 1993:799.

shed light and truth on the greater significance of his work, without reducing the texts to a readily consumable digest of themes and symbols which might tempt impatient readers to refrain from engaging with the actual text. Joyce might have indulged in the role of the High Priest of Aestheticism, in charge of the *Urim* and *Thummim*, the keys that transmitted his divine will, yet he did not entirely refrain from playing the part of an everyday self-advertiser, not dissimilar to his street-walking protagonist, the canvasser Leopold Bloom. In this way, Joyce ensured that the Homeric parallels were both communicated and withheld, revealed and concealed, posited and omitted, as if the Odyssean allusions were too crucial to ignore yet too provisional to last. Like a parenthesis.

Parentextuality

For Gian Biagio Conte, allusion ought to be understood as a trope, that is, as a figure that links "two different realities," a literal sense (the *verbum proprium*) and a figurative sense (the *improprium*), resulting in "the simultaneous co-existence of both a denotative and a connotative semiotic."[54] Allusion can be said to operate parenthetically insofar as the denotation, what is literally meant "in" the text, also contains the connotations found "alongside" it, producing a parenthetic tension between outside and inside. "What is recalled is *extraneous* to the new poem because it is irrevocably embedded in the other poetic situation. But the previous poetic context necessarily carries over *into* the new" (25; my emphasis).

Allusive practices confirm the constitutive power of intertextuality in literature whereby "a text can be read only in connection with, and in opposition to, other texts" (29). As Conte elaborates, intertextuality proffers that every specific verbal performance ought to be likened to Ferdinand de Saussure's *parole*, an actual and finite verbal instantiation, whose significance derives from its relationship to the transcendent system or *langue* that is strictly absent and hovers alongside the text at hand.[55] Derived from the Greek παραβολή, which denotes a "throwing to the side" and hence a "juxtaposition" or "comparison," the term *parole* retains its indicative function, pointing to other words to produce significance, as in a *parable*. The *parole* in the text evokes the *langue* that rests to the side. In Roman Jakobson's oft-cited, structuralist terms, the *parole/langue* distinction motivates the distinction between the horizontal, combinatory or syntagmatic axis of linguistic expression—the γραμμή or "line" that produces the literal, narratable sense—and the vertical, selective or paradigmatic axes that "point

54 Conte 1986:24.

55 Ferdinand de Saussure, *Course in General Linguistics* [posth. 1915] (1959:13–15).

beyond" (παραδείκνυσιν), away from mere denotation.[56] Through intertextuality, the planar surface of the verbal message acquires a third dimension, just as the parallactic effect of our two eyes provide us with a sense of depth, a sense, however, constituted by the presence of what is not there. Thus, for Michel de Certeau, intertextuality effects "a lapse" that "insinuates itself into language. The territory of appropriation is altered by the mark of something which is not there and does not happen (like myth)."[57]

Intertextual allusiveness constantly courses through Joyce's *Ulysses* and produces the novel's textual density; yet, as seen in the case of the Hebraic catalogue from "Ithaca," the paradigmatic coordinates are more palpably absent, manifestly present, preserved in brackets.[58] By means of parentheses, Joyce puts intertextuality on display. The "patterns" or "blueprints" (παραδείγματα) retain their transcendence while appearing quite immanently in the text. As a consequence, the parenthesized inserts alert us to the poetics that generates *Ulysses* as a whole. Through Bloom's sleepy consciousness, the reader is offered a rare but important glimpse behind the scenes, a chance to see the gears that *parentextually* motivate the entire work.

My neologism *parentextuality* mindfully evokes the work of Gérard Genette who methodically distinguishes and assesses various kinds of "transtextual relationships"—that is, the many ways in which two texts appertain to and thereby affect each other, how Text A stands in relation to Text B. Indulging in his typical flair for innovative terminology, Genette identifies five major types of transtextual relationships, with the form and function of each type discernible by the prefixes in each term.[59] To begin, Genette lists *intertextuality*, a concept already broached above and initially coined by Julia Kristeva with reference to phenomenological accounts of intersubjectivity. Drawing on the work of Ferdinand de Saussure and Mikhail Bakhtin, Kristeva employs intertextuality to explore the effects of multiple quotations in a given text and the constitutive efficacy of what she calls *paragrams*.[60] For Genette, intertextuality refers explicitly to "the actual presence of one text *within* [*inter*-] another," as in quotes, allusions, and plagiarized passages. With *paratextuality*, Genette instead focuses on material that is somehow *without*, texts that frame or appear "beside" (*para*-) the work at hand. Paratexts therefore function as "thresholds of interpretation," including book covers and advertisements, title pages and subtitles, frontispieces and epigraphs, footnotes and endnotes, prefaces and postfaces, everything that stands, to varying degrees, apart from

56 See Jakobson 1964:350–377.

57 de Certeau 1984:154.

58 For an extended discussion of intertextuality in *Ulysses*, see Rickard 1999:169–180. De Certeau is cited on p. 170.

59 Genette 2018:2–6.

60 See Julia Kristeva, "Towards a Semiology of Paragrams" [1969] (1988:25–49); and "Word, Dialogue and the Novel," (Kristeva 1986:35–61). On the historical development of the term, see Martin 2011.

the main body of the text. A *metatext*, in turn, refers to critical commentaries, glosses, and interpretive essays that lie *beyond* (*meta-*) the work, while an *architext* designates the generic markers that guide the reading *in principle* (*archi-*), markers that come first, have precedence and therefore provide the rule or program for interpretation. Finally, *hypertextuality*—the main focus of Genette's study—attends to the manners in which later works are connected to earlier works, that is, how the *hypertext* exists *on top of* (*hyper-*) the *hypotext* which persists *beneath* (*hypo-*). According to Genette, hypertextuality encompasses two major sub-types: indirect "imitations," for example, how Vergil's *Aeneid* recasts the Homeric epics; and direct "transformations," exemplified by the way Joyce's *Ulysses* revamps the *Odyssey*.[61]

The cogency of Genette's taxonomy relies on selecting a single prefix for each category. Of course, by his own admission, the list is hardly exhaustive. Moreover, the terms allow many overlaps and nuanced distinctions. Still, despite his unquenchable love for prefixed terms, what Genette's structural analyses overlook yet nonetheless admit, is the potential of two opposing prefixes operating simultaneously, that is, *paren-textual* practices in literary reception. By adducing the concept of parentextuality, the aim is not to replace Genette's categories or discount his astute and compelling analyses, but rather to complement them by sharpening the contours of the precedent and subsequent components under question. Hence, distinct from hypertextuality, which implies the hypotactic subordination of one text to another, parentextuality describes transtextual relationships that include but cannot be entirely reduced to imitations, transformations, and creative commentaries, nor to the subversive hypertexts like burlesque or parody. Granted, parody (παρῳδία) would appear to pertain well to what Joyce is doing, yet only when a prior text is held *alongside* and not *within* a present text. Parody, that is, does not sufficiently acknowledge the lateral text's *insertion*. As already mentioned, parentextuality is effectively closer to intertextuality. Tellingly, Quintilian reverts to the same prefix in translating the Greek parenthesis into the Latin term, *interpositio*, a "positing in the midst" (*Institutes of Oratory* 9, 3.23). Genette's account of intertextuality is helpful but only provided that "the actual presence of one text within another" is also understood as involving a kind of apartness or present absence, provided that the inserted text retains its sidelined qualities, that the parathetic is also acknowledged as enthetic.

The Latin prefix *inter-* is but an approximation of the doubled Greek prefix par-en, which more concretely expresses the dual status of the parenthesis as simultaneously and indissolubly external and internal. Other cases of the par-en prefix are illustrative. In addition to parenthesis, Quintilian provides the synonym παρέμπτωσις, a phrase that "falls" (πίπτει) within a discursive unit, which he translates as *interclusio*, a harsher intrusion that opens what is otherwise "closed" (*clauditur*). Whereas a parenthesis or

61 Genette 2018:6.

interpositio "places" (τίθει, *ponit*) a phrase within a sentence, a παρέμπτωσις or *interclusio* implies that the interruption comes from elsewhere, perhaps despite the author's control, an intervention that arrives at a distance and one that presumably engages more critically with the host.

The verbal form of parenthesis, παρεντίθημι is usually translated as "interpolate," meaning that an utterance of a different nature has been introduced into a statement while still retaining its difference, while the cognate noun παρενθήκη signifies a stray "addition": a piece of supplemental information, as when Herodotus apologizes for a digression on the Rhegians and Tarentines: ἀλλὰ τὰ μὲν κατὰ Ῥηγίνους τε καὶ Ταραντίνους τοῦ λόγου μοι παρενθήκη γένοε, "but those things relating to the Rhegians and Tarentines digressed [*parenthēkē genoe*] from my account" (*Histories* 7, 21.2). The *parenthēkē* may therefore refer to something one does during a pause or interval, for example, in Plutarch's description of the Roman general Pompey: ἑτέρας δὲ τοῦ πολέμου παρενθήκας ἐποιεῖτο καὶ τὸν χρόνον εἷλκεν, "And he occupied himself with other things [*parenthēkas*] during the interval of the war and dragged out his time" (*Pompey* 41).

Relatedly, the rare compound παρεμφέρω, "to bear what is apart within," occurs in the Longinian treatise *On the Sublime*:

> Ἔτι γε μὴν ἔσθ' ὅτε περὶ προσώπου διηγούμενος ὁ συγγραφεὺς ἐξαίφνης *παρενεχθεὶς* εἰς τὸ αὐτοπρόσωπον ἀντιμεθίσταται, καὶ ἔστι τὸ τοιοῦτον εἶδος ἐκβολή τις πάθους.
>
> *On the Sublime* 27.1

> Yet again at times a writer, while speaking about a character, suddenly impersonating [*parenechtheis*], changes into the character himself, and this sort of figure is some release of emotion.

In such fits of passion, the orator becomes an actor, the speech a dramatic performance.[62] the audience is thus faced with two semiotic systems, the verbal signs that constitute the message as well as the speaker himself who serves as a physical sign for the character represented—a double vision that registers one person as another without, however, dissolving the distinction between the two, all accomplished through the force of the *paren-* prefix.[63]

62 For an illustrative example, Pseudo-Longinus refers to *Iliad* 15.346–349, where the author assumes the voice of Hector—an effect that Pseudo-Plutarch explains as a slip from a "diegematic" to a "mimetic" mode (ἀπὸ γὰρ τοῦ διηγηματκοῦ μετέβαλεν εἰς τὸ μιμητικόν, *On Homer* 57.3). On ancient impersonation and its perceived effects, see Grethlein 2021:218–219.

63 For a semantic overview of the paren- prefix, see Schwyzer 1939:4–7.

By adducing something accessory, parentheses disrupt what is being presented yet also offer a means for negotiating one of the principal formal constraints of verbal description: *sequentiality*. Linguistic formulations unfold along a temporal line; and although sense is attained through the exercise of retention and protention, more than one unit of sense cannot occur at the same time. Grammatical arrangement cannot escape the line or γραμμή that produces meaning over a temporal continuum, as in prose, which proceeds straightforwardly (L. *prorsus*) from beginning to end. A parenthesis, however, precisely as a disjunctive constituent, allows an effective, even if only partial, solution to this timebound limitation, insofar as it intimates the coincident transmission of two or more thoughts.[64] To adopt the terms that Gotthold Ephraim Lessing famously employed in his essay on the *Laokoon* (1766), the parenthesis allows a *Nacheinander*, a sequential "one-after-the-other," to conjure the *Nebeneinander*, the spatial "one-beside-the-other" that is traditionally applied to the visual arts. Although, as many scholars have demonstrated, Lessing's terms are far from unproblematic, it is noteworthy that Joyce, at the head of the third episode of *Ulysses*, has Stephen Dedalus reflect on this explicit distinction while rambling on the strand, a meditation on the distinction between the "*nebeneinander*," which Stephen relates to the Aristotelian "ineluctable modality of the visible," and the "*nacheinander*," the "ineluctable modality of the audible" (*U* 3, 31).

The resultant simultaneity within a sequential process correlates to the functional value of the parenthesis, which is capable of placing two divergent thoughts beside each other without incorporating one into the grammatical order of the other. Hence, the figure is exceptionally versatile, expressing an emphatic interjection or fervid exclamation, an explicative addendum or apposite amplification, a qualification, a proviso, or limiting stimulation. A parenthetical remark may affirm the writer's position or mark critical distance. It can be interpreted as superfluous or pivotal, sincere or ironic, serious, comic, or bathetic. It can be read as a learned allusion, a passing comment, a fleeting aside, or a witty observation, summarily succinct or perplexingly digressive. Despite this demonstrable variety, John Lennard divides parenthesized clauses into two basic categories: on the one hand, a conventional usage, whereby the bracketed phrase is subordinate to the main sentence and plays a supporting role; and on the other hand, an exploitative usage, which is bolder, more emphatic, and at times blatantly antagonistic.[65] An entire novel's worth of affect can be neatly condensed into a brief parenthesis, as in one of the most well-known examples, the searing flash that jostles against Humbert Humbert's parrhesia in Nabokov's *Lolita*: "My very photogenic mother died in a freak accident (picnic, lightning) when I was three"[66]—a perverse epitaph, an

64 Cf. Schneider 2015:279.

65 Lennard 1991:25 et passim.

66 Vladimir Nabokov, *Lolita* [1955] (1970:10).

exhibition of emotional distance, or even perhaps a classical allusion: to the Heraclitean bolt that steered the narrator towards his criminal path or to the myth of Semele which would account for his Dionysian style.

Following Quintilian, classical rhetoricians have declined to regard the parenthesis as a *trope*, which changes the meaning of a word or phrase, and have instead treated it as a verbal figure or *schema*, which merely changes the order of words. Accordingly, the parenthesis is often understood merely as a species of *hyperbaton*, a "transposition," something that "steps over" (ὑπερβαίνει) the bounds of conventional syntax, employed particularly for the sake of emphasis, as in "This task I must do"; or as a type of *anacolouthon*, an inconsistent or anomalous change from one grammatical sequence to another, a non sequitur or rejection of the expected "path" (κέλευθος), often used to represent perplexity or an overwrought emotional state, as in the oft-cited passage from Shakespeare's *King Lear*, where the confused monarch berates his daughters, Gonerel and Regan:

> No, you unnatural hags,
> I will have such revenges on you both,
> That all the world shall—I will do such things—
> What they are yet I know not, but they shall be
> The terrors of the Earth!
>
> *King Lear*, II.iv

Yet, analogous to the way it allows paradigmatic simultaneity within a syntagmatic sequence, the parenthesis also collates the distinct functions of trope and schema. Although the purely syntactic nature of the parenthesis was prominent in rhetorical treatises, metaphorical usages are already discernible among English writers beginning around 1600. In Ben Jonson's satirical comedy, *Every Man out of his Humour* (1599), one reads: "I ne'er knew Tabacco taken as a parenthesis before." A century and a half later, in *Fanny Hill: Memoirs of a Woman of Pleasure* (1748)—a work notoriously recognized as the first English pornographic novel, penned by John Cleland while serving time in a London debtor's prison—one finds: "Charles, give me an account, interrupted by many a sweet parenthesis of kisses, of the success of his measures."[67] In both cases, *parenthesis* serves as a metaphor for a temporary interval, a hiatus or break from ordinary, level-headed activity. In other European languages, while the strictly literal-syntactic sense abides, the trope is also prominent, though with somewhat different connotations. For example the French *parenthèse* and the Spanish *paréntesis*

67 The citations are taken from the *Oxford English Dictionary*, s.v. "parenthesis."

may be used figuratively to denote a "digression" or a "break" from arduous work, while the Italian plural *parentesi* may designate an "extended pause."

Paradigms

A consideration of parentextual effects would demonstrably enhance the study of classical reception. To begin, parentextuality would appear to temper the opposition between aestheticist and historicist viewpoints which has come to characterize many ongoing debates.[68] Precisely through the positing of what is simultaneously both outside and in, the parenthetic form negotiates a pure aestheticism, which argues for the continued relevance of antiquity in modernity, with the claims of strict historicism, which insists that the past remains utterly separate from the present. Most recently, a renewed focus on exemplarity has served a similar purpose. Appealing to time-honored examples within modern contexts betrays a parenthetic form insofar as paradigmatic content from long ago is made to bear on current situations. That is to say, An exemplum is always a part of and apart from the receptive moment, a text that, as Simon Goldhill describes it, "interrupts the context of the present with the claim as an elsewhere and another time."[69] The dynamics of exemplarity demonstrate how classical reception "requires an explicit hypostatization—which need not be positive—of a particular past; it requires a sense that the present is disrupted from the past, while it is also genealogically linked to it, and that the present needs this ancient past to find itself; it needs its sense of untimeliness to find self-expression."[70] The mechanism may be elaborated. For Constanze Güthenke, the exemplar's claim is produced through modern acts of selection, "a mode of knowing and of organizing knowledge of the past," and thus discloses a "double ontology"—singular yet repeatable, here but also there, particular yet universal.[71] The gesture towards universal applicability, however, although afforded by the exemplum, is also undermined by it. For an exemplum is but a single element within a set that exhibits a recurrent feature and only in this sense can it represent a general characteristic of that set. Hence, paradeigma, taken as a Greek synonym of the Latin *exemplum*, translates into "pattern," a pattern that emerges through the recognized likeness between what is prior and what is presently existent. An exemplum or *paradeigma* has the capacity to make something discernible and intelligible, in a manner, moreover, as Aristotle emphasizes, that differs from both deductive and inductive methods:

68 For a useful account of the historicist-aestheticist divide, see Hiscock 2020:323–324.

69 Goldhill 2017:422.

70 Goldhill 2017:424.

71 Güthenke 2020:49–52.

Φανερὸν οὖν ὅτι τὸ παράδειγμά ἐστιν οὔτε ὡς μέρος πρὸς ὅλον οὔτε ὡς ὅλον πρὸς μέρος, ἀλλ' ὡς μέρος πρὸς μέρος, ὅταν ἄμφω μὲν ᾖ ὑπὸ ταὐτό, γνώριμον δὲ θάτερον.

Prior Analytics 2.25, 69a15–16

It is therefore evident that the paradeigma exists neither as part to whole nor as whole to part, but rather as part to part, where both fall under the same while one is known more than the other.

Whereas induction entails the movement from the particular instance to the universal rule and deduction from the universal to the particular, the paradigm entails a third approach, based on the relationship from particular to particular.[72] Unlike an axiom, which is presumed to subsist in an eternal, non-contingent realm where it exerts external authority from without, the paradigm persists as a part apart, that is, as something from a historical *without* that operates historically *within* the material under present consideration.

Although the example gives the rule by being removed from a past corpus, it nonetheless still belongs to that corpus, or in the words of Giorgio Agamben, it is "excluded through the exhibition of its inclusion."[73] *Paradeigma* may therefore also be translated as a "legal precedent," a guiding example from a previous, singular case that pertains to the singular case at hand, participating in the current proceedings as a component that is, however, not directly involved. It is on this basis that paradigms can be understood as suspending the referential function accorded to personal communication. In language instruction, for instance, morphological paradigms are rehearsed without being understood as subjective statements. The student who recites *amo, amavi, amabo* in the classroom is or at least is not presumed to be personally expressing a present, past, and future love in this world, no more than one expects to reside in an architectural blueprint rather than in the house that has actually been constructed.

Typically by way of citation, the exemplum or paradeigma consists in a manifestation (δεῖξις) of what persists off to the side (παρά). The paradigm points away from itself (παραδείκνυσιν), operating as a present sign that evokes a non-presence, a *praesentia in absentia*, which, again, fully correlates to the parenthetic mode. Yet whereas exemplarity in the conventional sense implies willful adaptation and profitable application, the parentextual encounter of past and present tends not to harmonize. On the contrary,

72 For a concise overview and discussion, see Agamben 2009:9–32. The passage from Aristotle's *Prior Analytics* is cited on p. 19.

73 Agamben 2009:24.

parenthetic interference causes a disjunction, even if by way of conjunction, a disjunction, in turn, that accords with modernist notions of progress or development, as well as a post-modernist suspicion of grand narratives. Certainly, in ancient historiography, motivated by different conceptions of temporality, the exemplum is often beset by contingencies and read as disjunctive, as a failure of contemporary acts to measure up to prior achievements.[74] Precisely as a parenthesis, the paradigmatic instance resists integration. With the mutual qualification of past and present—of what is *para* and what is felt to be *en*—the parenthetic form troubles any straightforward, positive use. Analogies and affinities are suggested, but only through delimitation, only insofar as the suggestiveness remains bracketed.

The effect is discernible across Joyce's *Ulysses*, where productive failures are generated by an inordinate number of allusions, insinuations, and provocations, a legion of references to learned, scientific, artistic, and popular materials from multiple cultures and epochs. Truant lines of meaning compound with dizzying effect and can hardly be reduced to either Hellenic or Hebraic exempla. Accordingly, Ariela Freedman remarks that Bloom's alternative Biblical scheme "is not meant to displace the Homeric analogue, or simply to undercut it humorously. Rather, it is meant to indicate that the narrative contains multitudes, numerous doors left open for alternate schemas, parallactic texts, and parallel universes."[75] Myriad keys to a plethora of doors and limitless passageways. A narrative at once realist and porous, intersected at every point by lines leading to echoic correspondences, near and far, both clearly and vaguely. As Joyce famously quipped, "I've put in so many enigmas and puzzles that it will keep the professors busy for centuries arguing over what I meant."[76] Specifically as an act of reception, the novel constitutes a receptacle as inexhaustible as the legendary sack of Fortunatus, as a site for swarms of parasites—for noisome disturbances or useless superfluities or raucous guests who, like the *parasitus* of Roman Comedy, are the life of the party. In sum, the novel forms a voluminous vessel for the piles of indissoluble fragments that are contained between the brackets of the book's blue cover.

Rather than attempt to provide a comprehensive account of practices that by definition elude comprehensive integration, the subsequent chapters present a series of illustrative, if not exemplary, episodes from twentieth-century German literature and philosophy, where a long Philhellenic tradition had come into serious question. particular focus falls on four major figures: Martin Heidegger, Theodor Adorno, Günter Grass, and Paul Celan—writers who represent the *period* as well as its critical *disruptions*. Throughout, attention is paid to their varied engagements with antiquity and the mutual

74 See Grethlein 2011.

75 Freedman2009:68.

76 Cited in Ellmann 1982:521.

confrontations these engagements inspire, with a focus on the nuanced seams that at once import material and sustain its extraneousness—moments that should prove to be especially fruitful for investigating the ramifications of parenthetic interferences in reception history overall.

Chapter 2

Philology in a Destitute Time

Epiphanies

Throughout *Ulysses*, Bloom and Stephen wander across Dublin like uncanny Doppelgänger, each matching the other in their desultory movements as in a mirror, until they finally collide in Nighttown. With their "parallel courses" having united (*U* 17, 544), they wend their way back to the kitchen where Bloom set off earlier that morning over a pan of pork kidneys. Unlike his Homeric parallel, Bloom does not truly return home because he never left his home city, at least not in the physical sense. Regardless, he arrives back with his Telemachian counterpart, Stephen, and the two, still mirroring each other, engage more in an adversarial confrontation than a charitable conversation.

A reflection furnishes a parallel image, a two-dimensional representation, but otherwise fairly accurate, which moves alongside the reflected figure. Yet the replicated surfaces and movements only obtain provided the mirror's plane is not breached. In attempting to unite with the specular image, one risks shattering the glass.[1] Damage ensues when the parallels intersect, when the *para* is also *en*. The collision of Bloom and Stephen thus actualizes the programmatic metaphor given at the very head of the novel where, glaring at Buck Mulligan's shaving mirror, Stephen quipped: "A symbol of Irish art. The cracked lookingglass of a servant" (*U* 1, 6).

The conception of art as a mirror is, of course, a long and hallowed tradition, most famously presented in Book 10 of Plato's *Republic*, to rekindle what Socrates refers to as "the ancient quarrel between poetry and philosophy" (παλαιά τις διαφορὰ φιλοσοφίᾳ τε καὶ ποιητικῇ, *Republic* 10, 607b). The confrontation between poetic traditions and rational critique amounts to an act of reception, yet one that constitutes a troubling interruption. At times with imperious force, time-honored texts impinge on the present day, suspend proceedings, and call for an interpretation that accords with contemporary understanding and current horizons of sense. In order to proceed, reception necessitates a translation that would negotiate the fundamental "difference" or "variance" (διαφορά)

1 See Steven Connor's provocative reflections (2015).

between the two types of discourse, the poetic and the philosophic. More specifically, the translative management consists in taking the *what-is* of the past and conceiving it in terms of a present-day *what-for*. Hence, Socrates' interrogation of poets in absentia turns on the general question of purpose: *What are poets for?*

The query is rather pernicious: first, because it has already been raised and settled earlier, with the conclusion that poetry, which should play an educative role, must be tightly regulated and that poets who purvey falsehoods and distractions, however brilliant and pleasurable they may be, have no place in the ideal city (*Republic* 3, 398a–b); and second, because, in rehearsing the question, Socrates intends to place mimesis itself on trial. It is here that the charge is made, that art merely reflects nature, that the artist or craftsman (δημιουργός) need only take a mirror (κάτοπτρον) and carry it about everywhere (*Republic* 10, 596d), which suggests that all art, including poetry, only reproduces phenomena (φαινόνενα), that is, how things appear (φαίνονται) and "indeed not what they are in truth" (οὐ μέντοι ὄντα γέ που τῇ ἀληθείᾳ, 596e). Whereas a manufactured couch, modeled on a transcendent form, serves a clear purpose, a painting of a couch or a poetic representation of one provides no physical repose. Thrice-removed from truth, art appears to be useless.

In its most basic sense, the concept of utility posits a subject who proves capable of converting any object, natural or manufactured, into an instrument. To formulate it in grammatical terms, a subject in the nominative case lords over an object in the accusative. The case system as developed by Hellenistic grammarians in the third century BCE was conceived hierarchically, explicitly as a "fall" (πτῶσις, *casus*), as a "turning away" (*declinatio*), downwards, from the top-ranking nominative to the lowest-ranking accusative, a hierarchy, moreover, that fully correlates with Platonic metaphysics. According to the *Commentaries* by Ammonius (ca. 435–517 CE), Aristotle did not even consider the nominative to be a "case" at all, since it names being before any grammatical *fall*.[2] Unfallen, then, nominative subjects seem warranted to make use of accusative objects that fall before them. To doubt, then, the usefulness of poetry and art, to question their instrumental availability, leads to two related consequences: an interrogation of art's ontological status as merely phenomenal, not real, and thus a challenge to the subject's presumed mastery, for what is a subject without a corresponding object?

The twentieth-century turn to phenomenology, founded and elaborated by Edmund Husserl, offers an important critique that undermines the validity of the subject-object dichotomy. It disputes the utter separation between the subject who views and the objects viewed. Rather than maintain a *nominative-accusative* structure, phenomenological description, with its precise focus on perceptual experience, ostensibly deals with the oblique cases, the *genitive* and the *dative*, insofar as a phenomenon is

2 Ammonius, *On Aristotle's Categories* 1a12.16–24 (1991:32).

always an appearance *of* something *for* someone.[3] In this regard, the phenomenon is parenthetic: a manifestation of things which is simultaneously *para* and *en*, outside of consciousness and within.

Parenthetic, but not parenthetical, for as Husserl explains, in order to recognize phenomena as such it is necessary to exercise an *epochē*, a "suspension," "abstention," or "bracketing" of what he calls the "natural attitude" (*natürliche Einstellung*). The natural attitude proceeds by way of unquestioned assumptions, takes existence for granted, and most especially tends to view particular objects with a subjectively willful purpose, an intention that prevents phenomena to appear as phenomena. In the *epochē*, Husserl breaks free of the usual, goal-oriented engagement with things, he brackets out the "always already" aspect of the world and thereby regards it afresh.

> I abstain from "living into" the world (suffering, doing), into the constantly perceived world, being interested in things, being busy with them, planning something with them, being awake, being active, living in the world as always performing new acts, always planning something new, taking up old plans again, pursuing interests that one already has, creating new interests—in the world that is always already in existence.[4]

By bracketing out our plans for things, the phenomenologist teaches us to see.

Husserl demands that we should not rest content with the natural attitude, which he describes as a kind of blindness, but rather allow the *epochē* to open a "reflexive attitude," a "disposition" or "mindset" (*Einstellung*) that "bends back" upon itself, as in a mirror yet in a way that attends to the intentional act itself, an adjustment that is less concerned with *what* is seen and more absorbed in *how* one perceives. The German *Einstellung* is closely synonymous with διάθεσις, which the Hellenistic grammarians employed to refer to verbal "voice"—active, middle, or passive; and the reflexivity that Husserl calls for reminds us that the term *phenomenon* derives from a participle in the Greek middle voice, from φαίνεσθαι, "to appear," in contrast to the active φαίνειν, "to cause to appear" or "give light." In general, the middle voice expresses an action

3 Cf. Zahavi 2003:98.

4 "Ich enthalte mich meines in die Welt, in die ständig warhnehmungsmäßige Welt „Hineinlebens" (leidend, tuend), für Dinge interessiert-, mit ihnen beschäftigt-sein, mit ihnen etwas vorhaben, wach sein, aktiv sein, in der Welt leben als immer neue Akte vollziehen, immer wieder Neues vorhaben, alte Vorhaben wieder aufnehmen, Interessen, die man schon hat, verfolgen, neue Interessen stiften—in der Welt, der immerfort schon seiend geltenden." Edmund Husserl, *Die Krisis der europäischen Wissenschaften und die transzendentale Phänomenologie* [posth. 1954] (1962:470). Although this appendix does not appear in the standard English translation, one may consult §39 ("The peculiar character of the transcendental epochē as a total change of the natural attitude of life") in *The Crisis of European Sciences and Transcendental Philosophy* (1970:148).

that simultaneously redounds to the agent, one that concerns or implicates the subject. For example, the verb for "giving" in the active (δίδωμι) denotes "ransoming" in the middle, a giving in order to be given someone or something in return. The act of "planning" or "devising" (βουλεύω), when inflected in the middle voice, signifies "deliberate" or "consider for oneself," while ἄρχω, which can be used to describe the active sense of "ruling" or the passive sense of "being ruled," in its middle form means to "begin." It is noteworthy, in this regard, that the verb of "perceiving," αἰσθάνομαι, only occurs in the middle voice, which underscores how in acts of perception the perceived impinges on the percipient's consciousness, how in touching the world we are simultaneously touched by it, medially.[5]

Husserl's most famous student, Martin Heidegger, broaches this fundamental distinction in §7 of *Being and Time* (1927), on "the concept of the phenomenon," by translating the active-voice φαίνειν as "to bring to the light of day" (*an den Tag bringen*) and "to put into brightness" (*in die Helle stellen*), which stress the "bright light" (φάος or φῶς) at the root of the verb, while rendering the middle-voice φαίνεσθαι reflexively as "to show itself" (*sich zeigen*).[6] Heidegger, whose habilitation thesis (1915) employed Husserlian concepts to explicate the thirteenth-century *Grammatica speculativa* of Duns Scotus, astutely distinguishes between the active and middle voices rather than the active and passive, which is the modern convention. In this regard, it is noteworthy that Heidegger's translations of the active form both feature prepositional phrases with the accusative case (*an den Tag, in die Helle*), which underscores how the active voice typically involves a relationship between nominative subjects and accusative objects, a system that correlates to the active-passive distinction that marks the difference between "the doer" and "the done to."[7] In contrast, the middle voice evades the strict division between subjects and objects, to the point where the nominative agent is coincident with the accusative object, as in Heidegger's translation, *sich zeigen*, which denotes how something shows itself, reflexively, as in a mirror, yet a reflection that occurs within.

In attending to the medial disposition—its diathesis, its *Einstellung*, its voice—phenomenology dismantles the nominative-accusative polarity which deludedly proffers that the world is an object under the subject's control, that everything is measurable and knowable, available for use and abuse, manipulation and exploitation, that subjective action can be effective without simultaneously being affected. With an eye trained solely on utility, efficiency and efficacy, one closes off other forms of questioning, one fails to open oneself up to thinking and confront what is not pre-determined, not useful and therefore, perhaps, fruitful. Poetry and art may still to some extent hold a mirror up

5 On the middle voice in relation to Husserlian phenomenology, see Hogrebe 2020.

6 Martin Heidegger, *Sein und Zeit* [1927] (1993:28) [*Being and Time* (1962:51)].

7 Peradotto 1990:133.

to natural and societal reality, it may still present an image that runs parallel to the experiential world, yet in transgressing the threshold that would maintain its distinctness, art and poetry become *disclosive*, not merely *world-reflecting*, where reality is presumed to be the a priori model for the work, but rather *world-creating*, with art showing itself capable of revealing essential aspects of experience not otherwise perceptible.[8] Analogous to the cosmological vision in Lucretius, the cosmos remains timelessly inert until the series of atoms, which fall like raindrops in parallel and separate lines, suffer an unpredictable swerve (*clinamen*), an interference or collision or *declination* that generates the world of forms in time (*De rerum natura* 2, 216–224).

Verbs "decline" by way of conjugations, by means of an enclisis (ἔγκλισις) that converts the absolute sense of a word into meanings that apply to perceived reality. The grammatical term ἔγκλισις παρεμφατικός is therefore the common name for the *indicative* mood, where the dual *paren-* prefix marks the verb *parenthetically*, as an "utterance in itself" (ἐν + φῆσις) that simultaneously indicates qualities which lie "in addition" or "alongside" (παρά), namely, the conjugated limitations of person, number, tense, voice and mood. A verb that neglects to provide these supplementary coordinates is consequently designated by an alpha-privative as an ἔγκλισις ἀπαρεμφατικός, which Latin grammarians translated as the *modus infinitivus*, the infinitive form stripped of all the ancillary information that would bind it to finite specificity. As Heidegger expounds it in his 1935 seminar, *Einfürhung in die Metaphysik* (*Introduction to Metaphysics*, publ. 1953), the infinitive, explicitly as an enklisis aparemphatikos, detracts the verbal function of "bringing things to appearance" (*zum Vorschein bringen*).[9] Confronting the phenomenon, as it appears in the world, not only implies a medial disposition but also one that is emphatically *paremphatic*.

The spirit of Husserl's phenomenological concerns, including Heidegger's subsequent grammatical elaboration of the same, are hardly limited to philosophical meditations but rather relate to broader trends in the early twentieth century, which challenge the human subject's intellectual hegemony over a purportedly objective and presumably stable reality. Advances in physics, mathematics, psychology, and sociology, which unmask fields of existence that evade conventional comprehensibility, correspond with literary and artistic endeavors that grapple with profound flux, with a world that does not stand still, an autonomous world that cannot be adequately captured by linguistic expression, one that rebuffs the subject's own attempts to maintain autonomy while caught in the maelstrom of urbanization and consumerism, secularization and nationalism, mass industrialization and bureaucratic disenchantment.

8 Stephen Halliwell traces the persistent tension between world-reflection and world-creation throughout the ancient history of mimesis (2002:118–148).

9 Martin Heidegger, *Einführung in die Metaphysik* (1953:51–52) [*An Introduction to Metaphysics* (1974:67–69)].

Joyce's early formulation of the *epiphany*, quite evidently cognate with Husserl's medial *phenomena*, addresses this newly perceived milieu.[10] Given its traditional theological import, which concerns the illuminating revelation of a deity, the showing forth of a god (ἐπιφάνεια), as well as its esteemed Romantic and post-Romantic pedigree, the epiphany is poised to re-enchant, albeit in a thoroughly secular manner. In *Stephen Hero*, an early draft of *A Portrait of the Artist as a Young Man* (1916), the epiphany is described as "a sudden spiritual manifestation, whether in the vulgarity of speech or of gesture or in a memorable phase of the mind itself," causing a recognition "that is that thing which it is," whereby "its soul, its whatness leaps to us from the vestment of its appearance," a quidditas captured in a moment "most delicate and evanescent"[11]—not as an accusative object subordinate to the instrumental will of a subject, but rather as an appearance *of* something *for* someone. The epiphany was Joyce's attempt to see without subjective presuppositions, to let things come into appearance without purposive designs.[12]

Joyce's epiphanies overlap with his brief stay in Paris. He arrived in the French capital on December 1, 1902 —the twenty-year-old's first trip abroad, arranged with the intention of studying medicine. A few months earlier, the burgeoning German poet, Rainer Maria Rilke, seven years Joyce's senior, had likewise taken up residence in Paris, explicitly to prepare a monograph on the sculptor Auguste Rodin. The experience would inspire Rilke's first and only novel, *Die Aufzeichnungen des Malte Laurids Brigge* (*The Notebooks of Malte Laurids Brigge*, 1910), which places his protagonist, an aspiring Danish poet, in the Latin Quarter, in the rue Toullier, only a few streets away from Joyce's residence in the rue Corneille. Staying in Paris at the same time, Joyce unwittingly lived alongside Rilke and his fictional double, forming parallel courses that never met yet nonetheless shared an open disposition for epiphanic revelation:

> I am learning to see. I don't know why it is, but everything enters me more deeply and doesn't stop where it once used to. I have an interior that I never knew of. Everything passes into it now. I don't know what happens there.[13]

The resemblances between Joyce's and Rilke's aesthetic enterprises outweigh the differences in articulation and tone. Both offer a substantial illustration of Husserl's

10 For a full discussion, see Fournier 2018.

11 James Joyce, *Stephen Hero* (pub. posth., 1963:211). For a comprehensive volume of examples with notes and commentary, see MacDuff, McFadzean, and Beja, eds. 2024.

12 See Ziolkowski 1961 and Beja 1971:71–111.

13 Rainer Maria Rilke, *The Notebooks of Malte Laurids Brigge* [1910] (1990:5). "Ich lerne sehen. Ich weiß nicht, woran es liegt, es geht alles tiefer in mich ein und bleibt nicht an der Stelle stehen, wo es sonst immer zu Ende war. Ich habe ein Inneres, von dem ich nicht wußte. Alles geht dorthin. Ich weiß nicht, was dort geschieht" (1930:vol. 2, 9).

phenomenological approach to seeing reality as if for the first time, an approach that weakens the subject's capacity both for self-knowledge and instrumental reason, a disposition in the midst of things which breaks with the traditional mimetic program and instead gives the initiative to things and the words they evoke.[14]

Paralysis

> Every night as I gazed up at the window I said softly to myself the word paralysis.
>
> —James Joyce, *Dubliners*

With phenomenology, the ancient quarrel between philosophy and poetry appears to be overcome; for both manners of discourse are hereby shown to participate in world-disclosive reflection. Other contemporary projects attend a related program, including above all Ernst Cassirer's *Philosophy of Symbolic Forms* (1923–1929). Throughout, it is demonstrated that both philosophy and poetry exhibit a medial disposition, that both proceed along similar paths.

It is perhaps for this reason that, on December 29, 1926, the writing of poetry and the act of thinking, *Dichten und Denken*, suffered a paralyzing setback. In the early morning hours of this winter's day, at the Clinique Valmont, a sanatorium nestled in the Swiss Alpine landscape of Glion-sur-Montreux, Rainer Maria Rilke passed away gently in the arms of his doctor. Three days later, on the New Year, Martin Heidegger learned of the poet's death while paying a visit to Karl Jaspers in Heidelberg. It had been Heidegger's intention to finish correcting the galleys of the first volume of *Sein und Zeit*, as well as complete the draft of the project's continuation; but that plan suddenly came to a halt. Fourteen years later, in 1941, during his lecture course on the *Metaphysics of German Idealism*, Heidegger interrupted his conceptual presentation to recount what happened:

> (The decision to break off the publication [of *Sein und Zeit*] was made on the day when the news of R. M. Rilke's death reached us. —Certainly, at the time I was of the opinion that over the course of the year I could say everything more clearly. That was a delusion.) [15]

[14] Robert Weninger outlines the many parallels between the two authors (2012).

[15] "(Der Entschluß zum Abbruch der Veröffentlichung wurde gefaßt an dem Tage, als uns die Nachricht vom Tode R. M. Rilkes traf. – Allerdings war ich damals der Meinung, übers Jahr schon alles deutlicher sagen zu können. Das war eine Täuschung.)" Martin Heidegger, *Die Metaphysik des deutschen Idealismus* (1991:40).

The casual remark to his students, sequestered within a parenthesis, is striking. Heidegger's terseness and the light cover of the passive voice, the misguided conviction and the acknowledged self-deception—all invite conjecture. What purpose, we might ask, does this parenthesis serve?

The bracketed reminiscence poses at least three principal questions.

The first is *intrinsic*: How should we read the coincidence, in 1927, between Rilke's death and Heidegger's decision to stop writing? Is the relation causal or are the two events merely fortuitous? Is the intrusion from real life simply accidental or does it not, perhaps, point to something more essential, something more substantive in regard to the philosophical work?

The second question is *extrinsic*: How does this personal anecdote connect to the 1941 lecture in which it is recounted? Is the autobiographical information useful, meant to illustrate the matter under discussion, or is it just a curious digression, possibly seductive, which may lead us down a false path or *Holzweg*? Incidental or not, it appears that both questions, the intrinsic and the extrinsic, entail an interruption of sorts. Just as the death announcement in 1927 interfered with Heidegger's publishing agenda, so does the personal recollection in 1941 detain the philosophical presentation at hand. Just as Rilke's passing co-occurred with the suspension of Heidegger's project, so does the recollection of this postponement, fourteen years later, temporarily delay the professor's explication of German Idealism.

The brief story from 1941 about an interruption in the past thus interrupts the philosophical argument, which leads to a third question: How do these two disruptions relate to each other? Are they thematically analogous, somehow complementary, or are they merely structurally similar?

The complexity lies in the general nature of parentheses, whose double aspect, at once in and off to the side, makes it difficult to ascertain how the bracketed contents relate to the main argument. Is Heidegger willfully trying to confuse us or be obscure? What are the grounds for this encapsulated account, which ventures to overstep the very boundaries of the discourse in which it is embedded? Does the anecdote offer anything more than a simple case of synchronicity, a somewhat uncanny concurrence, a *by-the-way* that Heidegger pauses to say on the way to thinking?

On the face of things, the interruption in 1941 is perfectly justified. Within the context of his lecture on the "concept of existence," the parenthesized anecdote helps Heidegger explain why his mode of ontological inquiry became subject to gross misinterpretation. The reason, he claims, is quite simple: He never published the subsequent parts of *Being and Time* because by early 1927, he came to the realization that his draft for the continuation of *Being and Time* was "insufficient" (*unzureichend*). If only he had persisted, he might have pre-empted the confusion that followed. Heidegger then interrupts himself with the inserted aside that he shelved the project on the day he learned of Rilke's death. Yet it is unclear whether this news directly led Heidegger to recognize his project's insufficiency or whether his present recollection of that sad day might remedy the failure. Perhaps Rilke's passing gave Heidegger sufficient reason for thinking differently, a *zureichender Grund* for a project deemed *unzureichend.* The question now is not, *What is the poet for?* But rather, *What is the poet's death for?* What ground might it supply, for pursuing a different track or even for making a turn?

However one reads the relation or non-relation between Rilke's death and Heidegger's project, the turn to this autobiographical episode is odd insofar as Heidegger opened this very lecture by warning explicitly against conflating the concept of existence with ontic notions of human "subjectivity" and "personality." Thinking, Heidegger just insisted, must be directed towards Being and not towards the personality of the thinker. The philosopher's life must be bracketed out in considering the philosopher's work. And yet, despite this programmatic statement, it is not long before he disrupts his lecture on German Idealism with a bracketed account from his personal life.

Scholars often assert that Heidegger consistently discouraged appeals to biography in philosophical investigations. Evidence is invariably taken from the introductory lecture to his course on the *Basic Concepts of Aristotelian Philosophy*, held during the summer semester of 1924 at Marburg: "Regarding the personality of a philosopher, this alone is of interest: he was born at such and such a time, he worked and died."[16] The particular circumstances of the thinker's life are taken to be inconsequential, irrelevant for understanding what is being thought since, in a medial-phenomenological mode, the thinker is not a master subject in full control any more than the matter of thinking is a controllable object. All the same, for later critics of Heidegger, divorcing the philosopher's work from his personal history can only be seen as a ruse. The political stakes, needless to say, are high. Should one dismiss the news of Rilke's death as an insignificant coincidence in regard to the trajectory of Heidegger's thinking, then one might go so far as to feel justified in separating all of Heidegger's work from the circumstances of his life, including, above all, his complicity with the National Socialist regime. To this day, Heidegger's many detractors would argue otherwise. That Heidegger's parenthetical reminiscence occurs in 1941 should alone give one serious pause. Even if, or especially because, Heidegger would reject seeing any causal link between his work and his personal life, the fact that he inscribes an autobiographical remark, parenthetically, in the midst of his lecture, should be taken into account. After all, what Heidegger wants to bracket out, still appears, even if it only appears in brackets. An *epochē* is performed, not merely so that one may regard a matter more purely or openly, but also with the result that what is bracketed stands out in full view, hiding in plain sight.

16 "Bei der Persönlichkeit eines Philosophen hat nur das Interesse: Er war dann und dann geboren, er arbeitete und starb." Heidegger, *Grundbegriffe der aristotelischen Philosophie* (2002:5). [*Basic Concepts of Aristotelian Philosophy* (2009: 4; translation modified)].

From a certain perspective, insofar as a parenthesis constitutes some kind of intrusion, the news of Rilke's death has always been parenthetical: first concretely, in 1927, at the moment when Heidegger abandoned his plans; and then as a memory, in 1941, at the moment when he digressed from his lecture. In both the recounted episode and the recounting, Rilke's death, including the impact it might or might not have had on Heidegger's personal life, infringes on thinking. But what, then, can this interruption tell us about the connection between poetry and thinking, *Dichten und Denken*, or, for that matter, between thinking and life or thinking and death?

Foundations

> I have nothing against ontology, but I have never had toward that which presents itself under this name anything but questions, reservations, very conditional hypotheses, interminable parentheses.
>
> —Jacques Derrida, "We Other Greeks"

Regarding the personality of a philosopher, this alone is of interest: he was born at such and such a time, he worked and died. As mentioned, Heidegger's oft-cited restriction on biographical criticism appears in the introductory session of his 1924 course on Aristotle's fundamental concepts or *Grundbegriffe*. The opening methodological comment on Aristotle's life is intended to dissuade his students from striving to construct a coherent philosophical system based on the notion that the philosopher exerted complete technical control over his concepts. Instead, Heidegger wants to investigate how many of Aristotle's terms came to be formed from words that already existed in customary usage and how this common usage, rooted in a distinctively Greek experience, continued to qualify the terminological usage in essential ways. Heidegger thus endorses an approach that is distinct from conventional philosophy:

> What must be seen [*Es muß gesehen werden*] is the *ground* [or *soil*: *Boden*] out of which these fundamental concepts have grown, and *how* they have grown, i.e., the fundamental concepts should be considered in their *specific conceptuality*, so that we may ask, *how the matters themselves meant here are seen, whereupon they are addressed, in which way they are determined.* If we bring this point of view to bear on the matter, we shall enter into the setting [*Milieu*] that is meant by concept and conceptuality. The fundamental concepts are to be understood in regard to their conceptuality, and specifically with the purpose [*Absicht*] of *gaining insight into the fundamental demands of all scholarly research.* Here, it is not philosophy being offered or even a history of philosophy. If *philology* means: *the passion for knowledge of what*

has been expressed [*and of what expresses itself*], then what we are doing is philology.[17]

The phenomenological thrust of these remarks is evident. The concepts that are to be examined—"the matters themselves," *die Sachen selbst*—must be allowed to show themselves. This passive imperative—*es muß gesehen werden* ("it must be seen")—cannot be accomplished by regarding Aristotle's key terms solely as abstract expressions that are cognitively deployed and instrumentally managed by the philosopher. Rather, the words must be seen as subsisting within a concrete context and possessing a certain degree of agency. In Heidegger's view, the aim is not *philosophical* but rather *philological* insofar as it engages in a reading that directs us towards the midst of things, towards the living *milieu*, where we may attend to the very soil that underlies and nourishes philosophical research. It enables us to draw closer to what Aristotle confronted, to enter upon the path that his thinking has opened up for us. We must detect not simply meaning but rather grasp the manner by which meaning initially came to be formed. The *How* is more important than the *What*. As Heidegger underscores throughout the lecture course, we are too distant from the being-in-the-world that pervades Aristotle's language. Motivated by nostalgia, we must approach the distinctive soil that gave rise to the concepts that appear in his texts; we must draw near to the original Greek experience of Being; and we must do so, finally, from our own historical position, motivated by philology, by "the passion for knowledge of what has been expressed and of what expresses itself."

For Heidegger, the task of the translator does not simply consist in transposing concepts from one language into another. Rather, it is the translator who must be translated, transported into a foreign domain of experience, while remaining aware of the gap that prevents any perfect, transparent translation.[18] The dismissal of the thinker's biography and personality, therefore, does not reject the role of history or especially the meaning that history should have for us. On the contrary, the philological aim is most

[17] "Es muß gesehen werden der *Boden*, aus dem diese Grundbegriffe erwachsen, und *wie* sie erwachsen sind, d.h., die Grundbegriffe sollen betrachtet werden auf ihre *spezifische Begrifflichkeit*, so daß wir fragen, *wie die da gemeinten Sachen selbst gesehen sind, woraufhin sie angesprochen werden, in welcher Weise sie bestimmt sind.* Wenn wir diese Gesichtspunkte an die Sache heranbringen, werden wir in das Milieu dessen gelangen, was mit Begriff und Begrifflichkeit gemeint ist. Die Grundbegriffe sind im Hinblick auf ihre Begrifflichkeit zu verstehen, und zwar in der Absicht, *Einblick zu gewinnen in die Grunderfordernisse jeglicher wissenschaftlichen Forschung.* Es wird hier *keine Philosophie* oder gar Philosophiegeschichte geboten. Wenn *Philologie* besagt: die *Leidenschaft der Erkenntnis des Ausgesprochenen* [*und des Sichaussprechens*], dann ist das, was wir treiben, Philologie." Heidegger, *Grundbegriffe* (2002:4 and 333; emphasis in text). The bracketed phrase is taken from Heidegger's handwritten note.

[18] See Heidegger's remarks in his 1942/1943 lectures on *Parmenides* (1982:16).

emphatically *our* aim, *our* passion. It encourages us, rather, to read what is there in its being-there within the limits of our own facticity, which together comprise the "hermeneutic situation." Philology, Heidegger would say, is *historical* without being *historiographical*. It does not strive to accumulate information objectively and neutrally in a technical, calculating manner.[19] Instead, philology proceeds as an impassioned enterprise that remains fully aware of its "presuppositions," including above all a pronounced "faith in history," by which "we presuppose that *history and the historical past, insofar as the way is made clear for it, have the possibility of giving a jolt to the present or, better, to the future*."[20] For Heidegger, this collision of the present and the past is precisely what motivates the "passion"—the *Leidenschaft*—that is philology.

Thus, Heidegger reiterates his approach:

> The lecture has no philosophical aim at all; it is concerned with understanding fundamental concepts in their conceptuality. The aim is *philological*; it intends to bring the *reading* of philosophers somewhat more into practice.[21]

Heidegger's intention to replace philosophy with philology belongs to an overarching project that would continue to characterize his career—namely, the dismantling or de-structuring (*Destruktion*) of the philosophical and theological systematizations that have been layered upon original events of thinking. The case of Aristotle is exemplary insofar as the Aristotelian corpus has been entirely integrated into a formidable metaphysical tradition beginning with Aquinas and continuing across the centuries. Aristotle, so to speak, has been buried alive; and Heidegger, in an Orphic key, wants to recover the event through thinking—to bring the ancient philosopher, and with him the Greek experience of being-there, back to the light of day.

To this end, Heidegger explicates key terms through textual cross-references and etymological speculations. At times, he turns to the ancient glosses of Themistius or the late antique commentaries by Simplicius of Cilicia; he occasionally considers the critical apparatus prepared by modern textual critics; yet he brackets out all the scholastic interpretations and philosophical histories that have gathered around Aristotle's language and smothered it beneath the weight of cogent erudition. Heidegger's philology therefore is not only Orphic but also resonates with the Lutheran criterion of *sola scriptura*.

19 Heidegger's definition of the historiographical is provided in the Parmenides course (1982:94).

20 "den *Glauben an die Geschichte* in dem Sinne, daß wir voraussetzen daß *Geschichte und geschichtliche Vergangenheit, sofern ihr nur die Bahn frei gemacht wird, die Möglichkeit hat, einer Gegenwart oder besser Zukunft einen Stoß zu versetzen*" (Heidegger 2002:6).

21 "Die Vorlesung hat gar keine philosophische Abzweckung, es handelt sich um das Verständnis von Grundbegriffen in ihrer Begrifflichkeit. Die Abzweckung ist *philologisch*, sie will das *Lesen* von Philosophen etwas mehr in Übung bringen" (Heidegger 2002:5).

Aristotle thus comes across as "his own interpreter" (*sui ipsius interpres*).[22] Leery of any universal or Catholic authority that strives to fix the discourse and stabilize its terms, Heidegger insists on listening to the text as he hears it, philologically and passionately, in the hope of catching some trace of Being, even if Being, like Eurydice, withdraws at the moment of self-revelation, disappearing in her sudden appearance, an epiphanic moment, precisely as Joyce described it: "most delicate and evanescent."[23]

By considering Aristotle's terminological usage in vital relation to customary usage, Heidegger's philology follows a different path of thinking, a poetic *Denkweg* that departs from the method of formal logic which was established by scholasticism and upheld in the work of Immanuel Kant. According to Heidegger, logic distinguishes between *intuition* and *concept*. Whereas an entity perceived by intuition is a mental representation of the singular (*representatio singularis*), an entity understood as a concept is a generalized representation based on features held in common among multiple entities (*representatio per notas communes*). The concept thus acquires a definition, which determines the purpose or use of the entity. To illustrate, Heidegger paraphrases Kant's own example:

> A savage sees a house, whose *what-for* [*Wozu*] he does not know, quite different from us [...]. To be sure, he sees the same entity, but the knowledge of the *use* escapes him; he does not understand what he should do with it. He forms no concept of house.[24]

Logic requires bifocality: The definition comprises both intuition and concept, it sees the entity in its singularity and simultaneously understands its technical purpose, its *Dasein* and its *Wozu*, the *What-is-there* together with the *What-for*. In a phenomenological mode, however, Heidegger charges that this scholastic definition causes the singularity of *What-is-there* to dissolve entirely into the technical possibilities of the *What-for*. The scholastic definition of definition is a reduction and hence "a symptom of decline, a mere technique for thinking [*eine bloße Denktechnik*] that was once the basic possibility

22 Cf. Michalski 2005:65–80.

23 As cited *supra*: Joyce, *Stephen Hero* (1963:211).

24 "Ein Wilder sieht ein Haus dessen *Wozu* er nicht kennt, ganz anders als wir [...]. Er sieht zwar dasselbe Seiende, aber ihm fehlt die Kenntnis des *Gebrauchs*, er versteht nicht, was er damit soll. Er bildet keinen Begriff von Haus." Heidegger, *Grundbegriffe*, 11. Heidegger is referring to Kant's introduction to his lectures on Logic: "In jeder Erkenntniß muß unterschieden werden *Materie*, d. i. der Gegenstand, und *Form*,d. i. die Art, wie wir den Gegenstand erkennen. — Sieht z.B. ein Wilder ein Haus aus der Ferne, dessen Gebrauch er nicht kennt: so hat er zwar eben dasselbe Object wie ein Anderer, der es bestimmt als eine für Menschen eingerichtete Wohnung kennt, in der Vorstellung vor sich. Aber der Form nach ist dieses Erkenntniß eines und desselben Objects in beiden verschieden. Bei dem Einen ist es bloße Anschauung, bei dem Andern Anschauung und Begriff zugleich." *Werke*, (Kant 1900ff: vol. 9, 33).

of human speech."[25] Scholastic logic traffics with a repertoire of definitions that have been abstracted from the purposes once embedded in a distinctive context. The original *technē*, which once revealed an entity's use within historical, concrete experience, has become a merely technical operation, a *Denktechnik* that obstructs the *Denkweg*.

In contrast, philology is involved with the incipient ground that continues to determine concepts in a concrete and vital sense.[26] A philological reception of the ancient philosophical text is called for in order to attend to each concept's "autochthony" or *Bodenständigkeit*. Aristotle's fundamental concepts are emphatically indigenous, having grown from the native Greek soil (*Boden*). To take a single brief example, when Aristotle says οὐσία, it should be heard as a word still rooted in customary usage, in the particular lifeworld of ancient Greek culture, where it denotes "property or real estate, a personal possession." In order to come closer to what Aristotle meant by *ousia*, it is necessary to explore the common ground which continues to govern the concept's meaning. As Heidegger concludes: "It can only be a matter of understanding the customary meaning in such a way that we take from it *directions* on the terminological meaning."[27] In other words, the concept in its conceptuality is set in the ground and yet detached, both embedded in customary *life* and removed in terminological *work*: Life and Work, intertwined yet apart, parenthetically.

The Abyss

To mark the twentieth anniversary of Rilke's death, on December 29, 1946, a small group of acquaintances gathered in Heidegger's cabin in Todtnauberg to listen to an informal lecture from their host. Although the theme announced was Rilke's poetry, Heidegger chose for his title the well-known line from Friedrich Hölderlin's elegy, *Brod und Wein*, composed around 1801: *Wozu Dichter in dürftiger Zeit?* ("What are Poets for in a destitute time?"). Hölderlin's poetic question concisely rehearses the conditions for Heidegger's earlier philological investigations—namely, how the technical conception of purpose (the *Wozu*) should be seen within the factical experience of a specific epoch and culture. Here, however, it is not some historically distant time that must be read but rather the present time of the thinker himself, a time, moreover, that is represented as somehow deficient, impoverished, and feeble, *eine dürftige Zeit*.

Heidegger's postwar German audience would hardly need to be persuaded that the present moment was one of profound indigence and spiritual turmoil. Certainly, on a more personal level, the aftermath of hostilities had particularly catastrophic for

25 "eine Verfallserscheinung [...], eine bloße Denktechnik, die einmal die Grundmöglichkeit des Sprechens des Menschen gewesen ist." Heidegger 2002:13.

26 For further discussion, see Kisiel 1993:286–95.

27 "Es kann sich nur darum handeln, die geläufige Bedeutung so zu verstehen, daß wir bei ihr *Anweisungen* auf die terminologische entnehmen" (Heidegger 2002:24 [2009:18–19]).

Heidegger. In addition to seeing the old town of Freiburg lying in rubble, in addition to witnessing the confusion and the desperation, the intolerable guilt and the unfathomable shame, in addition to having part of his home requisitioned by the French occupying forces, Heidegger was dismissed from the faculty, banned from all university buildings, and had his teaching license revoked. Although the French Denazification Committee initially voted to treat the philosophy professor with leniency, the University Senate pushed for a harsher sentence, having been compelled by the testimony of Karl Jaspers who denounced his old friend's pedagogical approach as "unfree, dictatorial and uncommunicative."[28] Twenty years before, it was at Jaspers' home that Heidegger resolved to curtail the publication of *Sein und Zeit*; and now it was Jaspers himself who played a direct role in parenthesizing Heidegger's academic career. As a result, by the spring of 1946, Heidegger suffered a complete mental and physical breakdown. It would take months to recover, and then, only after submitting to a prolonged course of psychosomatic treatment in the Sanatorium Hausbaden under the care of Victor Baron von Gebsattel, a former student of Ludwig Binswanger, whose own brand of phenomenological psychiatry was explicitly indebted to Heidegger's earlier work.[29]

Meanwhile, the thinker further despaired, disingenuously or not, over misrepresentations and crude generalizations of his philosophy through facile appeals to his personal life. In the private pages of the so-called *Black Notebooks*, Heidegger expressed the wish that such biographical matters be bracketed out—a wish underscored, once again, by his own parenthetical gesturing:

> That a thoughtful grounding again becomes a sort of collection of sayings, well protected against idle talk and unharmed by all hurried misinterpretation; that the works of twenty or more volumes including all the concomitant snooping into the author's life and utterances (I mean the usual "biographies" and collections of correspondence) disappear and the work itself will be strong enough and kept free from the disfavor of being explained by the inclusion of the "personal," i.e., from being dissolved into base generalization [*Vergemeinerung*].[30]

[28] Cited in Ott 1988:65.

[29] See Mitchell 2016.

[30] "Daß dann das denkerische Gründen wieder eine Art Spruchsammlung wird, gut verwahrt gegen das Gerede und unverletzlich durch alle eilige Mißdeutung, daß dann die 20-und-mehrbändigen Werke samt den beigegebenen Lebensbeschnüffelungen und Äußerungen (ich meine die üblichen „Biographien" und Briefsammlungen) verschwinden und das Werk selbst stark genug ist und freigehalten von der Ungunst, durch das Zutragen des „Persönlichen" erklärt, d. h. aufgelöst zu werden in die Vergemeinerung." Heidegger, *Überlegungen II–VI*. Schwarze Hefte 1931–1938 (2014:328).

Inevitably, after appeals to the indigenous German soil (*Boden*) had lost any and all innocence, the publication of these carefully preserved notebooks in 2014 re-ignited debates over the complex relationship between the philosophical project and the philosopher's life. At last coming to light, the stray entries exerted acute force, like a series of parentheses, too irrelevant to incorporate into the main line of thinking yet too illuminating to ignore. Destined, according to the author's own instructions, to be published as the final volume of his *Gesamtausgabe*, his most personal and at times most shameful admissions were included within the work precisely by remaining to the side, yet in the opinion of his critics, not merely as a negligible aside but rather as the damning last word.[31]

Back in 1946, although barred from the lecture hall and consigned to the margins of Todtnauberg, Heidegger continued to intervene, both as an insider and as an outlier—that is, as a self-styled philologist in a destitute time. Yet the impoverished time that Heidegger evokes in his Rilke lecture only indirectly alludes to the recent misery of the postwar period. For he views the present nocturnal state as the culmination of a much longer, more essential history. As Hölderlin's elegy proposes, the destitute time began with the disappearance of the gods—Dionysus, Herakles, and Christ—a time of mourning, waiting, and vague expectation.

> Aber Freund! wir kommen zu spät. Zwar leben die Götter,
> Aber über dem Haupt droben in anderer Welt.
> Endlos wirken sie da und scheinens wenig zu achten,
> Ob wir leben, so sehr schonen die Himmlischen uns.
>
> ...
>
> Donnernd kommen sie drauf. Indessen dünket mir öfters
> Besser zu schlafen, wie so ohne Genossen zu seyn,
> So zu harren und was zu thun indeß und zu sagen,
> Weiß ich nicht und wozu Dichter in dürftiger Zeit?
>
> Hölderlin, *Brod und Wein*, 7.
> Strophe, vv. 109–112; 119–122[32]

> But friend! we come too late. True, the gods live,
> But over our heads up there in another world.
> Endlessly they act there and apparently pay little attention
> Whether we live, so much the Heavenly Ones protect us.

[31] See, for example, Enno Rudolph's review (2015). For a broader discussion, see Espinet, Figal, Keiling and Miković, eds. 2018.

[32] Hölderlin 1953: vol. 2, 93–99.

...

Thundering they will come to it. Meanwhile I often think,
Better to sleep than to be without companions,
To abide and meanwhile what to do and say
I do not know and what are poets for in a destitute time?

In Heidegger's reading, what makes the present moment especially abysmal is that the absence of God—not the gods—is not recognized as such, that "God's failed presence" (*der Fehl Gottes*), is no longer even perceived as a failure or fault.[33] This obliviousness, according to Heidegger, is symptomatic of rampant, all-encompassing technologization, the relentless exploitation of the earth at the will of the metaphysical subject. Heidegger's well-known critique of technology, which he will develop over the remainder of his philosophical career, is announced here, in his first attempt to re-engage with poetry after Germany's defeat, having just emerged from what was arguably the most severe personal crisis of his life.

The critique of technology from this point forward is fairly consistent. Modern technology regards nature as a "standing-reserve" (*Bestand*), which reduces *what is* to something ready-to-hand, something available for human use and human purposes, and insofar as this technological reduction has left human being without ground: *Dasein* thus stands upon an abyss or *Abgrund.* To be sure, technology in itself is not the problem. For τέχνη, like ποίησις, allows beings to appear and therefore very much belongs to the phenomenology of Being. Aristotle is explicit on this point: ἔστι δὲ τέχνη πᾶσα περὶ γένεσιν ("All art [technē] is concerned with bringing into existence [genesis]," *Nicomachean Ethics* 6, 1140a10–11). Yet, whereas "poetic making" (ποίησις) lets something come forth of its own accord, τέχνη renders it conducive to a determined end. Τέχνη, in other words, is pragmatic. It is clearly a part of human being-in-the-world to the extent that it enables human beings to make ordered sense the world and produce things that are serviceable. In Heidegger's account, when τέχνη is allied to ποίησις, it manifests itself as a craft or an art, as a mode of unconcealed truth (ἀλήθεια) that is inherently differential. Yet, modern technics foregoes its poietic kinship and thus imposes itself as a reductive totalization.[34] Indeed, the current era has reached the point where technical, calculative thinking dominates over all other possibilities for interacting with the world. The middle ground is lost in the abyss, the *Mittelgrund* is swallowed up by the *Abgrund.* With increasing persistence, modern technics is occluding alternative ways of alethic unconcealment, above all, by suppressing ποίησις. And

[33] Martin Heidegger, "Wozu Dichter?" (1946) in *Holzwege* (1977:269) ["Why Poets?" (1971:200)].

[34] Cf. Fóti, 1992:xvi.

precisely by precluding poietic and other modes of transacting with the world, technology leaves us with a yawning deficiency, lost in a meager and needy nighttime.

To address this desperate situation, Heidegger turns the technical question, *Wozu* ("what for"), back on itself: *What are poets for in a destitute time?* Heidegger's response is both immediate and simple: True poets, like authentic thinkers, do not avoid or deny the present abyss but rather reach into it, into the present absence itself. Analogous to the *philological aim* outlined in the early lecture course on Aristotle, the *poetic aim* returns to the ground of being, where the *what-for*, the *Wozu* of technical conception, is concretely bound to the *being-there*, to the historical *Dasein* that determines this conception. Heidegger's legerdemain is as brilliant as it is seductive: If the thinker is a philologist rather than a philosopher, then the philologist is also a poet.

Thus, on the first page of his essay, Heidegger has already answered the title question, *Wozu Dichter?* In fact, he is less concerned with the answer since, in his view, we have not yet understood the question properly. Hence, Heidegger poses a fresh question: "Ist Rilke ein Dichter in dürftiger Zeit?" ("Is Rilke a poet in a destitute time?" 274). Does Rilke's poetry, like Hölderlin's, trace the absence of the gods? Can it guide us to the ground or soil, where thinking may encounter the revelation of Being? Can Rilke assist us in "turning away from the abyss" that has resulted from the total technologization of the world? To think on this series of questions, Heidegger adduces a poem from Rilke's *Sonnets to Orpheus*:

> Wandelt sich rasch auch die Welt
> wie Wolkengestalten,
> alles Vollendete fällt
> heim zum Uralten.
>
> Über dem Wandel und Gang,
> weiter und freier,
> währt noch dein Vor-Gesang,
> Gott mit der Leier.
>
> Nicht sind die Leiden erkannt,
> nicht ist die Liebe gelernt,
> und was im Tod uns entfernt,
>
> ist nicht entschleiert.
> Einzig das Lied überm Land
> heiligt und feiert.

Rilke, *Sonette an Orpheus*, I, 19[35]

[35] Cited in Heidegger 1977:274–275 [1971:204–205].

Even if the world swiftly changes
like shapes of clouds,
everything consummated falls
home to the primeval.

Above change and passage,
farther away and freer,
your fore-song still endures,
you god with the lyre.

Not recognized are the sorrows,
nor is love learned,
and what removes us in death,

is not unveiled.
Only the song above the land
sanctifies and celebrates.

In Heidegger's view, the sonnet suggests that Rilke has certainly understood the destitution of the times, when the tyranny of technical, calculative thinking detaches us from nature, when we are deluded into believing that we stand *apart* from the world rather than *in* the world. Technical thinking is *parathetic* without being *enthetic*. In a destitute time, sorrows are not recognized, love is not learned, death is not unveiled. Like Rilke, Heidegger has always insisted that death individuates human being authentically by defining the finite temporality of human existence. And in its attempt to master nature, modern technology presumes to triumph over death, to gloss over its inevitability. Enthralled to technology, Dasein acquires but an illusory immortality. Thus, the sonnet's movement from transience to endurance should not be confused with the calculated ordering that characterizes technical thinking, since Orphic song unveils the finitude that technology conceals. What remains is poetic song. What endures is poetic language, attending to the trace of the holy, abiding mournfully until, like Orpheus himself, it reaches into the abyss to retrieve what has been buried, even though Being, in its unconcealment, withdraws from the Orphic gaze that strives to grasp or comprehend it.

The concept of reception implicitly casts received poetry as a gift, as a tradition, "given across" time (*tradita*). Accordingly, for Heidegger, with an etymological link he consistently evokes, reception should not only elicit giving thanks (*Danken*) but also stimulate thinking (*Denken*).[36] Beginning with his first lecture course on Hölderlin in

[36] See, e.g., Martin Heidegger, *Was heißt Denken?* (1984:158) [*What is called Thinking?* (1968:138–139)].

1934, held immediately after he resigned from the university rectorate, Heidegger's engagement with poetry exhibits a thinker's gratitude by employing his own idiosyncratic brand of philology, one that eschews a comprehensive reading of the text and instead limits itself to focused comments. His parenthetic-philological method is tellingly selective in that he cites specific verses for his interpretation while bracketing out the rest. Accordingly, his discussion of Rilke's sonnet readily yields a message that accords closely with the account of death that Heidegger outlined in *Being and Time*, death as "one's ownmost and uttermost potentiality for Being" (307), but also death as one's ultimate impossibility, when being-there is no longer there. For Heidegger—and ostensibly for Rilke—death is, so to speak, parenthetical, standing within our Dasein by remaining outstanding. Death is projected into a future that never arrives, neither phenomenologically (for it never appears) nor ontologically (for it does not exist).[37] In reading Rilke's sonnet, Heidegger attends to the poet-as-Orpheus who reaches into this abyss but fails to grasp the love he aims to retrieve. What Heidegger overlooks in the poem, however, is the death of Orpheus himself. It is the slaughtered Orpheus, whose scattered limbs spread "farther and freer." It is Orpheus's death that results in an apotheosis, where the poet, post-mortem, is transformed into a heavenly constellation, *la lyre d'Orphée*, the "god with the lyre." For Rilke, death is not something forever unachievable, forever beyond grasp, but rather a completion, a sublimation.

In this essay composed in the aftermath of the war, Heidegger curiously rehearses the gesture made five years before: setting Orpheus's and thus the poet's death in brackets. Just as in 1927 and reported in 1941, the death of the poet coincides with an interruption in thinking. And again, now in 1946, the bracketing allows his thinking to take a fresh turn—namely, towards the essence of modern technology, which assertedly evades the ontological structure of death. The move ultimately leads Heidegger to enlist Rilke, justifiably or not, in the metaphysical tradition. *What are poets for in a destitute time?* Rilke has been invited to respond to Hölderlin's question, but only when the response stays extrinsic to the question.

Sorrows Not Known

If philology, as Heidegger once formulated it, is truly "a passion for knowledge"—*eine Leidenschaft der Erkenntnis*—then the aim of philology, its *Wozu*, may be to counter the destitute time, in which, as Rilke writes, "sorrows are not known" (*Nicht sind die Leiden erkannt*). Heidegger's philology and Rilke's poetry share this conjunction of suffering and knowledge, *Leiden and Erkennen*. And should philology be understood as a passion, it would be impossible to divorce the philologist's work from the philologist's life, however much one might wish to place one's own life into brackets.

37 Cf. Gosetti-Ferencei 2014.

For the 1953 edition of his 1935 seminar, *Introduction to Metaphysics*, Heidegger explains in a prefatory note that he has used square brackets to distinguish new additions from those passages printed in round brackets, which, he claims, belonged to the original manuscript. This typographic matter, however, despite sounding rather innocuous, came to cause graver concerns towards the end of the book, where one reads the following passage:

> What today is being passed around entirely as the philosophy of National Socialism, but what hasn't the slightest to do with the inner truth and greatness of this movement (namely with the encounter of planetary determined technology and modern man), does its fishing in the troubled waters of "values" and "totalities." (199; translation modified)[38]

The parenthesized amplification, though not blatantly critical, could suggest that Heidegger, already in 1935, was suspicious of the Nazi regime insofar as it rested on a fateful and fearful alliance of modern humanity and planetary technologization. In citing one of Hitler's favorite tags—"the inner truth and greatness of the movement"—Heidegger could be interpreted as undercutting the purported grandeur with a parenthetical aside. One may, for example, stress Heidegger's subtle use of the demonstrative pronoun—"the greatness of *this* movement"—like the use of *iste* in classical Latin, already seems to signal the thinker's critical distance. At any rate, soon after this edition was published, in an open reply to Jürgen Habermas's denunciation of Heidegger's complicity with National Socialism, Christian Lewalter cited this very passage as sufficient evidence for exonerating the old philosopher. Heidegger himself was so grateful for Lewalter's intercession that he fully endorsed his interpretation in a letter published in *Die Zeit* in September 1953.

The ensuing debate hinged on a decidedly philological matter. Did Heidegger in fact write the parenthetical remark in 1935, proving that he already held the regime in some contempt? Or was it inserted only much later, after the catastrophe, for the 1953 publication? How is it that Heidegger would have employed the phrase "planetary-determined technology" in 1935, when he adopted this phrase consistently only in the 1950s? Heidegger, in the 1966 *Spiegel* interview, would again refer to these "explanatory brackets," insisting they were, without question, written down in 1935.[39] Still, at

38 "Was heute vollends als Philosophie des Nationalsozialismus herumgeboten wird, aber mit der inneren Wahrheit und Größe dieser Bewegung (nämlich mit der Begegnung der planetarisch bestimmten Technik und des neuzeitlichen Menschen) nicht das Geringste zu tun hat, das macht seine Fischzüge in diesen trüben Gewässern der "Werte" und der "Ganzheiten" (Heidegger 1975:152).

39 "Nur noch ein Gott kann uns retten." Interview with Rudolf Augstein and Georg Wolff, September 1966. In *Der Spiegel* (May 31, 1976:193).

least since Lorenzo Valla, anachronisms have always triggered philological suspicion. The doubts would eventually lead Otto Pöggeler, in 1983, seven years after Heidegger's death, to consult the archives in Marbach.[40] Although the archived manuscript from 1935 was in excellent condition, the page in question was the only one that was mysteriously missing. The parenthetical critique of technology might have acquitted the thinker, but the positive evidence is gone. Concrete proof will forever remain wanting, *dürftig*—and that, perhaps, after all, may be precisely what philologists are for.

[40] Otto Pöggeler, "Heideggers politisches Selbstverständnis." In *Heidegger und die praktische Philosophie*. A. Gethmann-Siefert und O. Pöggeler, ed. (Frankfurt am Main: Suhrkamp, 1988), 17–63.

Chapter 3

In the Wake of Catastrophe

Parataxis

Parentextuality, how distance affects present discourse, motivates Heidegger's etymological reflections. To claim that something has come to light, epiphanically, implies that it is otherwise hidden. The premise motivates Heidegger's thinking as parenthetic in that it strives towards an authentic encounter with disclosed meaning by attending to the *parasemantic* properties inherent in the words we employ. Whereas calculative approaches tend to have little patience with interruptions or digressions, with malfunctions or glitches, in brief, with anything that might obstruct the achievement of its goals, Heidegger seems to welcome all resistance as a goad to thinking. Whereas technological purposiveness by far prefers the beeline over the byway, Heidegger disdains the shortcut and instead allows himself to stray along distracting and possibly misleading *Holzwege*. For him, "the planetary determined technology" of modernity proceeds as though on a flattened plain, a *planum*, wandering like a *planet*, freely, without anything to block its already set path. It is, in fact, precisely this kind of etymologizing that energizes Heidegger's thinking, an insistence on encountering the vertical depths and heights that intrude upon the two-dimensional surface, on grappling with the meanings that one's willful track while also turning it into a three-dimensional phenomenon. Etymologizing in all its variants—whether it is validated by linguistic science, by folkloric traditions, or merely by alliterative accident—trips up instrumental intentions. Words no longer serve as amenable vehicles for the subject's designs but rather become *problems* (προβλήματα), like large stones that "have been hurled in front" (προβεβλημένα) and impede the trail as planned. With etymologies disclosed, words evade the subject's nominative control, they frustrate use and demonstrate that, in speaking, it is language that speaks.[1]

1 "Die Sprache spricht." Heidegger's well-known claim comes from his 1950 lecture "Die Sprache," published in vol. 12 of the *Gesamtausgabe: Unterwegs zur Sprache* (1959:10).

Although hardly a proponent of instrumental reason or timesaving technology, and certainly not an advocate of clear and simple prose, Theodor Adorno found Heidegger's style of thinking and its implications to be intolerably self-contradictory, if not utterly dangerous. Particularly troubling for Adorno was the way Heidegger reverts to post-Romantic, mystical language to conjure a dense cloud for concealing seductively impoverished thinking: a tyrannical imposition camouflaged as the humble piety of thought, endorsements of identity perniciously posing as the destruction of metaphysics, a reception of the cherished "pre-Socratics" that amounts to a gross deception; in sum, a dazzling screen that projects a "jargon of authenticity." [2]

From the lexicon of Existentialist buzzwords, Adorno singles out "authenticity" (*Eigentlichkeit*) as the central tenet of this latest installment of German ideology, a term that connotes ideas of ownership (*eigen*), property (*Eigentum*), and an individual's singularity or peculiarity (*Eigentümlichkeit*). Authenticity therefore speaks to a felt sense of being genuine, being committed to one's convictions, solely responsible for one's actions, and resilient against tides of conformism. Yet in Adorno's assessment, authenticity exacerbates the very problems it is assumed to solve. Although it seems to provide a dependable source for supreme values after the demise of religious faith, it is premised on an untenable fetishization of one's identity and proffers an exaggerated trust in self-possession and self-integrity, while further importing a particularly German nationalist brand of mystical aura. In gesturing towards what is deemed original or primal—as in Heidegger's etymological meditations—on a societal level, it inflates notions of autochthony, which grants undue privilege to a land's earliest settlers while nourishing nostalgia for a lost, supposedly primeval wholeness. By militating against abstractions and essentializing concepts, it promulgates a lethal anti-intellectualism and instigates the kind of oblivious cultic devotion witnessed under fascism. Finally, authenticity purportedly rejects the status quo yet is in fact entirely complicit with bureaucratization and the market economy, that is, with mechanisms that hide the concrete content of social relations beneath the cover of quantification and the sheen of the commodity.

Adorno's attack on Heidegger had publicly commenced a year before *The Jargon of Authenticity* was published. On June 7, 1963, at a special meeting of the Hölderlin Gesellschaft in West Berlin to commemorate the hundred-twentieth anniversary of the poet's death, Adorno presented "Parataxis: On Hölderlin's Late Poetry," which aimed to salvage Hölderlin's work from the undeniably influential and, to Adorno's mind, highly perilous obscurantism that had been disseminated by the society's most prestigious member, Martin Heidegger.

Beginning with his opening sentence, Adorno's intervention centers on the issue of reception: "There is no question that the understanding of Hölderlin's work has grown along with his fame since the school of Stefan George demolished the conception of

2 Theodor W. Adorno, *The Jargon of Authenticity* [1964] (1973:49–89).

him as a quiet, refined minor poet with a touching life story."[3] The implicit reference is to Norbert von Hellingrath, a young member the George Circle, whose critical edition of Hölderlin's poetry and inspired prolegomena to the poet's translations of Pindar (1911) liberated the poet from the confines of a silencing definition. From that point forward, Hölderlin would no longer be regarded merely as rather sensitive friend of Schelling and Hegel who drafted several poems of note before succumbing to aphasiac madness and spending the entire second half of his life in an attic room overlooking the Neckar in Tübingen. Instead, Hellingrath's philological efforts established the urgent importance of the erstwhile forgotten poet, brought the work to light, out of concealment, promoted Hölderlin as a bold thinker who courageously confronted the ardent flame of archaic Greece and Pindar in particular, and thereby cleared the path for receiving in the present this exemplary recipient of the past.

Adorno concedes that, whereas philology is indispensable in preserving and preparing a readable text, it invariably does so by placing unsound belief in determining authorial intention, a procedure that ignores a work's objective—and thus, non-subjective—form, what his old friend Walter Benjamin and Heidegger as well called *das Gedichtete*, that which is poetically composed apart from the poet's plan and that which alone can bring to light the poem's "truth content" (*Wahrheitsgehalt*, 447–448/109–110). Philosophy is therefore required as crucial interpretive medium for addressing this productive tension, yet it fails as soon as it attempts to "confiscate" or "seize possession of it" (*beschlagnahmen*, 452/113). In Adorno's view, Heidegger foists "phrases from the jargon of authenticity" and thereby violently reformulates the poetry in a kind of "pseudo-poetry" that is fundamentally unaesthetic (452–53/114). That is, despite his acknowledgment of *das Gedichtete* and despite his suspicion regarding ontic concepts of subjectivity and personality, Heidegger simply replaces Hölderlin's intention with his own. With ample citations from the commentaries, Adorno demonstrates how "Hölderlin is skewered [*aufgespießt*] on the alleged key phrases or control words [*Leitworte*] selected by Heidegger for authoritarian purposes" (455/116). In the name of receptive openness, Heidegger betrays his appropriative will. The mighty critic of technology turns out to be the greatest technician of all.[4]

Adorno does not restrict himself to discrediting postwar Germany's most famous philosopher but rather devotes the second half of his talk to outlining what he presents as a more legitimate approach. Philosophy, he reiterates, should address the tensional relationship between content and form, that is, between poetry's "musical" aspects, which are non-propositional, non-conceptual, and non-logical, and a poem's opposing "verbal"—propositional, conceptual, and logical—aspects: A collision that produces

3 Theodor W. Adorno, "Parataxis: Zur späten Lyrik Hölderlins" [1963] (1998:447; 1992: vol. 2, 109).

4 Whether Adorno's critique is fully justified remains an open question. On this topic, see Mörchen 1983 and Düttmann 1991. For a more recent assessment, see Waldanger 2018.

a "non-conceptual synthesis against its medium," a "constitutive dissociation" that disrupts the verbal-propositional ordering driven by subjective intention (471/130). The result is "parataxis," an arrangement (τάξις) that sets and maintains what lies apart (παρά) and resists logical subordination or *hypotaxis*. As in a parenthesis, paratactic form suspends the "logical train of thought," it dispenses with predication, refrains from connections, rebels against harmonization, and thus short-circuits subjective designs (472–473/132). Yet, although disruptive, parataxis does not destroy language, for "to destroy the unity of language would constitute an act of violence equivalent to the one that unity perpetuates" (476/136). Instead, with form paratactically fragmenting content, Hölderlin's late poetry stages the dethronement of the subject and thus the violent subjection of nature, including the self-subjection of human nature.

With parataxis, Adorno appears to reach back to Norbert von Hellingrath's work on Hölderlin's Pindar translations, which he cited at the head of his presentation. In his introductory essay, Hellingrath refers to Dionysius of Halicarnassus who describes Pindar's lyric style as featuring an "austere construction" (ἁρμονία αὐστηρά), translated as *harte Fügung*, a "hard fitting" as opposed to the "smooth" (*glatte Fügung*, ἁρμονία γλαφυρά).[5] For Dionysius, in the austere harmony, words are "fixed securely in place," the parts of the sentence are "held distinct, separated by conspicuous distances" and forming "harsh and dissonant combinations," "like uneven, unpolished blocks of stone, unworked and rough-hewn."[6] In Hellingrath's terms: the rhythms of words, phrases, and phonetic sounds exhibit rigorously discrete formations that are "more irrational, less clear, less bound," with each single word constituting a "tactical unit [*taktische Einheit*]" to create an archaic, jarring effect, especially for modern readers who approach poetry from a "conceptual, non-sensual angle," unlike the smooth style, which subordinates words to "the image or mental context," a style more in accordance with modern tastes, where sensuality is less dominant.[7]

5 Norbert von Hellingrath, *Pindarübertragungen von Hölderlin: Prolegomena zu einer Erstausgabe* (1911), 1–2, with reference to Dionysius of Halicarnassus, *De compositione verborum*, 21.

6 ἐρείδεσθαι βούλεται τὰ ὀνόματα ἀσφαλῶς καὶ στάσεις λαμβάνειν ἰσχυράς, ὥστ᾽ ἐκ περιφανείας ἕκαστον ὄνομα ὁρᾶσθαι, ἀπέχειν τε ἀπ᾽ ἀλλήλων τὰ μόρια διαστάσεις ἀξιολόγους αἰσθητοῖς χρόνοις διειργόμενα· τραχείαις τε χρῆσθαι πολλαχῇ καὶ ἀντιτύποις ταῖς συμβολαῖς οὐδὲν αὐτῇ διαφέρει, οἷαι γίνονται τῶν λογάδην συντιθεμένων ἐν οἰκοδομίαις λίθων αἱ μὴ εὐγώνιοι καὶ μὴ συνεξεσμέναι βάσεις, ἀργαὶ δέ τινες καὶ αὐτοσχέδιοι. *De compositione verborum* 22.

7 "diese drei parallelen rhythmen [der worte, des melos, der laute] werden in harter fügung irrationalere minder übersichtliche minder gebundene (nicht etwa minder gehaltene) und in höherem grade einzige bildungen aufweisen. für uns/ die wir von der begrifflich unsinnlichen seite herkommen/ wird als wesentlich erscheinen dass in harter fügung möglichst das einzelne wort selbst taktische einheit sei/ in glatter dagegen das bild oder ein gedanklicher zusammenhang meist mehrere wörter sich unterordnend. die glatte fügung ist also minder unmittelbar und wird daher leicht bei fortschreitendem schwinden der sinnlichkeit der alleinherrschaft in der dichtung sich nähern" (Hellingrath 1911:2).

Hellingrath's underlying premise is that it was Hölderlin's translations of Pindar's odes that influenced the syntactic anomalies in the late poetry. The resemblance to Adorno's thesis regarding parataxis is unmistakable: how musical or rhythmic form maintains an objective autonomy that resists the subject's control, how the language withstands subordination to a vehicular function, how sensuality overwhelms conceptualization. Yet the resemblance is not only to Hellingrath's syntactic thesis: In returning to philology to counter Heidegger's philosophical approach, Adorno essentially performs what Heidegger has urged all along. In this regard, it is noteworthy that Heidegger dedicated his 1936 lecture, *Hölderlin und das Wesen der Dichtung* to Hellingrath, who arguably inspired him to structure the presentation with five discrete "key phrases" (*Leitworte*) from Hölderlin's œuvre, a colliding series of paratactic lines that emulates the *harte Fügung* by disrupting an overriding train of thought—the very *Leitworte* that Adorno accused Heidegger of using to "skewer" the poet.

Whatever the polemical divergences or clandestine convergences with his target, Adorno's parataxis, precisely as a suspensive disruption or "constitutive dissociation," accomplishes a parenthetic effect, one, however, that is not facilely marked by brackets which, for Adorno, would betray an authorial will to subordinate what is recalcitrantly insubordinate. Thus, Adorno's comments in an earlier essay from 1956:

> Brackets take the parenthesis completely out of the sentence, creating enclaves, as it were, whereas nothing in good prose should be unnecessary to the overall structure. By admitting such superfluousness, brackets implicitly renounce the claim to the integrity of the linguistic form and capitulate to pedantic philistinism.[8]

For Adorno, brackets confine paratactic outliers to a "prison" with the aim of defusing their energy and rehabilitating them to comply with the purposes of the main sentence. But above all, lunulae are unaesthetic eyesores, nothing but a barbaric attempt to control the suspension, a desperate gesture performed by a subject blindly convinced of its hegemony and therefore ignorant of its weakness, unaware of its socially mediated status.

As for the "Parataxis" lecture, Adorno sparked a hefty scandal. Reports vary. According to Jochen Schmidt, a significant portion of the audience interrupted the presentation by storming out in protest, while Emil Staiger recalls that only one man stood to denounce what he regarded as an unfair and impudent attack, given that Heidegger was not in attendance. Staiger goes on to say that Peter Szondi rose to Adorno's defense, pointing out that Heidegger's work was cited at length, which therefore legitimized the critique. Yet Bernhard Böschenstein insists that the reproaches took place on the

8 Theodor W. Adorno, "Satzzeichen" [1956] (1998:111) ["Punctuation Marks" (1990:304)].

following day, during the open discussion of the plenary lectures—a session that Adorno chose not to attend. In any event, Adorno would dedicate the published version of his talk to Szondi, a telling gesture of gratitude after the Hölderlin Gesellschaft broke its customary practice and refused to print "Parataxis" in its Yearbook. As for Heidegger, although he did not deem Adorno's article worthy of rebuttal, he immediately canceled his membership, outraged that the Society had invited "that man" to speak out against him publicly.[9] Of course, as Robert Savage emphasizes, "Adorno's polemic against Heidegger demands dissent and would have missed its target had it been greeted with polite applause."[10] Which is to say, the confused accounts of what happened on the afternoon of June 7, 1963, confirm the paratactic or parenthetic force of Adorno's intervention insofar as it marked an unsettling caesura in how Hölderlin and poetry in general had hitherto been received.

Receptivity

Apart from Adorno's polemical intervention, Heidegger's reflections on the essence of poetic language—his relentless mode of questioning, his idiosyncratic vocabulary and style, his creative obsession with etymology—enjoyed broad appeal among West German writers. The most important case by far is Paul Celan, a poet of Jewish descent and Holocaust survivor, whose innovative and often disquieting approach to lyric form has secured his position at the forefront of postwar German literature.

Born Antschel, Celan was twenty-one years old when Nazi soldiers invaded his home in Romania in 1941. While Celan's parents and closest relatives were immediately deported and soon perished in nearby camps, Celan himself was consigned to hard labor and remained under confinement until the Soviet army liberated the region in 1944. Three years later, when the Soviet-backed communist party seized power in Bucharest, Celan fled to Vienna where he fell in love with Ingeborg Bachmann, at the time a twenty-two-year-old student of philosophy and burgeoning poet who was completing a doctoral dissertation on the critical reception of Martin Heidegger. What ostensibly motivated Bachmann's exegeses and analyses was a desire to reconcile her sincere admiration for Heidegger's reflections on poetic language with the thinker's complicity in Nazi ideology. After Celan moved to Paris in 1948, he maintained a steady correspondence with Bachmann, often discussing Heidegger's work, grappling with their shared feelings of ambivalence and suspicion, and sending each other copies of Heidegger's books and essays.[11]

9 For a full account with bibliography, see Savage2005:287–288.

10 Savage 2005:288.

11 For the biographical details, I have borrowed liberally from James Lyon's comprehensive monograph, *Paul Celan and Martin Heidegger* (2006).

Celan's intense engagement with Heidegger spans his all too brief career, beginning with a diligent study of *Sein und Zeit* in 1952, the same year he presented his poem "Todesfuge" before the Gruppe 47, a most vibrant and pivotal collective of authors in postwar West Germany. Celan's reading gained him broad recognition across the Republic, a prestige shared by Ingeborg Bachmann who was also invited to read. Her first collection of poems, *Die gestundete Zeit* ("Borrowed Time"), was awarded the Group's poetry prize the following year, a volume that warranted comparison with Celan's first major collection, *Mohn und Gedächtnis* ("Poppy and Memory"), published in late 1952. Light traces of Heidegger's poetics may be discerned in the later poems included in this collection, in particular themes derived from Heidegger's essay *Wozu Dichter?* yet the effect the thinker had on the poet is more clearly pronounced in Celan's acceptance speech for the Bremen Prize in January 1958 which opens in a decidedly Heideggerean mode: *Denken und Danken sind in unserer Sprache Worte ein und desselben Ursprungs* ("Thinking and Thanking in our language are words from one and the same origin").[12]

Given Adorno's excoriating critique in "Parataxis," coupled with his earlier and most notorious claim from 1949 that "to write a poem after Auschwitz is barbaric,"[13] one may be tempted to cite Celan's achievement as a decisive rebuttal. Yet, as John Zilcosky astutely points out, such a conclusion would be misleadingly naïve. Hardly a rehearsal of Plato's banishment of the poets by philosophy, Adorno's statement, when considered in context, reads more like a challenge, one certainly drenched in pessimism, but a challenge nonetheless: What form can culture produce which could address the Shoah?[14] As for Celan, he clearly regarded Heidegger's work as a powerful catalyst in developing his own unique, hermetic and tentative voice, as a serious and often troubling problem to deal with and not baldly as an authoritative source to mimic. If gratitude is discernible in Celan's reception, it is a sentiment directed towards the thinking that makes him think. As he inscribed in the margins of his copy of *Was heißt Denken?—Rezeptivität als Grundverhalten beim Dichten* ("Receptivity as basic comportment in poetizing").[15]

Through occasional correspondence, the conversation-cum-confrontation proceeded apace, however disturbed by worries and fears: an increase in 1959 of anti-Semitic incidents across West Germany and Celan's growing conviction that the government and universities were being led by former Nazi officers; and in Paris, where Celan lived and worked, the denunciations of Heidegger following the published translation of his 1933 Rector Address. 1959 also marked a highly publicized debate between

12 Originally published as: Paul Celan, *Ansprache bei Verleihung des Bremer Literaturpreises an Paul Celan* (Stuttgart: Deutsche-Verlags-Anstalt, 1958). For an English translation, see Celan, 2001a:395–396.

13 From Adorno's essay, "Kulturkritik und Gesellschaft" [1949] (1955:31).

14 Zilcosky 2005:672.

15 Cited in Lyon 2006:45.

Heidegger and Martin Buber on the essence of language, with the famed author of *I and Thou* expectedly defending the thesis that language was inherently dialogic and Heidegger insisting instead on its fundamentally monologic character. Avidly reading journalistic accounts of the debate, Celan found himself wholeheartedly agreeing with Heidegger's position, while also condemning Buber for publicly offering reconciliation with a man once loyal to the Nazi Party, or so he admitted to Otto Pöggeler, who was in Paris to conduct archival research for his habilitation thesis under the direction of Heidegger's former student, Hans-Georg Gadamer.[16] Pöggeler—who, as we have seen, would later search for the suspiciously missing page in the 1935 manuscript of *Introduction to Metaphysics*—would henceforth serve as the key intermediary between Celan and Heidegger.

Through Pöggeler, Celan and Heidegger maintained a steady exchange of inscribed books, essays, and poems, a conversation of ideas and reflections which finally found the chance to become a full-fledged confrontation on July 24, 1967. For on that day, upon attending Celan's reading in the grand lecture hall at the University of Freiburg—whose main entranceway, incidentally, is flanked by statues of Homer and Aristotle, *Dichten und Denken*—Heidegger invited the guest speaker to his forest cabin at Todtnauberg. Although Celan, unlike Buber, refused to be photographed with Heidegger, although he, the bereaved Central European Jew, found it difficult to meet with a man whose tainted history was ineradicable, the poet reluctantly accepted the thinker's proposal.[17] Gerhard Neumann, who drove Celan to the meeting, would report his memories of that day, recounting the long periods of "painful silence" as Celan pressed Heidegger to acknowledge his involvement with the Third Reich and publicly denounce current extremist movements.[18] Soon after the meeting, Celan provided his wife Gisèle with a terse report:

> Heidegger had approached me — The day after my reading I went, with M. Neumann, to Heidegger's cabin (Hütte) in the Black Forest. Then, in the car there was a serious dialogue, with very clear words on my part. M. Neumann, who witnessed this, told me afterwards that for him the conversation had had an epochal aspect. I hope that Heidegger will take up his pen and write a few echoing and also warning pages, as Nazism rises again.[19]

16 Lyon 2006:97–98.

17 As reported in the memoires of Celan's host, Gerhart Baumann. For a full account, see Baumann 1986:59–82.

18 Cited in Otto Pöggeler (1989:76). See also Lyon 2006:159–172.

19 "Heidegger était venu vers moi – Le lendemain de ma lecture j'ai été, avec M. Neumann, dans le cabanon (Hütte) de Heidegger dans la Forêt-Noire. Puis ce fut dans la voiture un dialogue grave, avec des paroles claires de ma part. M. Neumann, qui en fut le témoin, m'a dit ensuite que pour lui cette conversation avait eu un aspect épochal. J'espère que Heidegger prendra

While Heidegger never wrote those pages, Celan memorialized the encounter in "Todtnauberg," a poem initially published by Éditions Brunidor in a limited edition, which appeared on January 12, 1968, the day, incidentally, that Celan attended Adorno's guest lecture at the Collège de France.[20] Two weeks afterwards, Celan sent a signed copy to Heidegger and would later revise it for what would turn out to be his last collection, *Lichtzwang*, published in 1970, posthumously.

TODTNAUBERG

Arnika, Augentrost, der
Trunk aus dem Brunnen mit dem
Sternwürfel drauf,

in der
Hütte,

die in das Buch
— wessen Namen nahms auf
von dem meinen? —,
die in dies Buch
geschriebene Zeile von
einer Hoffnung, heute,
auf eines Denkenden
kommendes
Wort
im Herzen,

Waldwasen, uneingeebnet,
Orchis und Orchis, einzeln,

Krudes, später, im Fahren,
deutlich,

der uns fährt, der Mensch,
der's mit anhört,

sa plume et qu'il écrira quelques pages faisant écho, avertissant aussi, alors que le nazisme remonte" (August 2, 1967; Celan 2001b:550).

20 As reported by Werner Hamacher (2011:50–51). My subsequent reading of the poem is highly indebted to Hamacher's insights throughout.

die halb-
beshcrittenen Knüppel-
pfade im Hochmoor,

Feuchtes,
viel.

Lichtzwang version, 1970[21]

TODTNAUBERG

Arnika, eyebright, the
drink from the well with the
star-die on top,

in the
cabin,
into that book
— whose name did it register
before mine? —
into this book
the inscribed line about
a hope, today,
for a thinking-man's
coming
word
in the heart,

forest-turf, unleveled,
orchis and orchis, singly,

something crude, later, while driving,
distinctly,
he who drives us, the man,
who listens in,

the half-
trodden bludgeon-
path on the high moor,

[21] Celan 2000: vol. 2, 255–56.

something moist,
much.[22]

The single sentence, spread across twenty-six terse lines, features no finite verb apart from those that appear in subordinate clauses, an almost motionless description that nonetheless moves from outside (the flowers, *Arnica* and *Augentrost*, and the well with star-shaped ornament), into the cabin (focusing on the guest book), outside again (more flowers), and then, while being driven away along a bumpy path upon the high moorland, a "distinctly crude" conversation, an exchange that the driver listens to but one that we are not given to hear.

Having received the speaker into his forest hut, the host performs a kind of non-reception, which reflects his guest's own non-engagement. Quite unusually for Celan's lyric style, the poem does not have any explicit addressee, no *Du*. Correlatively, the sole trace of the first-person singular appears obliquely in the possessive pronoun, as part of a question, moreover, set off by long dashes: "— whose name did [the book] register / before mine? —" (vv. 7–8). The parenthesis contains the only instance of a verb in the preterite (*nahm*), which closely rhymes with its object, *Namen*, altogether comprising a thought about the past and consequently a "hope" for the future (*Hoffnung*, v. 11), a hope already evoked at the head of the poem, the *Arnica* and the *Augentrost* ("eyebright," v. 1), two flowers known for their healing properties. When the would-be interlocutor finally emerges, however, he is reduced to or abstracted into a verbal substantive with an indefinite article (*eines Denkenden*), a stark relegation of the potential second-person to a third-person form, which seems to undercut all expectation for a vital or productive exchange. The parenthesized, interrogative reflection on the past—who was the previous guest and did a proper conversation ensue?—implies that any honest dialogue will remain but an internal conjecture. As for the crude conversation in the car, it is reserved solely for the one listening in, for the third person, the one there but absent from the discourse. The scene does suggest some connection by evoking the first-person plural (*uns*, v. 20), but again in the accusative case, as opposed to nominative subjects of speech or action. Austere harmony, indeed.

Every attempt to get inside, to become intimate, to reach the "heart," is soundly disrupted. The line-break, *in der / Hütte* (vv. 4–5), is iconic, representing a trip or near stumble on the threshold, and also programmatic. As Werner Hamacher points out, through splitting the phrase, the *in* literally remains outside.[23] Thus, every attempt to get inside, to become intimate, to reach the "heart" (v. 15), is soundly disrupted. The syntax is likewise perplexing. The *die* that follows (*in der Hütte, die* ...) is likely to be heard at first as a relative pronoun, with *Hütte* as the antecedent ("in the cabin, *which* ..."), until, reading on, it is seen to function as a definitive article governing *Zeile* ("line,"

22 I have modified Michael Hamburger's translation for literalness (1978:58–59).

23 Cf. Hamacher 2011:24.

v. 10), stretched across an extended attributive clause ("the into-this-book-inscribed line"). An entry contained or held up by an entrance. The speaker enters within without the encounter he longed-for or perhaps feared.

The line in Heidegger's guest book, preserved in the archives, reads:

> Ins Hüttenbuch, mit dem Blick auf den Brunnenstern,
> mit einer Hoffnung auf ein kommendes Wort im Herzen
> am 25. Juli 1967
> Paul Celan.[24]
>
> Into the cabin-book, with the view of the well-star
> with hope for a coming word in the heart
> on July 25, 1967
> Paul Celan.

The poem reprises the original entry and thereby doubles and divides it, which is precisely what "Todtnauberg" conveys: a differential repetition between the line inscribed "into *that* book" (*in <u>das</u> Buch*, v. 6, i.e., the guest register) and "into *this* book" (*in <u>dies</u> Buch*, v. 9, i.e., the printed poem). The distinction is amplified in the poem by the parenthetic reflection, which increases the distance between "that book" and "this book," which of course matches the temporal gap between visiting the cabin and writing the poem. In the earlier, Brunidor version of the poem, which Celan sent to Heidegger, another parenthesis appears in rounded brackets:

> [die] Zeile von
> einer Hoffnung, heute,
> auf eines Denkenden
> kommendes (un-
> gesäumt kommendes)
> Wort
>
> Brunidor, ed., 1968, vv. 10–15
>
> [the] line about
> a hope, today,
> for a thinking-man's
> coming (un-
> delayed coming)
> word

[24] The text is found in Pöggeler 1986:165.

The parenthesized wish, that the "word"—presumably, an acknowledgment, a confession, and/or a denunciation—may arrive "without delay" (*ungesäumt*) trips through a deflatingly dilatory syntax, holding the hope and the hoped-for word far apart in a troubling syncope. The line-break that splits the adverbial *ungesäumt* exposes the "seams" (*Säume*) that cause the desire for promptness to stutter and threaten to distort the scene into one of "delinquency" or "default" (*Säumnis*), "neglect" or "dereliction" (*Versäumnis*). The opportunity to speak may prove to be a fatally missed opportunity. Still, although a parenthesis interrupts the discursive momentum, it is generally taken to be a provisional disturbance. A final word will occur, one that will either grant or demolish hope. Clearly, by the time he revised the poem for publication in *Lichtzwang*, Celan had decided that the wait for a heartfelt avowal from Heidegger was not only temporary but also utterly delusional, that the coming word would never come.

Too much violence, too much wounding, too much death seem to stand between the guest and host in "Todtnauberg," as well as between Celan and Heidegger in Totdtnauberg. As Hamacher underscores, the rare term *Wasen* ("sward" or "patch of turf," v. 16) not only distorts Heidegger's *Wesen* ("essence," as in *Das Wesen der Dichtung*, "The Essence of Poetry"), but also refers, according to the Grimms' historical dictionary, to "the land where the skinner or *Wasenmeister* disembowels and buries the cattle."[25] The gory image is perpetuated by the word *Krudes* ("something crude," v. 18), from Latin *crudus*, "bloody, dripping with blood," and the fractured *Knüppel-pfade* ("bludgeon-path," v. 23–24), which likely refers to the thick clubs that stud the wooded trail, while conjuring the crude weapon, an "unleveled" path (v. 16), littered with deeply troubling *problemata*, and finally, the *Moor* itself, a homonym of "death" (*mort*) in the language of Celan's adopted home which hearkens back to the "death" (*Tod*) in the titular *Todtnauberg*. The innocent, Hellenic *Orchis* (v. 17), which can denote either an "orchid" or "testicle" (ὄρχις), summons the dark and dreary Orcus. Two *testes*—two eye-witnesses whose testimony ought to inseminate discourse—face each other, *Orchis und Orchis*, yet remain separate, alone, apart (*einzeln*).

In an early draft of the poem, Celan opens intertextually with a citation from Hölderlin's hymn, *Friedensfeier* ("Celebration of Peace"): *Seit ein Gespräch wir sind* ("Since a conversation we have been"), one of the five *Leitworte* or, pace Adorno, "skewers," which organized Heidegger's 1936 essay, "Hölderlin and the Essence of Poetry":

> Seit ein Gespräch wir sind,
> an dem
> wir würgen,
> an dem ich würge,

25 "das land wo der abdecker oder wasenmeister das vieh ausweidet und verscharrt," Jacob Grimm and Wilhelm Grimm, *Deutsches Wörterbuch*, s.v. Wasen.

das mich
aus mir hinausstieß, dreimal,
viermal.

Im Ohr
wirbelnde
Schläfenasche, die
eine, letzte
Gedankenfrist duldend,
Feuchtes, viel[26]

Since a conversation we have been,
on which
we choke,
on which I choke,
which I
cast out, three times,
four times.

In the ear
whirling
temple-ashes, which
one, last
thought-deadline enduring,
something moist, much.

What should have been a "conversation" (*Gespräch*), a concurrence that would have sealed the bond of the first-person plural pronoun (*wir*), like the reconciliation described in Hölderlin's "Celebration of Peace," was in fact a choking fit: In this preliminary version, the *wir* modulates to *würgen*, a strangulation that would require three or four attempts to set the experience into a poem. The words whirled troublingly in the old thinker's ears half concealed by ash-gray hair at the temples (*Schläfenasche*) as one final "deadline" (*Frist*) was granted for a "thought" (*Gedanke*). For the poem's final version, nothing from this earlier draft was retained saved for the last line, *Feuchtes / viel* ("something moist, much," vv. 25–26). Now split into two lines, the conclusion may allude to the drenched path on the moor or to the tearful moisture that possibly "fell" (*fiel*) yet probably did not, a potential atonement that instead left "much" (*viel*) to be said, on one's own, on their own.

[26] Paul Celan, *Lichtzwang: Vorstufen–Textgenese–Endfassung* (Tübinger Ausgabe; 2020:49).

Jargon

Günter Grass met Celan in Paris in December 1956. The twenty-nine-year-old sculptor, graphic artist, and dramatist, originally from Danzig, had moved from West Berlin to the French capital only several months before with the primary intention of completing his first novel-in-progress, *Die Blechtrommel* (*The Tin Drum*). Celan, aged thirty-six, had not only been living in Paris for eight years but had also been recognized as a prominent poet since the publication of "Todesfuge" in 1952. In addition to their different standing in the literary world, and in addition to the age gap between them, at a point in history when being a mere seven years older made a horrifically fateful difference, there were of course radical contrasts in upbringing and temperament, with Celan's immediate family having been exterminated by a regime to which Grass had sworn absolute loyalty until his seventeenth year. Nonetheless, the two men found sufficient common ground: Two German-speaking artists from the East now living in France, united in their commitment to find a poetic language in the wake of utter catastrophe.

Decades afterwards, Grass would recollect: "I had the most intense contact with Paul Celan, although we were as different as people can be. And yet it worked; it worked in a sometimes exhausting but wonderful way."[27] In one sense, Grass regarded the relationship as one between neophyte and mentor: "Here and there [*Zwischendurch*] conversations [*Gespräche*] with Paul Celan; or rather, I was an audience for his monologues"; while, in another sense, it led to heated disputes: "Right at the start I told him, I'm not a wall you're talking to. And then we had real arguments [*Streitgespräche*]."[28] Grass appears to have found these conversations-*qua*-confrontations especially important, as he acknowledges in his lecture for the Frankfurt Poetics series, "Writing after Auschwitz" (1990): "I owe a lot to Paul Celan: stimulation, contradiction, the concept of loneliness, but also the realization that Auschwitz has no end. His help never came directly, but was given in passing [*in Nebensätzen*], for example on walks in the park."[29] All in all, the biographical accounts depict an inspiring and fruitful exchange driven by contradiction, one that preserved the solitariness of both participants, a drawing near

27 "Den stärksten Kontakt hatte ich mit Paul Celan, wobei wir beide so unterschiedlich waren, wie Menschen nur unterschiedlich sein können, und dennoch ging es; es ging auf eine manchmal anstrengende, aber doch wunderbare Weise." From a radio interview (1996), in Grass 2020: vol. 24, 491.

28 "Zwischendurch Gespräche mit Paul Celan; oder besser, war ich Publikum seiner Monologe" (NGA 21, 383); "Ich habe ihm gleich zu Anfang gesagt, ich bin nicht die Wand, zu der du sprichst. Und dann hatten wir richtige Streitgespräche" (Grass 2020: vol. 24, 481–482).

29 "Ich verdanke Paul Celan viel: Anregung, Widerspruch, den Begriff von Einsamkeit, aber auch die Erkenntnis, dass Auschwitz kein Ende hat. Seine Hilfe kam nie direkt, sondern verschenkte sich in Nebensätzen, etwa auf Spaziergängen in Parkanlagen" (Grass 1990:30). For a fuller account of the friendship and the many themes and motifs that link their work, see Frizen 2024:105–152.

that also drew them apart, a communication *in Nebensätzen*, as though in the form of asides or *Nebenbemerkungen*, almost parenthetically.

Celan recommended authors and titles that were unfamiliar to Grass who grew up in an era of severe censorship. Most significantly, there was Rabelais, an author who fueled his picaresque adventures with an overblown, heteroglossic mix of erudition and bawdiness, sophistication and vulgarity, in a resolutely anti-classical, unsolemn manner that would play an exceptionally strong role in shaping Grass's burgeoning style. As informal mentor, Celan read and commented on the chapter drafts for *The Tin Drum* before Grass presented his work and won the annual prize at the 1958 meeting of the Gruppe 47. And the older poet remained a vital resource as the younger writer began drafting his second large-scale novel, *Hundejahre* (*Dog Years*). In sum, Celan encouraged Grass as he, Celan, drove himself: to continue to write, to persist in the aftermath of disaster, and thus to contest the pronouncement that invariably oppressed every serious German writer of the era. To speak what is already speakable is hardly a challenge, unlike attempts to testify to an unspeakable hell in all its ugly, evil horror. *Hoc opus, hic labor est*. In Grass's formulation: "Adorno's commandment [*Gebot*] struck me as a downright unnatural prohibition [*Verbot*]; as if someone, like God the Father, had presumed to forbid the birds to sing."[30]

Perhaps because birds cannot or should not be silenced, in *Dog Years*, Grass named the most prominent of the three narrator-protagonists Eddi Amsel, after the common word for "blackbird." Born near Danzig in 1917, Amsel pursues his artistic inclinations by making shockingly effective scarecrows. His expressionist style, coupled with his status as a "half-Jew" (*Halbjude*) under Nazi ordinances, singles him out as a target of excessive violence, even at the hands of his former "blood-brother" and protector, Walter Matern. After Amsel produced a group of nine scarecrows dressed up as paramilitary SA men, Matern leads a gang of nine hooded ruffians to beat the degenerate, half-Jewish artist to a bloody pulp, a thrashing that knocks out every one of Amsel's thirty-two teeth. Subsequently, through a variety of aliases—including Haseloff, Mr. Brooks, and the repaired Goldmäulchen ("Goldmouth")—Amsel evades Nazi persecution as a ballet and theater impresario and, after the war, now as Brauchsel, Brauksel, or Brauxel, he emerges as the wealthy owner of a large factory that mass produces mechanical scarecrows. It is Brauchsel-Amsel who has commissioned two other Danzig-born authors, Harry Liebenau and his boyhood friend Matern, to prepare chronicles covering the years 1917 to 1961, which he will gather along with his own memoirs in the single volume that comprises Grass's *Dog Years*.

A manufacturer of scarecrows, Amsel is a blackbird whose business is to drive away birds, an auto-apotropaic operation, as it were, a mode of artistic expression

30 "Geradezu widernatürlich kam mir Adornos Gebot als Verbot vor; als hätte sich jemand gottväterlich angemaßt, den Vögeln das Singen zu verbieten" (Grass 1990:15).

designed as if to frighten off an essential, avian part of the artist himself or perhaps a sublimated birdsong that motivates or is motivated by its own absence. Amsel's artistic practice in part explains his fascination with *Geschlecht und Charakter* (*Sex and Character*), the infamously popular study by the Viennese philosopher, Otto Weininger, first published in 1903. A young man of Jewish descent who converted to Christian Protestantism, Weininger interprets Anti-Semitism as the projected desire to shed unwanted personal shortcomings, to rid oneself of the without within. In Weininger's view, grossly outlined, the desire stems primarily from the feminine-passive principle that he ascribes to Jewish self-consciousness, a negative core that, once articulated and exorcised, can reinforce the positive, masculine-active principle purportedly underlying Aryan consciousness. Published only months before the author's suicide at the age of twenty-three, Weininger's *Sex and Character* attracted a broad readership across the Austro-Hungarian Empire. Its theses were seriously considered even by leading Jewish thinkers and artists, including Karl Kraus, Ludwig Wittgenstein, and Franz Kafka.[31] James Joyce as well is known to have consulted the 1906 English translation of Weininger's work as a key resource for the characterization of Leopold Bloom in *Ulysses*.[32] By 1933, *Sex and Character* had been foraged to yield Nazi-propagandist sound bites that effectively contributed to the hate-driven jargon broadcast throughout the "dog years." In *Dog Years*, a copy of the book belongs to Eddi Amsel's father, who has underlined many passages in red pencil, especially from the chapter that focuses on "Jewry" (*Das Judentum*)—a "standard reference" that is shown to have shaped collective beliefs of the age: "the standard work, six-hundred-page-work, a work unparalleled, devil's work, Weininger's work,"[33] a work moreover that chillingly elucidates young Amsel's scarecrow-making agenda. Particularly telling is the following passage from Weininger's study, cited verbatim in the novel:

> Provisionally speaking, Judaism's world-historical significance and immense merit is none other than its capacity to make the Aryan constantly aware of himself, to warn [*mahnen*] him of himself. This is what the Aryan has to thank the Jew for; through him he knows what to beware of: Judaism as a possibility within himself.[34]

31 For a critical overview, see Sengoopta 2000.

32 See Elbay 2016.

33 "das Standardwerk, Sechshundertseitenwerk, Werksondergleichen, Teufelswerk, Weiningers Werk." Grass, *Hundejahre* (1963), 220. Subsequent citations from this edition are marked *HJ*.

34 "Es ist, vorläufig gesprochen, vielleicht die welthistorische Bedeutung und das ungeheure Verdienst des Judentums kein anderes, als den Arier immerfort zum Bewußtsein seines Selbst zu bringen, ihn an sich zu mahnen. Dies ist es, was der Arier dem Juden zu danken hat; durch ihn weiß er, wovor er sich hüte: vor dem Judentum als Möglichkeit in ihm selber." Otto Weininger, *Geschlecht und Charakter: Eine prinzipielle Untersuchung* [1903] (1920:405); cited verbatim in Grass *HJ*, 220. See Neuhaus 1992:86 and Minden, 2013:30–31.

Amsel's art is thus viewed as an admonition, one that elicits a terrifying reaction from his Aryan neighbors. Through mimetic production, the artist reveals the hated tendencies lodged in the souls of his audience.

The motif of admonition (*Mahnung*) is pertinent. Although the common blackbird (*Amsel*, L. *merula*) is generally taken to be a bird that sings, it also recalls the crow or jackdaw that caws and therefore warns, as emphasized by the Latin name for the jackdaw, *monedula*, from *monere*, "to warn, admonish." The Czech word for "jackdaw" is *kavka* and thus summons Franz Kafka, whose Hebrew first name was *Amschel*—a line that not only returns us to Grass's Amsel but also, provocatively if not altogether troublingly, to Paul Celan's given family name, the cognate *Antschel*, a connection that Celan himself explicitly made.[35] To the extent that an author's memory can be trusted, it was Celan who emboldened Grass to develop complex Jewish characters, including Eddi Amsel, "to insert not noble but ordinary and eccentric Jews into my petty-bourgeois novel-world."[36] The unsettling jargon culled from Weininger's study and mimicked by Amsel the blackbird emphasize the essence, so to speak, of *jargon* itself—a term possibly derived from Late Latin *gaggire*, an onomatopoetic verb to describe the incomprehensible chattering of birds. The history of this usage in English has been consistent, from the word's first appearance in Chaucer, who depicts the pleasant twitter of a speckled magpie ("ful of jargon as a flekked pye"),[37] to the "little birds" which excite Coleridge's Ancient Mariner "with their sweet jargoning,"[38] while in early-twentieth-century German, the term can denote Yiddish dialect, as in Kafka's "Introductory Lecture on Yiddish" (*Einleitungsvortrag über Jargon*, 1912) or his reference to the Yiddish Theater in Prague as *das Jargontheater*.[39]

Weininger's *Sex and Character* is hardly the sole text that is taken up and parodied in *Dog Years*. Besides Grass's typically wide-ranging allusive style, there are several books that consistently intervene on the narrative, including, most importantly, Martin Heidegger's *Being and Time*. Heidegger's shadow lurked palpably in the background as Grass composed the novel between 1959 and 1962. The now elderly philosopher not only inspired and unnerved Celan, especially as the poet prepared *Meridian*, his key poetological text which he presented on the occasion of receiving the Büchner Prize in October 1960 but also held prominence as the grand enchanter whose so-called jargon of authenticity continued to echo across high German culture. In Grass's treatment,

35 "Kafka hieß mit seinem jüdischen Vornamen *Amschel*, Antschel ist eine Nebenform davon; mittelhochdeutsche heißt *amschel*—Amsel." Celan to Reinhard Federmann, March 1962, cited in Hillard 2007:305.

36 Grass 1990:29–30.

37 Geoffrey Chaucer, *The Canterbury Tales* "The Merchant's Tale," v. 636.

38 Samuel Taylor Coleridge, *Rime of the Ancient Mariner*, Part 5.

39 The Kafka citations, as well as the references to Chaucer and Coleridge, are taken from Marjorie Garber's discussion on "jargon" (2009:105–106).

Heidegger's presence is conjured through Eddi Amsel's difficult friend, Walter Matern, who kept a copy of *Being and Time* in his rucksack during the war, even after he had been dishonorably discharged from the Wehrmacht on charges of alcoholism and theft. Together with the Catholicism of his childhood and the lyric poems of Gottfried Benn, Heidegger's fondness for neologisms and etymological figures, pronounced under the rustic cover of a pointed stocking cap (*Zipfelmütze*), supplies Matern with a peculiar dialect. As Harry Liebenau, the narrator of the novel's second part, explains: Matern "mixed liturgical texts, the phenomenology of a sleeping cap [*einer Zipfelmütze Phänomenologie*] and worldly curly lyric poetry into a salad flavored with the cheapest juniper schnapps" (*HJ* 285). Heidegger-German (*Heideggerdeutsch*) punctuates Matern's dilatory account with satirical syntagms, for example, *Der Mensch menscht* ("The human being humans") and *Das Ding dingt* ("The Thing things"), along with a nearly constant surge of vocabulary entries: *Unverborgenheit* ("Unconcealment"), *Nichtung* ("Nihilation"), *Seinsstand* ("Stance of Being"), *Hergestelltheit* ("Producedness"), *Fernsinn* ("Distance-Sense"), and so forth.[40]

Matern is the protagonist-narrator of the third and final part of *Dog Years*, the "Materniad," where devastation and shame are exacerbated by his inner conflicts, his simultaneous attempts to admit and suppress his guilt, above all, the guilt over having instigated a gang of thugs to knock the teeth out of his old blood-brother, Eddi Amsel. After Germany's defeat, however, as Matern wanders across the war-torn landscape, he redirects his aggression outward, now blaming Heidegger for the rise of National Socialism; the philosopher in the cusped stocking-cap (*Zipfelmütze*) is thus placed on an equal footing with the mad Führer, who had his "umbilical cord cut in the same cusped-stocking-cap-year [*Zipfelmützenjahr*]" (*HJ* 474). With inebriated delirium, Matern grinds out a rage-filled litany: *Zipfel, Ge-zipfel, Zipflung, entzipfelt, Gezipfelheit* ("cusp, cusp-frame [modeled on the Heideggerean *Ge-stell*], cusping, de-cusped, cuspness," *HJ* 476). He has decided to hunt down the fabled thinker, first in Freiburg and then at his cabin in Todtnauberg, but like *alētheia*, the cusped-cap withdraws upon every approach, and Matern must rest content with demolishing the garden gate (*HJ* 477).

While resuming his Rabelaisian drift from one city to the next, Matern soon learns that his former comrades all speak in a like cusped manner. Accordingly, a stray black dog, believed to have been the Führer's favorite, is absurdly interpreted à la Heidegger as a "hole" (*Loch*): *Ein schwarzes laufendes vom Fernsinn durchstimmtes Loch offenbart das Nichts in seiner ursprünglichen Offenbarkeit* ("A black running hole tuned by Distance-Sense reveals the Nothing in its original revealability," *HJ* 418). Grass's parodic critique is clear: As with Weininger's hideously misogynist, anti-Semitic theses, Heidegger-German provides a jargony screen or even a "speech-grille" (*Sprachgitter*) that frames or parcels or distorts the hard reality: another paragrammatic discourse that

40 For a comprehensive overview with citations, see Kiefer 2002:246.

intrudes upon a more realistic account and thus dubiously allows an entire generation to evade shame, guilt, and responsibility, including, of course, the author's own.

Anti-Classicism

In drawing in what ostensibly ought to stay out, parenthetic interruptions frustrate classical ambitions towards symmetry, harmony, and integrity, balance, concord, and beauty. Hence, for authors who reject classicizing expectations, for those who emphatically wish to raise problems, parenthetic practices serve as a potently creative resource.

Günter Grass clearly numbers among those who have been especially attuned to this potential. In an essay from 1967, he attributes his explicitly "anti-classical" approach to techniques derived from the novels of Alfred Döblin. For Grass, "classical" and "anti-classical" do not designate any historical period or literary sensibility but rather involve specific treatments of narrative chronology. He therefore contrasts Döblin's anti-classical procedures with classical narrators like Thomas Mann and, rather surprisingly, Bertolt Brecht. In Grass's view, the works of the apparently conservative Mann and the blatantly radical Brecht both consciously exhibit a narrative design that "fits into the plan of classicism [*Klassizität*],"[41] a *plan* that Döblin boldly deployed by allowing multiple historical sequences to impinge on the story's flat line, its *planum*. In Grass's assessment, with Döblin, discontinuous paths cut through the chronological continuity. Marginal vectors obstruct the smooth recounting. Closed systems are broken open to admit the noxious noise of parasitic interferences, to include the excluded and thereby host a spectral *absentia in praesentia*.[42]

Rather than reading "absolutely" or "flatly"—Grass's word is *platterdings*—an engagement with Döblin's novels must attend to the disruptions that reveal three-dimensional depth, a volume that enriches, complicates and challenges the two-dimensional storyline. Here, parenthetic incursions move well beyond their ascribed role as dismissible, eminently removable parcels of speech and instead emerge as cognitive invasions that must be addressed in all their recalcitrance, in all their resistance to being smoothly integrated into the main body of the text.

According to Grass, the simultaneity of multiple, competing temporal dimensions produces deictic vividness in that a story from the past becomes an event in the present and the reader becomes a witness. The effect is one of ἐνάργεια or *illustratio*, which conjures the past and the future before the readers' eyes: a *Vergegenwärtigung* or *presentification*, whereby the present scene is infiltrated and inflated by what is

41 "Die Arbeit eines Thomas Mann, mehr noch die Arbeit des Bertolt Brecht, fügte sich bewußt in den von den Autoren entworfenen und im Detail vollendeten Plan der Klassizität." Günter Grass, "Über meinen Lehrer Döblin" [1967], in Grass 1997: vol. 14, 264.

42 For a provocative discussion, see Serres 2007.

absent. Through parenthetic interferences, Döblin's realist plots are punctuated by the no-longer and the not-yet, by elements that are part of the main narrative only by being apart from its chronological unfolding. Two discursive impulses are distinguished throughout: one that conforms to a straightforward narrative from beginning to end, and another that breaks with and upsets this path, skewing the primary temporal pulse by inviting other narrative vectors that cut through and depart from the principal story.

According to Grass, Döblin's parenthetic technique played a determinant role in the composition of his own work, beginning with *The Tin Drum* (1959). Presented as a confessional memoir, the main plot chronologically recounts the life story of the first-person narrator, Oskar Matzerath, from his mother's conception in 1899 to his thirtieth birthday in 1954. In stitching together this fifty-five-year-long narrative, additional material constantly protrudes from below and falls from above the story's flat surface. Imported material obstructs the reader's easy path. The persistent mythic and historical digressions, as well as Oskar's intrusive comments from the time of writing, interrupt the narrated time. Past and future discourses appear vividly—*enargetically*—as absences, absences that are nonetheless parenthetically present. They are quite literally *problems* or προβλήματα—large stones that get in the way, block the story's progression, and thereby compel us to navigate and renegotiate before we are permitted to resume along the main plot's direction. The autobiographic chronicle is thus rendered uneven, not smooth, not flat. Every element of the main plot is overburdened, oversaturated, and overdetermined, which prevents the reader from reading *platterdings*.

Parentheses accord well with Grass's conception of literary and critical writing. As he has repeatedly claimed, a writer is someone who writes "against elapsing time" (*gegen die verstreichende Zeit*) or "against the tow" (*gegen den Sog*).[43] In other words, Grass sees himself as a literary artist who resists the tug of the chronological story; he breaks with the impulse to adhere to the principal plot by letting ghostly presences intrude—present absences that generate a surplus of meanings, undermine the chronicle, and potentially evade the narrator's control. For Grass, the writer should be someone who grants ample room to infiltrating disturbances, someone who seeks out turbulence rather than choose a flightpath that arrives at its planned destination without delay (*ungesäumt*) or without re-routing. In his view, the writer is someone who looks for problems.

Oskar Matzerath, of course, is nothing if not a problem child. His brash drumming aims to rouse people out of their conformist stupor. He imports differing rhythms—differing *tempi*—that trip up the dominant beat. A poignant example comes from the episode that depicts a Nazi rally in Danzig in 1933. As the procession into the arena files in, Oskar hides beneath the grandstand and bangs out a waltz that breaks the tug of the military band's march. It is not long before the strictures of disciplined movement

43 See Neuhaus 1992:118.

surrender to the loose and spiraling sway. Iconically, the tin-drummer is bracketed below the rostrum, a position that is hidden yet nonetheless present, which enables his non-participatory, three-quarter beats to hurl the main spectacle into utter disarray: "Law went down the drain and sense of order" (*Gesetz ging flöten und Ordnungssinn*, 154/109).[44] The German idiom, *flöten gehen*, literally means "to go piping" and therefore to go missing or be lost, to disappear with the wind, like the breath that passes through a flute (*Flöte*). The figure of speech likely derives from the same Hebraic-Jewish root that forms the German *pleite* ("bankrupt"), that is, when one's fortune is all spent.[45] Thus, in addition to the scene's bracketed staging and counter-rhythmic incursion, the formulation parenthetically broaches a Semitic current that thwarts a political ideology fueled by anti-Semitism, while also sounding an allusion to a legend that prominently appears throughout the novel, namely the legend of the Pied Piper (*Rattenfänger*) who lured the rats out of Hamelin in Lower Saxony—all tellingly articulated in a performative hyperbaton: "Law went down the drain and sense of order."

As a child who claims to have willfully stopped growing at the age of three, Oskar operates throughout as a parenthetical figure. His dwarf-perspective enables him to remain apart from the reality in which he participates—an outsider on the inside. The perpetual three-year-old presents himself as innocent, ignorant, and vulnerable, as possessing qualities that allow him to observe up close an especially fraught period in German history. Yet, until he begins to grow again, he rarely suffers the consequences of direct involvement. He intervenes in the world as a protagonist who is presumably and dubiously exempt from the world.

As a problem child, Oskar serves as the story's unreliable narrator, which is to say, he is reliably unreliable. The novel's very first word—*zugegeben*, "granted"—delivers a concessive force that qualifies every statement that follows. "Granted [*zugegeben*]: I am an inmate of a mental hospital [*ich bin Insasse einer Heil- und Pflegeanstalt*]" (9/3). His confinement as a court-ordered "inmate" (*Insasse*) underscores his parenthetical status, held or bracketed in a hospital that is located in everyday reality, protected by the bars of his bed. Moreover, the novel's incipit—*zugegeben*—broaches serious questions regarding the act of reading. In taking up "what is given" (*das Gegebene*) and "what is admitted" (*das Zugegebende*), every reader is invited to reflect on the promise and limits of reception, just as Oskar places himself in the recipient's role in order to *give* and *confess* the stories that constitute the novel. He is a reader, a witness, and a writer—someone who has received the mythic and historical material that he in turn passes along to his audience.

44 All references to the novel are from Günter Grass, *Die Blechtrommel* [1959] (2011) and *The Tin Drum*, Breon Mitchell, trans. (2010), with my modifications.

45 Jacob Grimm and Wilhelm Grimm, *Deutsches Wörterbuch*, s.v. "flöten" (woerterbuchnetz.de).

What results is a dynamic conglomeration of past, present, and future, a temporal collocation that produces uncanny effects of vividness. Early on in the novel, Oskar drums up a realist description of the banks of the Vistula as they appeared before he was born. The description sets the scene for the story of Oskar's grandfather Koljaiczek, who worked on the river as a raftsman, yet almost as soon as the flat or slightly hilly landscape is evoked, it serves as a broad screen upon which images of Poland's past and future are projected:

> flat [*plan*] between the scattered farms, just made for cavalry attacks, for a division of Uhlans to wheel in from the left onto the sand table, for hedge-vaulting Hussars, for the dreams of young cavalry officers, for battles long past and battles yet to come, for an oil painting: tartars flat [*flach*], dragoons rearing up, Brethren of the Sword falling, grandmasters staining their noble robes [...] the pretty tanks, dreaming of days to come when they too would be allowed to enter the picture, to come out onto the plain [*Ebene*] beyond the Vistula's dikes (18)[46]

The long conjuring, which continues unabated for two pages, interrupts the story of Koljaiczek's fate—an extended parenthesis that recalls the tour that Aeneas takes with King Evander in Vergil's *Aeneid* 8, a stroll through the wilderness of Latium, which is the future site of Rome. In both cases, the negative power of the no-longer and the not-yet intrudes upon the positivism of the present moment and thereby trips up the flow of the narrative at hand. Parallel planes from centuries past intersect with and rattle the otherwise pastoral environment of the current scene.

Niobe

A similarly strong parenthetic effect is found in the chapter entitled *Niobe*, though in a much more expansive form. As the penultimate chapter of the novel's first book, it is situated at a moment when the dramatic pulse of the primary plot is particularly strong. Overall, the first book recounts Oskar's early life, from childhood to adolescence, and culminates with the excruciating death of his mother Agnes—understandably, a major event in the autobiography, which propels the reader to the eve of the outbreak of war, which will be depicted in the novel's second part. After the burial of Oskar's mother, the

[46] "plan zwischen Einzelgehöften, geschaffen für Kavallerieattacken, für eine links im Sandkasten einschwenkende Ulanendivision, für über Hecken hetzende Husaren, für die Träume junger Rittmeister, für die Schlacht, die schon dagewesen, die immer wieder kommt, für das Gemälde: Tartaren flach, Dragoner aufbäumend, Schwertritter stürzend, Hochmeister färbend den Ordensmantel [...] die hübschen, vom kommenden Tage träumenden Panzer, da auch sie ins Bild, hinausdürfen auf die Ebene hinter den Weichseldeichen" (*Die Blechtrommel*, 30).

narrative drive is inexorable, moving headlong into disaster. Yet, suddenly, as we are being borne along the strong current, the *Niobe* chapter brings the narrative momentum to a halt. A drawn-out episode intervenes and features but a tenuous relation to the main story, very much like a parenthesis that can be removed without upsetting the autobiography's integrity. Not surprisingly, Volker Schlöndorff, in his film adaptation which otherwise remains very faithful to the novel, chose not to include this scene. The novel alone includes the exclusion, sets it in brackets, where it can exert its force before the plot proper may resume its forward itinerary.

If the name Niobe signals a moment of classical reception, its function in Grass's novel can only be understood as a parenthesis of reception. Readers who might expect some retelling or reworking of the classical myth would be frustratingly disappointed. The *Niobe* chapter is neither a transformation nor an imitation, neither a subversion nor a correction of the classical myth; it does not offer a parodic revision or a creative misprision of the ancient source, at least not in any immediately discernible way. Indeed, Grass neglects the traditional plot altogether. Instead of alluding to the beautiful and arrogant Phrygian queen who was punished by the gods, instead of evoking the cruel deaths of her fourteen children and her transformation into stone, Niobe in *The Tin Drum* is merely the name of a wooden figurehead that was once attached to the prow of a fifteenth-century Florentine merchant ship and ended up being displayed in the Maritime Museum in Danzig. Yet although her fate is non-mythic—modern and secular and driven by all-too-human greed—the Niobe figurehead is no ordinary museum exhibit and certainly not without significant mythical power. For she has long been ascribed magical powers that destroy men who are seduced by her charms. As Oskar affirms: "This woman [*dieses Weib*], this galleon figure, brought disaster [*Unglück*]" (240/171). Oskar thus disrupts his own life story to relate another, nearly five-hundred-year-long story about this lethal carving painted in green and fitted with amber eyes.

The *Niobe* chapter constitutes a novella in its own right, a parallel text, replete with historical detail and nested in *The Tin Drum* as if in brackets. As is often the case in Grass's novel, the parenthetic gesture installs a narrative window through which parallel contexts impinge on the primary context and thereby demonstrate that every context is permeable. It is this "permeability of contexts" that Ross Chambers views as prerequisite for digression, which allows other storylines to interfere with the principal plot, an interference that is "neither fully discontinuous nor wholly continuous," and therefore a distraction that disrupts disciplined attentiveness.[47] Although digressions, as moments of relaxed discipline, are generally perceived as pleasurable—like the pleasure exhibited by the uniformed soldiers who break with the military march at the rally and instead dance to Oskar's waltz—the distraction could just as well lead into frightening experiences, which is precisely what occurs in the *Niobe* episode.

[47] Chambers 1999:12.

The figurehead was sculpted around 1473 in Bruges and was modeled on a Flemish maiden who was subsequently convicted of witchcraft. Before being burned at the stake, the young woman threatened revenge. As a result, the Florentine banker who commissioned the figure for his ship, Tomasso di Folco Portinari, soon lost his mind and hanged himself. In response, the local Flemish authorities chopped off the hands of the sculptor. The curse next befell the galleon itself. While sailing off the coast of Zeeland, the ship was captured by a horde of Danzig pirates led by Paul Beneke, who brutally murdered Portinari's business partner, Angelo Tani, as well as the entire Florentine crew. The vessel was commandeered to Danzig, where Beneke was expeditiously sentenced to death by drowning in the courtyard of the city's Stockturm, after a mysterious fire had broken out in the harbor. Dozens of vessels had been destroyed, including the Florentine ship, but the Niobe figurehead miraculously survived unscathed.

Over the next centuries, every vessel to which Niobe was affixed suffered blood-soaked mutinies. Now known as the "green kitten," she was charged with causing the murderous insurrection in Danzig in 1522, the subsequent iconoclastic riots, and Danzig's naval defeat in the Swedish campaign during the Thirty Years' War. The poet Martin Opitz is said to have died in Danzig at the age of forty-two after he madly recited his verses to this green *femme fatale* with amber eyes. It was only towards the end of the eighteenth century that Niobe's dark power was contained, when the conquering Prussians locked her away in the old torture chambers of Danzig's Stockturm, the very site where the pirate Paul Beneke had been executed nearly four hundred years earlier. Here, the figurehead would have remained, if the director of the new Maritime Museum, which was established after the signing of the Versailles Treaty, had not retrieved her as an important historical artefact. The director soon paid for his ambition by dying of blood poisoning. The museum's second director understood Niobe as a menace. He tried to present the figurehead to the city of Lübeck, but the citizens of the North German port outright refused to accept the notorious gift. Writing from his hospital bed in 1954, Oskar intervenes to assert that this act of prudence would spare Lübeck from excessive damage during the wartime air raids.

Regardless, back in the 1920s, now firmly installed in Danzig's Maritime Museum, Niobe continued to claim more victims. A new director, an elderly priest, an engineering student, two recent graduates from St. Peter's Gymnasium, and four museum guards all took their lives in front of the enchanting, devilish artefact. Oskar implies that the Weimar Republic, in its liberal commitment to tolerance, similarly included the evil that should have been excluded. Hence, the wooden figure, which was designed to ward off disaster at sea, instead brought misfortune upon all those who trafficked in her allure. The final victim was Oskar's older friend, Herbert Truczinski, who accepted the job that no one else would take: Working the night shift as the museum guard. On the fourteenth day after he assumed his duties, Herbert Truczinski was found half-naked up on top of the figurehead; he had driven a double-ax into Niobe's back and impaled himself on the other blade.

As already suggested, Grass imports Niobe's identity without incorporating her ancient story. The myth is absent yet present, or present only in name, adducing the myth by omitting it. The gestures of separation are consistent: Grass detaches the Phrygian queen from her mythic context just as the Niobe figurehead has been removed from her initial installation on a Florentine ship, only to be torn yet again from her maritime service in the Netherlands and placed on exhibit in Danzig's Maritime Museum. It is likely that Grass developed this chapter after his visit in 1951 to the Museo Navale in La Spezia, which displays a wooden figurehead, painted pale green and identified as Atalanta. In 1923, a museum guard named Vegezi purportedly became so infatuated with the piece that he leapt to his death off a drydock. Subsequently, in 1944, a German officer named Erich Kurtz tried to have the figurehead moved to his quarters, but when his plan failed, he shot himself in the head. In his suicide note, he declared his love for Atalanta to whom he dedicated his life.[48] The details raise key questions: If the classical myth has no function in Grass's novel—if Niobe is merely a name that he inserted for some uncanny but vague effect—why, then, did he not simply call the figurehead Atalanta? Why is Niobe important? Important enough to include as the myth to be excluded?

Although the classical myth of Niobe is neglected in Oskar's account, several motifs appear to warrant its included exclusion. To begin, the figurehead that triggered rampant death and destruction clearly foreshadows the lethal violence about to be unleashed on September 1, 1939, in Danzig. The history of evil contained in the Niobe episode, although it bears no direct relation to Oskar's life story, nonetheless presages the ruinous war which will very much affect Oskar's biography. Oskar's poor friend, Herbert Truczinski, furnishes the pivot out of the Niobe parenthesis and back to the novel's principal plot. By striking the figurehead in the back with a double ax, with the upward facing blade penetrating his own abdomen, Herbert provides an ironic amplification of the notorious *Dolchstoßlegende*, the "stab-in-the-back" theory, which fueled Nazi support and which here is shown to amount to national suicide.

After Herbert was found impaled on top of Niobe, the figurehead was removed to an undisclosed cellar. "But disaster," Oskar writes, "cannot be sealed in a cellar."

> It drains through the pipes with the sewage, it seeps into the gas lines, invades every household, and no one who sets his kettle of soup on bluish flames suspects in the least that disaster is bringing his grub to a boil (181).[49]

[48] See Plard 1984.

[49] "Doch man kann das Unglück nicht einkellern. Mit den Abwässern findet es durch die Kanalisation, es teilt sich den Gasleitungen mit, kommt allen Haushaltungen zu, und niemand, der da sein Suppentöpfchen auf die bläulichen Flammen stellt, ahnt, daß da das Unglück seinen Fraß zum Kochen bringt" (253).

Bracketed behind the locked door of a cellar, Niobe injects evil into the city's utilities—a motif that Oskar elaborates in the subsequent chapter devoted to the Christian Advent season of 1938. *Er kommt! Er kommt!*—"He's coming! He's coming! And who came? The Christ Child, the Savior? Or was it the heavenly Gasman with the gas meter under his arm, ticking away?" (187).[50] From subterranean depths, the latency of the Niobe myth persists to undermine the Advent liturgy. Her destructive power cannot be confined simply by being stored away. Despite being set in brackets—or perhaps precisely because she has been set in brackets—she continues to be in play, just like the atrocities of the Second World War, which cannot be comfortably confined to the past.

A slight numerical detail already hinted at the fact that the classical myth, despite being neglected, was still in force: Herbert Truczinski's death on the fourteenth day summons Niobe's fourteen children who perished at the hands of Apollo and Diana to avenge the insult suffered by the gods' mother Leto. In *The Tin Drum*, the number seven assumes a sinister significance, which culminates in the number 49—seven times seven: 1949, the year when the Federal Republic of Germany was established and when, according to Grass, the nation hoped to place its guilt and shame in brackets for the sake of moving on.

Moreover, the tale of the hubristic mother punished in the name of a divine mother is preserved in the theme of motherhood that steers the main plot. We recall that the Niobe chapter intervenes directly after Oskar's mother Agnes has passed away. Tortured by an extra-marital, incestuous affair with her cousin, Jan Bronski, Agnes obsessively prayed to the Virgin Mary, who gave birth to the Christ-child, whom Oskar in turn reinterprets as the "heavenly Gasman" engendered by the sequestered Niobe maidenhead. Despite these points of contact, however, the two maternal figures—Mary and Niobe—perform opposing narrative functions. Whereas the Christian Virgin propels the main plot of Oskar's life story forward, the mythic queen exerts a force that pulls the plot backward. Precisely as a parenthesis, Niobe represents a countering resistance that works against the tow—*gegen den Sog*—a halting interruption of the chronological momentum, a broken conformity with the principal action, a difficult past that intrudes in the present without being reconcilable with the present. A significant moment occurs late in the novel, during the postwar period, when Oskar poses with his art-student colleague for a parodic image of the Madonna and Child. Here, the mother figure is painted green, which is to say, Mary is portrayed as Niobe, who holds Oskar as Antichrist in her arms. The painting, which became a scandalous success in West Germany, was titled after the year of its appearance: *Madonna 49*.

In his lectures on *Aesthetics*, Hegel makes a telling distinction: Both the Virgin Mary and Niobe, he acknowledges, are grieving mothers. Yet, whereas Niobe's essence

50 "Er kommt! Er kommt! Wer kam denn? Das Christkindchen, der Heiland? Oder kam der himmlische Gasmann mit der Gasuhr unter dem Arm, die immer ticktick macht?" (261)

is reduced to her corporeal existence, Mary's essence consists in pure soul. Hence, Niobe merely *has* love, while Mary's "whole inner life *is* love"; and it is precisely this difference between having and being that motivates Hegel's contrast: In witnessing her son's crucifixion, Mary "is emotional, she feels the thrust of the dagger into the center of her soul, her heart breaks, but she does not turn into stone."[51] As pure soul, Mary assimilates the pain of her grief, while Niobe, as body alone, resists assimilation. Niobe is present yet remains forever apart; she endures but only as a stone which can never be fully incorporated into the spirit. Whereas Mary inspires us to move on, Niobe holds us back. Thus, the queen who, according to Ovid would have been "most fortunate [*felicissima*] of mothers, had she not seen herself as such" (*Metamorphoses* 6, 155–156), is portrayed by Hegel as "the unfortunate [*die Unglückliche*]."

Nonetheless, Ovid's Niobe insists:

> sum felix—quis enim neget hoc?—felixque manebo
>
> *Metamorphoses* 6, 193

> I am fortunate—for who would deny this?—and fortunate I shall remain

The verse traverses from present indicative (*sum*) to future indicative (*manebo*), two verbs in the first-person, which frame the parenthetical intrusion in the third-person present subjunctive (*neget*). The proud containment achieved by the initial and final verbal statements at once admits and dismisses the potential contradiction. The containment, moreover, is reiterated through the repetition of the adjective *felix*, "fortunate," which likewise brackets the inserted aside while being bracketed by the first and last words: *sum* (*felix—quis enim neget hoc?—felixque*) *manebo*. By parenthesizing the parenthesis, the verse stresses the dynamics of containing and being contained, a movement that accords with the main theme of the *Metamorphoses*, however much Niobe insists on stability, however much she doubles down on a consistent identity that links present and future, what she now is and what she will always remain. The adjective *felix*, moreover, here alludes to the term's primary sense of "fruitful" or "productive," cognate with words linked to childbirth: *fecundus*, *fetus*, and *faenus* ("monetary interest on capital"), as well as *femina*. Her state of being "fortunate" thereby rests on what is contained and what issues from the womb. Regardless, the potential contradiction—"Who would deny this?"—in being contained, comes across as both a dismissal and an admission, a self-affirmation that is equally undercut. And indeed, the vertical aspiration of Niobe's haughtiness, ascribing to herself the stable consistency ascribable to the

[51] G. W. F. Hegel, *Aesthetics: Lectures on Fine Art* [publ. posth. 1835] (1975:826).

gods above, is soon leveled on the "flat and broad field" (*planus ... lateque ... campos*, 218), on the plain where her fourteen children are slaughtered. Niobe's felicity is met with the wrath of Apollo and Diana who flatten her *platterdings*. Transformed into stone, Niobe achieves stability but only by being relegated to the margins, bracketed out, so that the divinely sanctioned order can proceed.

That said, in Ovid's account, Niobe does not merely endure as stone but rather as a stone that weeps: a death animated by life despite being a life contained in death. Grass evokes this energy, a force that is simultaneously containable and uncontainable. Just as the sun in the *Metamorphoses* melts the snow on the Niobe stone, which makes it appear to shed tears, the sun in *The Tin Drum* catches the amber eyes of the Niobe figure and gives her the appearance of life.

> The afternoon crept across the pale, polychromatic façade of the museum. It swung from curlicue to curlicue, rode nymphs and horns of plenty, devoured plump angels plucking flowers, ripened ripely painted grapes beyond their prime, burst into the midst of a country fête, played blindman's buff, swung in a swing of roses, ennobled burghers bargaining in baggy breeches, caught a stag the dogs were after, and reached at last that second-story window through which the sun, briefly yet forever, illuminated an amber eye. (248/179)[52]

The relegated figure is resuscitated, the parenthetically immured is rendered most vivid in a resplendent burst of ἐνάργεια. The latent past has been made murderously present. For, when the repressed returns, it returns with much more formidable power. On the fourteenth afternoon, Herbert Truczinski assumes his post, which will be his last. And upon hearing the news, Mother Truczinski will sit at her window stone-faced and grieve herself to death. The parenthetic context that renders the Niobe figurehead vivaciously meaningful has turned the present context into a horrifying nightmare.

The Niobe episode in *The Tin Drum* broaches a world of violence from which mothers hope yet fail to protect their sons. Moreover, it exposes how a hyper-masculine society tends to demonize the feminine as the source for the evil that they themselves perpetuate. What cries out from within the confines of this extended parenthesis, is the violence that men perform against women, from the burning of the Flemish maiden on the preposterous charge of witchcraft to the double-ax that Herbert Truczinski drives

52 "Der Nachmittag kroch über die blaßbunte Museumsfassade. Von Kringel zu Kringel turnte er, ritt Nymphen und Füllhörner, fraß dicke nach Blumen greifende Engel, ließ reifgemalte Weintrauben überreif werden, platzte mitten hinein in ein ländliches Fest, spielte Blindekuh, die in Pluderhosen Handel trieben, fing einen Hirsch, den Hunde verfolgten, und erreichte endlich jenes Fenster des zweiten Stockwerkes, das der Sonne erlaubte, kurz und dennoch für immer ein Bernsteinauge zu belichten" (250).

into the wooden maidenhead.[53] In the novel as a whole, the masculine compulsion to move forward in life, from childhood through adolescence to adulthood, is countered by Oskar's incurable desire to find refuge beneath his grandmother's four skirts and crawl back into the womb. The *regressus in uterum* is a motif that constantly tugs against Oskar's obligation to live in the world. It accounts for his self-alleged decision to stop growing at the age of three, it attests to his wish to remain locked in a childish parenthesis in the midst of ruthless men, while giving him the opportunity to intervene in and disrupt their world if only as an included exclusion.

Already at the very start of the novel, the grandmother with her protective four skirts seems to anticipate the mythic Niobe as depicted in the famous statue attributed to Scopas and as portrayed by Ovid: How the Phrygian queen tried to save her last surviving daughter by "covering her with her entire body and all her garments" (*toto corpore ... tota veste tegens*, *Metamorphoses* 6, 298–299). But in the end, neither Oskar's grandmother Anna nor his mother Agnes is able to protect their offspring, no less than Niobe or the Virgin Mary. In Oskar's view, they are both *matres dolorosae*, both consigned to post-partem grief. They both fail to keep their fetuses safe within the parenthetical existence of the womb. Their love will always be insufficient, incapable of harboring the incipient life that is a part of them yet already, fatally, apart.

In the Dead of Night

In late January 1960, as he re-immersed himself in Heidegger's poetological essays, Celan suddenly terminated his relationship with Günter Grass, who at the time was drafting *Dog Years* while basking in the success that followed the publication of *The Tin Drum* that previous September. As Celan reports in a letter to his editor, Rudolf Hirsch, Grass arrived with "the old little big mendacities, multiplied by the self-satisfaction [*Selbstgefälligkeit*] that has meanwhile shot up even higher"; confronted by the author's "cold-blooded lies and vulgarities," Celan "had to break off my friendship with him and show him and his wife the door."[54] At the letter's conclusion, Celan inscribed a line from his translation of Shakespeare, *Sonnet* 90: "Then hate me when thou wilt, if ever, now"—*Mußt du mich hassen, haß mich ungesäumt ... Mein Herz, es trauert* (lit., "If you must hate me, hate me without delay … My heart, it mourns.") Without delay, *ungesäumt*, as Celan would soon emphasize in the parenthesized wish to Heidegger

53 See Krimmer 2008:282.

54 "Und [...] vorgestern [...] der Besuch von Grass ... Die alten kleinen großen Verlogenheiten, vermehrt um die mittlerweile noch höher ins Kraut geschossene Selbstgefälligkeit [...] er kam dann mit weiteren kaltblütig geäußerten Lügen und Gemeinheiten. Ich mußte ihm die Freundschaft aufkündigen, ihm und seiner Frau die Tür weisen." Celan to Rudolf Hirsch, January 29, 1960, in Celan 2004a:98.

from the early draft of "Todtnauberg," that the "thinking-man's word come (come un- / delayed)"—*auf eines Denkenden / kommendes (un- / gesäumt kommendes) / Wort.*

After January 1960, Celan and Grass would never meet face to face again.

For all its sprawling density, apart from presenting a grand and perplexing palimpsest on which to read a chronicle of twentieth-century German history, *Dog Years* essentially turns on the fraught friendship between the "half-Jewish" Eddi Amsel and the German-Catholic Walter Matern. In Amsel's account, the tension can be traced back to a primal scene when he and his friend were nine years old. Matern is found standing on the summit of the dike in Nickelswalde, outside Danzig, where he is desperately searching for a small stone—a *Zellack*—to hurl into the Vistula. As Amsel scurries up the sand dune, he sees that Matern, having failed to find a *Zellack*, has chosen to throw his pocket-knife, a pocket-knife that was in fact a gift from Amsel himself. No amount of argument can dissuade Matern: He absolutely has to fling something into the water and the only thing available is the pocket-knife (*HJ* 11–19). Throughout the description, emphasis is placed on the river's flow and the many things that have been caught in its current, not only common detritus, but also memories and personages from the entire history of the region, from Adalbert, the ninth-century bishop of Prague who converted the rural population, to Napoleon Bonaparte to the troops marching off into the Great War (*HJ* 10–11). Human-historical interventions into the inhuman, endless surge. In casting the pocket-knife, Matern takes a gift that was handed over to him, a *traditum* that he has received, uses it to disrupt the current that flows from past to present, and thereby abuses the friendship implicit in the gift.

In later reminiscences concerning his "difficult" friendship with Celan, Grass remained unusually cautious: "Did I say everything? — More than I wanted. Have I concealed anything important? — Certainly. Is there still a postscript to come? — No."[55] As for Celan, there is a haunting poem from May 1965, drafted the day before Celan was released from the psychiatric clinic, Le Vésinet:

Vom Anblick der Amseln, abends,
durchs Unvergitterte, das
mich umringt,

versprach ich mir Waffen.

Vom Anblick der Waffen — Hände,
vom Anblick der Hände — die längst

[55] "Habe ich alles gesagt? – Mehr, als ich wollte. Habe ich Wichtiges verschwiegen? – Bestimmt. Kommt noch ein Nachtrag? – Nein." Grass, *Rückblick auf die Blechtrommel* (1973), cited in Schenk 2016:102.

vom flachen scharfen
Kiesel geschriebene Zeile

— Welle, du
tragst ihn her, schliffst ihn zu,
gabst dich, Un-
verlierbare, drein,
Ufersand, nimmst,
nimmst auf,
Standhafer, weh
Das Deine hinzu —,

die Zeile, die Zeile,
die wir umschlungen durchschwimmen,
zweimal in jedem Jahrtausend,
all den Gesang in den Fingern,
den auch die durch uns lebendige,
herrlich-undeutbare
Flut uns nicht glaubt.[56]

From the sight of the blackbirds, in the evening,
through the unbarred space, which
surrounds me,

I promised myself weapons.

From the sight of the weapons — hands,
from the sight of the hands — the line written
long ago by the sharp, flat
pebble

— Wave, you
bore it hither, honed it,
consented yourself, un-
losable, to it,
shore's sand, you take,
take in,
sea-oats, blow
yours along — ,

[56] Published in Celan, *Atemwende* [1967] (2000: vol. 2, 94).

the line, the line,
through which we swim, entwined,
twice each millennium,
all that song at the fingers,
that even the flood that lives through us,
the glorious-uninterpretable
flood does not believe us.

The speaker catches sight of the blackbirds flying outside the window, through the "unbarred" space (*das Unvergitterte*) that "surrounds" him (*umringt*, vv. 2–3). The scene is striking. As Derek Hillard comments, "To be ringed in by the unbarred is to be enclosed by a ring but one that is composed by an Open. To be enclosed by an Open is to be open to the greatest threats."[57] A disquieting without that frames a fearful within. *Unvergittert* further evokes the title of Celan's 1959 collection, *Sprachgitter* or "Speech-grille," as if the "lattice" or "grid" (*Gitter*) of human language has been removed through the blackbirds' song. Yet, no longer protected by this verbal screen, the speaker now requires "weapons" (v. 4). A progression ensues, moving from the birdsong to the promise of weapons to the "hands" (vv. 5–6) which may be capable of writing a "line," one written "long ago" or "once" (*einst*) by "a sharp, flat pebble" (vv. 7–8). The pebble was deposited by the "wave" that, rushing past, summons an addressee (v. 9), someone who once bore the small stone, "honed it," devoted himself to it—the "un-losable" stone that "you" now "take up" (vv. 10–14), ready to inscribe a line that would join speaker and addressee, *ich und du*, into a partnership: "the line through which we swim, entwined" (vv. 17–18). It would be a weapon-line that they, together, can hurl into the "glorious-uninterpretable flood" (vv. 22–23). A sharp reply or a poignant aside that disturbs the flow of time which moves along augustly and meaninglessly—*herrlich-undeutbar*—and without acknowledging the individuals' intervention.

Celan unmistakably alludes to the last entry that Franz Kafka inscribed in his "diaries":

> Every word turned round in the hand of the spirits—this swing of the hand is their characteristic movement—becomes a spear turned against the speaker. A remark like this one in particular. And so on to infinity. The only consolation would be: It happens whether you want it to or not. And what you want only helps imperceptibly little. More than consolation is: You too have weapons.[58]

[57] Hillard 2007:305.

[58] "Jedes Wort, gewendet in der Hand der Geister—dieser Schwung der Hand ist ihre charakteristische Bewegung—, wird zu Spieß gekehrt gegen den Sprecher. Eine Bemerkung wie diese ganz besonders. Und so ins Unendliche. Der Trost wäre nur: es geschieht, ob du willst

At a particularly difficult and vulnerable moment in his life, Celan, whose birth name was Antschel, turns to Kafka, whose Hebrew name was Amschel—two blackbirds who together can withstand the flood of history and resist dissolution. Through reading, through reception, a transhistorical friendship becomes a source of consolation and a means for self-defense. Perhaps the same wish was held by Eddi Amsel, Grass's protagonist, who was as desperate for dialogue as Matern was for a pebble; Amsel who clambered up the "shore's sand" to join his friend, who, at least from one perspective (*Anblick*), was compelled to throw his friend's gift away.

The Cut

On July 21, 1968, on the walk to his office at the École Normale Supérieure, Celan sketched out two traditional tercets or a *sixain*:

Einmal die Klinge,
    einmal die Schneide,
    einmal keins
Nichts ist verloren,
    nichts ist erkoren
    Einer sagt eins. [59]

Once the blade,
    then the edge,
    then none
Nothing is lost,
    nothing chosen
    Someone says one.[60]

In terms of the history of poetic forms, the sixain is typically associated with the *epigrammes* of Clément Marot, the sixteenth-century poet accredited with the invention of the French sonnet, the final tercets of which feature Marot's signature innovation on the Petrarchan sonnet, namely, the rhyme scheme here adopted by Celan (aab-ccb).[61] Celan's fascination is understandable. In addition to inspiring the French

oder nicht. Und was du willst, hilft nur unmerklich wenig. Mehr als Trost ist: Auch du hast Waffen." Franz Kafka, *Tagebücher*, Hans-Gerd Koch, Michael Müller and Malcom Pasley, ed. (Frankfurt am Main: Fischer, 1990), 926.

59 Paul Celan, *Gedichte aus dem Nachlass*. Bertrand Badiou, Jean-Claude Rambach, and Barbara Weidemann, eds. (Frankfurt am Main: Suhrkamp, 1997), 479–480. 196.

60 I am especially grateful to Richard Sieburth for this translation.

61 See McClelland 1973.

poetic Renaissance of the Pléiade, Marot relied on his attachment to the court of Marguerite d'Alençon to support the Reformation, translate the Psalms and rail against the academics at the Sorbonne. In 1533 he audaciously edited the works of François Villon, whose employment of criminal argot further stained Marot's position vis-à-vis the Catholic establishment, before he was exiled to Italy for his outspoken Lutheranism. This anti-authoritarian vita no doubt allowed Marot's six-line stanza to persist across modern French poetry, from the romanticism of Victor Hugo to the Parnassian strains of Charles Leconte de Lisle to the symbolism of Paul Verlaine, whose famous "Chanson d'automne" (1866), composed in sixains, was used by the Allies' Special Operation Executive to inform the French Resistance on the precise timing of the Normandy Invasion, with the first tercet broadcast by the BBC on June 1, 1944, to announce a two-week frame, and the second tercet sent around midnight on June 5 to signal the invasion on the following morning.[62]

Les sanglots longs (a)
Des violons (a)
De l'automne (b)
Blessent mon cœur (c)
D'une langueur (c)
Monotone. (b)

Verlaine, "Chanson d'automne," vv. 1–6

The long sobs
Of the violins
Of autumn
Wound my heart
With a languor
Monotone.

In Celan's lines (vv. 1–2), the knife's "blade" (*Klinge*) and "edge" (*Schneide*) not only allude to Verlaine's wound to the heart (*blessent mon cœur*) but also, autobiographically, recall Celan's suicide attempt in early 1967, when he stabbed himself in the chest and only barely missed damaging his vital organ. Celan's repeated *einmal* ("one time"), moreover, may well recall Verlaine's *monotone*.

All the while, Marot's Protestant position seems to motivate the rhyme in Celan's second tercet, *verloren* ("lost") and *erkoren* ("chosen," vv. 4–5), insofar as it evokes the theological tension between mortal helplessness and divine grace as it is articulated in Martin Luther's great hymn, *Ein' feste Burg ist unser Gott* ("A mighty fortress is our

[62] Hall 2004:100.

God"), which the adamant reformer reportedly sang as he entered the Diet of Worms in 1521:

> Mit unsrer Macht ist nichts getan,
> wir sind gar bald *verloren*;
> es streit' für uns der rechte Mann,
> den Gott hat selbst *erkoren*.

Luther, *Ein'feste Burg ist unser Gott* 10–13
(my emphasis)

> With our might is nothing done,
> We are soon utterly lost;
> For us he fights, the right man,
> Whom God Himself has chosen.

Whereas the Christian hymn affirms that, though "lost" (*verloren*), we are nonetheless saved because God has "chosen" (*erkoren*) to sacrifice His only Son—that is, because He has chosen a self-sacrifice—in Celan's reworking, "nothing is lost" (*nichts ist verloren*) perhaps because "nothing is chosen" (*nichts ist erkoren*).

Celan composed the sixain nearly a year to the day when he had visited Heidegger in the Black Forest. As we have seen, the fraught encounter was memorialized in "Todtnauberg," where the poet restated the hope that he had inscribed in the philosopher's guest book, a hope initially qualified by an urgency in brackets:

> [die] Zeile von
> einer Hoffnung, heute,
> auf eines Denkenden
> kommendes (un-
> gesäumt kommendes)
> Wort

Celan, "Todtnauberg," Brunidor, ed., 1968,
vv. 10–15

> [the] line about
> a hope, today,
> for a thinking-man's
> coming (un-
> delayed coming)
> word

Now, in the summer of 1968, having recently deleted the parenthesized lines for the final version published in *Lichtzwang*, Celan revised the more recent sixain into couplets by setting it between brackets, first with the title "Reimklammer" ("Rhyme-bracket"), then with the title "Klammer auf, Klammer zu" ("Open parenthesis, close parenthesis"):

KLAMMER AUF, KLAMMER ZU

(Einmal die Klinge, einmal die Schneide, einmal keins.

Nichts ist verloren, nichts ist erkoren,
Einer sagt eins.)[63]

OPEN PARENTHESIS, CLOSE PARENTHESIS

(First the blade, then the edge, then none.

Nothing lost, nothing chosen,
Someone says one.)

Here, the title employs the convention used in oral presentations to alert the audience to a parenthesis in the written text and here directly refers to the opening and closing of the graphic marks that silently appear in the poem: a pronouncement of the unpronounceable. The parenthetic structure is perpetuated internally by means of multiple word repetitions and morphemic rhymes, which create a dynamic series of framings or inscribed edges and thereby recall the earlier title, "Rhyme-bracket":

<u>einmal</u> *die Klinge*, <u>einmal</u> ("*one time* the blade, *one time*")
<u>einmal</u> *die Schneide*, <u>einmal</u> ("*one time* the edge, *one time*")
<u>nichts</u> *ist verloren, nichts* ("*nothing* is lost, *nothing*")
<u>verloren</u>, nichts ist <u>erkoren</u> ("*lost*, nothing is *chosen*")
<u>einer</u> *sagt* <u>Eins</u> ("*one* says *one*")

Throughout, each opening calls for a closing that is re-opened in turn. The effect recalls the parenthetical lexis, cited above, in Niobe's speech as formulated by Ovid: *<u>felix</u>—quis enim neget hoc?—<u>felixque</u>* (*Metamorphoses* 6, 193). In a similarly formal manner, Celan's poem, now as a pair of couplets, unfolds across lexical parentheses whose overlapping confuses the openings and closings, the bracketed and the bracketing. Emphasis

[63] Celan, *Gedichte aus dem Nachlass*, 196.

is thus placed on the complementary states of containment and being contained or perhaps the un-containment implied in every containment.[64]

The blade's edge—the *Schneide* of the *Klinge*—can thus be seen as making the cuts that detach what is within from what is without. The cutting (*Schneiden*) separates two entities by causing a wound which may or may not close over and heal, the sharp edge creating the edges that keep parts apart or allow participation by way of apartness. In addition to the painful reminiscence of Celan's attack on his heart, it is tempting to recall the blade of the pocket-knife depicted at the head of Grass's *Hundejahre*, the gift that Eddi Amsel gave to Walter Matern to seal their friendship, yet also the gift that the friend selected and tossed into the river's current. In Celan's poem it is precisely selection and loss which are explicitly repudiated: *Nichts ist verloren, nichts ist erkoren* ("Nothing lost, nothing chosen"). Repudiated, but also inverted. Grass's novelistic account accords with our expectations: the pocket-knife is selected before it is lost, with the obvious implication that nothing would have been lost if nothing had been selected. Celan's poem, in contrast, reverses the order by summoning loss before selection: "Nothing is lost, nothing is chosen" suggests that loss is prerequisite for selection, that something must go astray before it can be taken up by oneself or another.

In this regard, Celan's parenthesized poem may serve as an allegory of parenthetic reception. Something that occurred "at one time" (*einmal*) may be selected to return a second time, but not without loss. Similarly, antiquity may be contained in an act of reception which "recovers" or "takes up again" what took place "once" (*einmal*), but not without acknowledging the "edge" (*Schneide*) that sets the two poles apart, even when or precisely because they "overlap" (*sich überschneiden*). Can the "boundary" or "separation"—the horos that different *horizons* demarcate—ever melt together, ever merge as one? Are not all efforts to contain the "once upon a time" (*es war einmal*) doomed to escape through the cut that defines and confines it?

"Nothing lost, nothing chosen." The statement gives way to the conclusion that *Einer sagt eins* ("One [man] says one"), where the saying (*sagt*) itself is bracketed by singular positions. It is noteworthy that the lyric gives neither a first-person speaker nor a second-person addressee. The potential dialogue—the very promise inherent to acts of reception—yields but two singularities, one in the third-person (*Einer*), the other in the neuter (*eins*), a rather ambivalent result, which describes a convergence of views or a reduction to monologue or a mute reification.

As every pupil learns, "one times one" (*ein mal eins*) only ever equals one. In German, *das Einmaleins* denotes the "times table" and therefore one of the "basics," analogous to the "ABCs": a rudimentary piece of knowledge that by extension may symbolize an identification (one times one produces one) or undermine any potential partnership (one times one never amounts to two). In Celan's poem, the latter

[64] For an extensive discussion of these ramifications, see Hamacher 2019:143–180.

interpretation seems to be affirmed in the opening verse by the jarring modification of the conventional *Einmaleins: einmal keins* ("one times none"), which arithmetically produces zero. To the extent that reception depends on some kind of repetition, Celan's parenthesized poem seems to demonstrate the vainness or vanity of any receptive project. The *einmal* repeated here fails to accumulate, fails to establish a fruitful collective, and instead sinks into stark one-sidedness, if not empty silence. As the common German proverb states, *Einmal ist keinmal*, "Once doesn't count"—one time is no time. All the same, Celan's *einmal keins* also dismisses the finality expressed by "once and for all" (*ein für allemal*), a dismissal affirmed by every act of reception, where closure (*Klammer zu*) gives way to fresh openings (*Klammer auf*), where the initial cut of the "blade" (*Klinge*) continues to "resound" (*nachklingen*).

Chapter 4

Iphigenia among the Germans

Reception of Reception

In staging his *Iphigenie auf Tauris*, Johann Wolfgang Goethe staged Reception itself. The story about a Mycenaean maiden who, exiled from her home in the South, was welcomed and sheltered by a barbarian people of the North, readily represents how the corpus of ancient Greek culture, detached from its native historical context, came to be received and curated by German artists, poets and scholars, including, of course, by Goethe himself. That is to say, Goethe's drama reflects on the very conditions of classical reception that made this classicist achievement possible. Begun in 1779 and first published in 1786, the *Iphigenie* should therefore still hold its privileged position in German literary and intellectual history not simply because it constitutes an exemplary accomplishment of the poet's classical style, but also because, through its classicizing form and content, it implicitly interrogates the very basis for any neoclassical enterprise.

Considering the *Iphigenie auf Tauris* as an allegory of reception raises a number of questions: How is ancient Greek culture depicted within a non-Greek setting and how does its foreign host receive it? What demands do Iphigenie, Orestes and Pylades make in the name of Hellenic mores and how are they acknowledged, adopted or rebuked in the northern climes? What can the recipient culture retain and what must it surrender? I would like to suggest that these and similar inquiries all turn on the issue of *aspect*. Embedded in Goethe's drama are varying subjective viewpoints that determine how received cultures appear and thereby shape what Hans Robert Jauß has characterized as the "horizon of expectation" (*Erwartungshorizont*).[1] Subsequently, readings of Goethe's *Iphigenie* come to reflect possible ways in which reception itself has been formulated and assessed. By turning to a representative, but by no means comprehensive selection of key German interpretations of Goethe's text by Theodor Adorno, Rainer Werner

1 The conception of the "horizon of expectation" is developed in Hans Robert Jauß, *Literaturgeschichte als Provokation der Literaturwissenschaft* [1967] ("Literary History as a Challenge to Literary Theory" [1970]).

Fassbinder, and Jauß himself, all emerging during the socially and politically tumultuous period of 1967–1973, the present chapter aims to give a critical account of a range of receptive options, an account, that is, based on an investigation into the diverse verbal aspects (perfective, imperfective, and aorist) that distinguish different historical receptions of reception.

In specifically denoting the act of taking in, absorbing, and understanding works of historically distant or foreign cultures, the term *reception* is a fairly recent concept. It acquired this definition explicitly in the "Aesthetics of Reception" (*Rezeptionsästhetik*), which was developed and promulgated by Jauß, Wolfgang Iser, and their students at the University of Constance in the late 1960s and early 1970s.[2] Although perceived at the time as revolutionary, reception, so understood, directly derives from the hermeneutic method of Jauß's teacher, Hans-Georg Gadamer, who in turn elaborated the philological-nostalgic approach of his own teacher, Martin Heidegger. As a result, the new *Rezeptionsästhetik* is almost invariably tainted on the one hand by a Heideggerean nostalgia for origins and a concomitant recognition of present distance from sources, and motivated, on the other hand, by Gadamer's reformulation of the "classical," a reformulation that challenges a traditionalist understanding of the classical as a normative repertoire of fixed meanings and ideals and instead as the "consciousness of something enduring, of significance that cannot be lost and that is independent of all the circumstances of time—a kind of timeless present that is contemporaneous with every other present."[3] A work, that is, that urges a fusion of distinct horizons and thereby instigates an interpretive response.

In his inaugural lecture at Constance, delivered in April 1967, Jauß called for a shift in attention from concerns regarding literary production to the subjective and social-historical conditions of how literature has been variously interpreted. The original title that Jauß chose for the occasion, *Was heißt und zu welchem Ende studiert man Literaturgeschichte?* ("What is, and to what end, does one study Literary History?"), directly alludes to Friedrich Schiller's inaugural lecture, presented in May 1789 at the University of Jena, entitled *Was heißt und zu welchem Ende studiert man Universalgeschichte?* By replacing Schiller's "universal history" with "literary history," Jauß already signals the kind of transformative repetition that constitutes the major object of study outlined in his Aesthetics of Reception. The instigation of focusing on the recipient as distinct from the authorial producer, also evident in "Reader-Response Criticism" as it was being promulgated in the United States, continues the path broached by Heidegger and Gadamer, a path paved by hopes for a fusion of past and present horizons. This theoretical provenance comes to the fore in Jauß's revised title: *Literaturgeschichte als Provokation der Literaturwissenschaft*, published in English

2 For a useful account of this academic movement, Holub 1995 and Semsch 2005.

3 Hans-Georg Gadamer, *Wahrheit und Methode: Grundzüge einer philosophischen Hermeneutik* [1960] (1990:293) [*Truth and Method* (2004):288].

as "Literary History as a Challenge to Literary Theory" in 1970. The "provocation," presented on the cusp of comprehensive university reforms in the Federal Republic of Germany, resonates further with Schiller's own intervention, made, as it turned out, on the eve of the French Revolution, which likewise aimed to pull down authorities of all kinds, save the authority of human reason.

The word *reception* not only emphasizes the importance of understanding understanding—that is, how any cultural artefact is viewed and therefore interpreted within particular horizons of sense from the standpoint or aspect of an individually-minded and socially-conditioned subject—but also indicates a crucial tension between two distinct gestures. On the one hand, reception refers to the punctual *act* of taking something in, while on the other hand, the prefix *re-* suggests an iterative *activity*, taking something up again and again. Reception, moreover, may also connote some notion of *return*: taking something back, regaining, recovering or retaking something that was lost or absent. Yet, although a text may be "received" at any point in time, reception as such unfolds over time under changing circumstances and with greater or lesser degrees of subjective cognition. A reading may wish to grasp a work of literature wholly and definitively, it may even desire to regain the original meaning of the text, but these dreams can only ever be utopian, requiring that one forget that reception necessarily takes place in linear, irreversible time. Reception, one could say in an Aristotelian key, is a potential activity (*dynamis*) that continues to be potential, irreducible to any conclusive act or actualization (*entelecheia*), which would terminate its potentiality as such, by causing it to rest in a determinate telos.[4]

As an allegory of reception, the plot of Goethe's *Iphigenie auf Tauris* reflects this tension between decisive acts and open-ended activity. Thoas, the Taurian king, has provided a hospitable haven for the Greek maiden, who was rescued from her father's sacrificial blade and brought to these northern climes by the goddess Diana. Under Thoas's command, Iphigenie has been received charitably, just as, one could surmise, *Iphigenie* ought to be received by a well-intentioned audience. Yet Thoas has ulterior motives. Having lost his former queen, he wants to wed Iphigenie in order to perpetuate his dynastic line. In this regard, Thoas appears as the perfect German Philhellenist by expressing a profound love or philia for a Hellenic beauty or ideal that he longs to possess. Both hope to marry into the classical culture of the South so that their barbarian culture of the North may flourish through enrichment and enlightenment. The benefits are clear. With Iphigenie's influence, the Taurians have suspended their custom of sacrificing any stranger who alights upon their shores, while also being afforded the promise of stable rule. In a similar fashion, Goethe envisioned that the neoclassical, humane clarity of his *Iphigenie* would rid German society of despotism, obscurantism

4 See, e.g., Aristotle's discussion in *Physics* 3.1.

and superstition.[5] And analogously, in the wake of 1945, German teachers and scholars consistently promoted Goethe's play in order to recall and reassert the humanitarian values and ideals that had been severely damaged by Nazi barbarism.

The ancient Taurian and modern German reception of Iphigenia and *Iphigenie*, respectively, place great stock in the dream of what Adorno, in his own reading of the drama, has called a "klassizistische Lösung"—a "classicist solution" that aims to contain an ideal as something completed in a definitive act of reception.[6] This act proceeds from a *perfective aspect*, which ostensibly characterizes any normative classicism. It aims to contain the past within the horizon of the present, to capture the para within the borders or horoi of the present, specifically as that which has been achieved from the perspective of the now. Understood as a repository of set accomplishments and universal standards, the classical ideal is what has been and shall ever be: eternal and unimpeachable, like the humanist virtues of enlightened emancipation from dogma and self-determination. Yet the desire to limit any person or any object to the status of completed action invariably suffers frustration. Thoas's political designs in receiving Iphigenie, no less than Goethe's poetic intentions in appropriating the Iphigenia myth or any reader's hermeneutic pursuit in understanding Goethe's drama, depend on the amenability of whom or what is being received. Yet, as Adorno points out, the "classicist solution" is "fragile, because [...] it balances [*ausgleicht*] where no reconciliation is possible."[7] The classicist balancing or *Ausgleichen* insists on making what is other the same, *das Gleiche*, which is to say, it dreams of obliterating the alterity that nonetheless persists, of recasting the without fully within.

According to the basic plot of the German tragedy, Thoas wants Iphigenie, but Iphigenie does not want Thoas. She resists succumbing to the king's aspectual plan, just as the textual material of Goethe's play arguably curbs the poet's or the reader's classicizing intentions. As the first word of Iphigenie's opening monologue, *Heraus*, already implies: the protagonist, and by extension the play, strives to break free from the circle of completion. Nonetheless, the resistance that disturbs such appropriative acts hardly defuses the activity of reception. On the contrary, it represents the kind of motivational failure that has always encouraged further endeavors to subsume what is desired within one's subjective aspect, to regain what has been lost, to retrieve what can never be fully recovered or retained. As Goethe himself commented on his *Iphigenie*: "Alles Unzulängliche ist produktiv" ("Everything inadequate is productive").[8] In the end, Iphigenie returns to her Greek homeland and thereby underscores the irreconcilable

5 Cf. Fowler 1982.

6 Theodor W. Adorno, "Zum Klassizismus von Goethes Iphigenie" [1967] (1998:506) ["On the Classicism of Goethe's *Iphigenie*" (Adorno 1992:160).

7 Adorno 1998:506 (1992:160).

8 Goethe to Friedrich Wilhelm Riemer, July 20, 1811 (Herwig, ed. 1969:677).

alterity that renders every act of reception impossible as a conclusive act but, precisely for this reason, possible as an ongoing activity. Thoas's final blessing, *Lebt wohl* ("farewell"), uttered just before the curtain falls, correlates to a mode of reception that respects the text's open-endedness. Here, the motivating aspect is not perfective but rather *continuous* or *imperfective*. It, too, contains the past within the horizon of the present, but in a way that acknowledges the contingencies and provisionality of what is received. Taken together, one can begin to see how each aspect informs and limits the other.

Iphigenie abandons her northern hosts, yet this incomplete reception does not leave the recipient culture entirely empty-handed. Rather, in Goethe's staging, the inability to hold on to the living maiden is countered by an important and innovative compensation or *Ausgleich*. Although the Taurians must say farewell to Iphigenie, they are allowed to keep the cultic image of Diana. With this consolation prize, Goethe radically rewrites the plot. Contrary to the Euripidean tradition, in which Iphigenia and her statue travel together, at the conclusion of Goethe's *Iphigenie*, the sacred sculpture emphatically stays behind among the barbarians. One could ascribe the failure (Iphigenie's departure) to the play's *active* dimension and the compensation (the retained possession of the statue) to the drama's *actualized* accomplishment. As an activity, reception falls short because the barbarians cannot possess the life it desires, while as an act, reception succeeds because they are able to hold on to and behold a lasting monument. The actualized accomplishment remains fragile insofar as it is still purchased with the disappearance of the living maiden. As a remembrance of things past, the monument is but a reminder of loss, the statue of Diana but a present marker of Iphigenie's absence or at least a bracketed presence. The incompletion or inadequacy of reception can be heard as a murmuring beneath the resplendent surface of classicism. These rumblings invariably discourage the ambitions of any receptive project bent on complete comprehension by breaking the perfect conjunction of living substance and its representational image, by adducing a temporal limitation that upsets the definitive establishment of the Same.

Ut Loqui

At least from a Greek perspective, barbarians are condemned to allegory insofar as they are heard "to speak otherwise" (ἄλλως ἀγορεύειν). To the Greek ear, they mumble and murmur, making no clear sense, speaking only *as if* they were speaking meaningfully, and therefore not truly speaking at all. One could say that the barbarian mumbling is incapable of putting verbal form and meaning, representation and substance, together into a clear and integrative whole. Elements found within the discourse remain fatally off to the side. In one of his typically fanciful etymologies, Varro addresses this issue by means of a pertinent illustration:

> Loqui ab loco dictum. Quod qui primo dicitur iam fari vocabula et reliqua verba dicit ante quam suo quique loco ea dicere potest, hunc Chrysippus negat loqui, sed ut loqui: quare ut imago hominis non sit homo, sic in corvis, cornicibus, pueris primitus incipientibus fari verba non esse verba, quod non loquantur. Igitur is loquitur, qui suo loco quodque verbum sciens ponit, et is tumprolocutus, quom in animo quod habuit extulit loquendo. Igitur is loquitur, qui suo loco quodque verbum sciens ponit, et is tum prolocutus, quom in animo quod habuit extulit loquendo.
>
> Varro On the Latin Language 6.56

> "To speak" [*loqui*] is said to be from "place" [*loco*]. Because whoever is said to speak now for the first time, says names and other words before he can say them each in their proper place [*suo loco*]; Chrysippus says that this man does not speak, but rather speaks as if [*ut loqui*]: therefore, just as the statue of a man [*imago hominis*] is not the man, so in the case of ravens, crows, and children beginning for the first time to speak, their words are not words, because they are not speaking [*non loquantur*]. Therefore he speaks [*loquitur*], whoever knowingly puts each word in its place [*suo loco*], and he has spoken forth [*prolocutus*], when he has proclaimed whatever he had in mind by speaking [*loquendo*].[9]

The paronomasia of *loqui* and *locus* suggests that the utterance of detached words will only sound like speech (*ut loqui*) when each word is put in its proper place (*suo loco*). In the Stoic theory of Chrysippus, syntactic ordering is required for communicating meaningful sentences; otherwise, individual "names and other words" (*vocabula et reliqua verba*) wander about aimlessly, dislocated or displaced, as though in exile. A single word may still have referential power, just "as a statue of a man" (*ut imago hominis*) presumably represents someone; yet this single act of reference fails to make sense unless it is properly set in some propositional arrangement, unless every word is guided into place in accordance with a rational, subjective aspect.[10]

Varro's illustration may appear sufficiently straightforward, yet, upon closer examination, the accretion of examples readily falls apart. To begin, the conflation of non-human animals, which *never* speak in the strict sense, and human "children," who are *not yet* speaking, glosses over the temporality that characterizes the latter. Here, speaking-as-such (*loqui*) results from leaving speaking-as-if (*ut loqui*) behind—that is, in the case of children, Varro's propositional logic localizes *ut loqui* at the beginning

[9] Varro, *On the Latin Language* (1938:222–25; translation modified.

[10] See Inwood 1985:74–75.

and *loqui* at the end: children begin by babbling and end by speaking. This temporal progression, however, conflicts with the illustration that clearly aligns *ut loqui* with the statue. The correlating proposition—just as a statue of a man is not the man, so the unordered words of children are not words—is undermined by temporality, to the extent that, precisely in terms of time, a statue will survive the man it represents. In the initial claim, *ut loqui* (as children's babbling) precedes *loqui* (as rational speech), while in the latter case, *loqui* (as the living human) is succeeded by *ut loqu*i (as the statue).

The contradiction emerges from the two different functions that Varro assigns to the human being. On the one hand, the human subject is the rational agent who puts each word into place, allowing whatever subsists in his mindful soul (*in animo*) to be expressed by speaking properly (*loquendo*); while on the other hand, he is also the physical body—the animated corpus—that serves as the model for the statue itself. In the first case, *homo loquitur*, the man speaks, by gathering discontinuous words within a rational aspect that produces sense. By contrast, in the second case, the man represents the very "as" (*ut*) that characterizes "the man's statue" (*imago hominis*) as *ut loqui*. Again, if the *ut loqui* is said to come before the symbolic conjunction of living thought and its representation, it must also be admitted that the barbaric *ut loqui* is what alone remains or survives after the loss of life—just as northern reception survives southern antiquity.

Throughout his extended stay in the Italian states, Goethe worked on giving a Hellenized form to his German drama, to inspire a modern representation with the living *animus* of antiquity. How might German culture be wedded to the classical spirit? How might German poetry overcome its barbaric otherness and thereby attain the level of timeless, universal humanism? How could it establish a meaningful *locus* for Hellenic ideals and thereby become *eloquent*? Goethe's own living presence on the Weimar stage would aim to ensure the meaning of concrete works of art. Tellingly, while still in Italy, Goethe encouraged the painter, Johann Heinrich Wilhelm Tischbein, his close friend and traveling companion, to include an ancient bas-relief depicting Iphigenia, Orestes, and Pylades in the famous portrait of *Goethe in the Roman Campagna*. The sculpted sarcophagus, which Goethe and Tischbein had seen in the Villa Ridolfi, would ultimately arrive to the Munich Glyptothek in 1817, where it remains to this day. Would the living spirit of classical antiquity likewise subsist in these northern climes? Would it ever speak properly? Or would it continue to speak only as if it were speaking—that is, by failing to speak in any proper sense?

Life in Exile

As noted, in the Euripidean tradition that Goethe inherited, the living Iphigenia cannot be separated from the cultic image. The two belong together. Both the maiden and the statue have suffered displacement in the barbarian realm and both must be restituted to Greece. Even though their current residence in the North is essentially hospitable, providing the basic necessities of shelter and nourishment, a sense of profound alienation persists. Iphigenia's brother Orestes has been sent to the Taurian land, together with his friend Pylades, to fetch the sacred image—a mission that promises to free him from the maddening Furies. Upon discovering his sister, whom he presumed to be dead, Orestes realizes that, in reclaiming the holy object, he will also save his sister from exile. When Iphigenia prays to the statue of the goddess, she speaks to herself as well:

> ἀλλ' εὐμενὴς ἔκβηθι βαρβάρου χθονὸς
> ἐς τὰς Ἀθήνας: καὶ γὰρ ἐνθάδ' οὐ πρέπει
> ναίειν, παρόν σοι πόλιν ἔχειν εὐδαίμονα.
>
> Euripides *Iphigenia in Tauris* 1086–88[11]

> But depart from this barbarian land
> for well-disposed [*eumenēs*] Athens: for it is not fitting
> to dwell here, when you can have a fortunate city.

The "barbarian land" is a place of non-belonging—a non-place or utopia, so to speak—and therefore meaningful only in appearance and not in fact. The imperative (ἔκβηθι), which again can be read both as an apostrophe to Artemis and as a self-address, is emphatically expressed in the *aorist aspect*, which here denotes a command to depart punctually and irreversibly, once and for all, in contrast to the continuous, progressive aspect of the present imperative. The aorist verb collapses time into a single moment, a moment of resolve or conclusiveness, a decision torn from the horizon (*horos*). In this mode, Iphigenia utters a command to travel to Athens, to move from a non-place to a place described as "well-disposed" (εὐμενής)—that is, as a city of good fortune that will not only welcome Iphigenia and her goddess warmly, but also a community where the haunting Furies will be transformed into the well-disposed Eumenides. As expected, Thoas will not allow his Iphigenia and her statue to leave. Has he not furnished them with caring protection? Has this barbarian land not served as a safe home, far from a land where fathers are ready to sacrifice their own daughters and where sons mercilessly kill their own mothers? In order to accomplish their mission, the Greeks must act covertly, deceiving the Taurian king. Once the deception is exposed, Euripides can resolve the struggle only by introducing Athena herself on stage, the *dea ex machina* who will set Thoas straight and free the passage for the Greek refugees to return to their native land together with their sacred image.

That this storyline may express the hope of liberation from tyranny was not lost on many modern European retellings. It is not surprising that Christoph Willibald Gluck's

[11] Cited from J. Diggle's edition (1981).

operatic masterpiece, *Iphigénie en Tauride*, which premiered in the same year as Goethe's initial production of the *Iphigenie*, was hailed as a celebration of Enlightenment values and would soon be regarded as representing civilization's freedom from the oppression of the *ancien régime*. For Goethe, the emancipatory promise of the plot was just as central. Yet this redemption is jeopardized by the activity of reception—for what rustles beneath the classicist dream of reconciliation is the persistence of the dream's partial success, which is to say, its partial failure: the North may retain the artefacts of ancient culture—its artwork, its poetry, its style—but it must surrender its breathing life.

Goethe's drama exacerbates the problem by delineating the ethnic differences between the Greeks and the Taurian-Germans—differences between Hellenic civilization and barbarian crudeness, between rhetorical skill and laconic severity, between democratic governance and authoritarian rule. Here, Goethe can draw on an equally long tradition. For example, in his *Iphigenia in Aulis*, Euripides is quite explicit on the hierarchical distinction, when he has Iphigenia explain:

> Βαρβάρων δ' Ἕλλενας ἄρχειν εἰκός, ἀλλ' οὐ βαρβάρους,
> μῆτερ, Ἑλλήνων : τὸ μὲν γὰρ δοῦλον, οἳ δ' ἐλεύθεροι.
>
> Euripides *Iphigenia in Aulis* 1400–01

> It is fitting for the Greeks to rule over the barbarians, but not for the barbarians,
> O mother, to rule over the Greeks: for the former are slaves, while the latter are free.

That this chauvinism soon became conventional wisdom, cited by Aristotle and others, rests on the idea that freedom was an exclusively Hellenic accomplishment that placed this culture above all the others.

The superiority of the South led Goethe, at the end of his Italian journey, to view his German homeland now as a barbaric place of exile. On the very last page of his *Italienische Reise*, Goethe gives the last word to Ovid:

> Cum subit illius tristissima noctis imago,
> Quae mihi supremum tempus in Urbe fuit;
> Cum repeto noctem, qua tot mihi cara reliqui;
> Labitur ex oculis nunc quoque gutta meis.
>
> Ovid *Tristia* 1.3.1–4[12]

> When the saddest image of that night appears,

[12] Cited from S. G. Owen's edition (1915).

Which was for me the last moments in the City ;
When I recall the night, on which I left behind so many things dear to me ;
Even now a teardrop falls from my eyes.

Goethe's long, autobiographical account does not end in German but rather in classical Latin. Ovid's elegy vividly rehearses the "saddest image" (*tristissima imago*) of his last night in the city of Rome when he had to leave behind so much that was dear to him. In recollection, the image "of that night" "appears suddenly" (*subit*) by sneaking into or beneath the inner space of thought. Again, the *imago* marks the absence of the beloved. Thus, for Ovid, the memory of the painful event of exile still brings a "tear" to his eye—"even now" (*nunc quoque*). Goethe's citational conceit is that his own pain in saying farewell to Rome is the very same pain that Ovid felt on the night of his banishment. The coincidence of location underscores the coincidence of emotion. The eighteen centuries that separate Goethe from Ovid have collapsed into a single timeless point. For Goethe, heading home to Weimar means being sent into time-bound exile, away from the utopian realm of eternity. That Goethe cites a Roman, not a Greek poet already refers to a rustling that disturbs the classical surface.

In a later poem from the *Tristia*, Ovid again articulates his longing to escape his banished condition, which he now likens to the fate of Iphigenia and Orestes:

cum vice sermonis fratrem cognovit, et illi
pro nece complexus Iphigenia dedit,
laeta deae signum crudelia sacra perosae
transtulit ex illis in meliora locis,
haec igitur regio, magni paene ultima mundi,
quam fugere homines dique, propinqua mihi est:
aque mea terra prope sunt funebria sacra,
si modo Nasoni barbara terra sua est.
o utinam venti, quibus est ablatus Orestes,
placato referant et mea vela deo!

Ovid *Tristia* 4.4.79–88

When in speaking she recognized her brother, and
instead of death, Iphigenia gave him an embrace,
joyfully she carried off the statue of the goddess, who hated cruel rites,
from this place to something better.
This therefore is the region, almost at the end of this great world,
which men and gods have fled, right here next to me:
and near my land are rites of death,
if a barbaric land can be Ovid's own land.

O, would that the winds, which carried Orestes away,
might bear my sails too, with the god appeased!

Goethe's utopian project posits classical freedom as liberation from death, as liberation from time itself, "from these places" (*ex illis ... locis*) that serve only as a reminder of loss. Still, by bringing his *Iphigenie* to Weimar, Goethe hoped to inspire the barbarian court with Hellenic life. Already after the first performance in 1779, Goethe noted in his journal: "A really good effect, especially on those who are pure" (*Gar gute Wirkung davon, besonders auf reine Menschen*).[13] The German production can thus be read as an achievement that *fuses* two distinct cultures. Hellenic freedom would have a civilizing effect on German coarseness, just as Iphigenia had a civilizing influence on the Taurians. In return, barbarian diligence could offer nourishment and protection. In his bid for Iphigenie's hand in marriage, Thoas stands for the German who promises to shelter Hellenic timelessness within the contingent sphere of human history. The dream of Weimar Classicism rests on the interrelationship of ancient Greek and Taurian-Germanic culture, which aspires toward the ideal of universal human freedom—an aspiration based on a marriage, which not simply conjoins two distinct peoples and two distinct epochs, but also unites time and timelessness, all by means of a resplendent fusion of horizons—a symbolic accomplishment par excellence.

Yet, despite the philhellenic labor, the dream invariably falls short. The desire for fusing the two cultures is disrupted by a return to present, wakeful circumstances. The marriage of ancient Greek spirit and modern German history can never be perfectly consummated. It cannot be consummated, because the Ideal is itself constituted by the very distance that keeps both cultures divorced. As Iphigenie laments in her opening monologue, she can never belong to this alien sphere: *es gewöhnt sich nicht mein Geist hierher* ("My spirit is not accustomed to this place," v. 6).[14] Gazing out towards the sea's horizon, she prays to Diana, who once saved her from death at Aulis, to save her now from a "second death": *rette mich die du vom Tod errettet / Auch von dem Leben hier, dem zweiten Tode* ("Save me, whom you have saved from death / also from this life here, from this second death," v. 52f). In the figure of Iphigenie, Greek culture may ultimately live on, but only after she has been released and allowed to return to antiquity. The final line of Goethe's drama, the terse *Lebt wohl* mumbled by Thoas, is but a concession to the dream's impossibility: Despite all efforts of hospitality, the living ideal resists being appropriated within the aspect of modernity.

Even though she is homeward bound, a harmonious reception or full recovery is equally under threat for Iphigenie. In recalling the Tantalid curse that haunts her family, she cannot be certain that a return to Mycenae would be inviting or beneficial,

13 Goethe 1989:168.

14 Goethe, *Iphigenie auf Tauris*, from the Hamburger Ausgabe (Goethe 1981: vol. 5, 7–67).

especially after she learns how her mother slaughtered her father and how her brother slew their mother. Time, of course, has not stood still since her miraculous redemption from Aulis. Return can never be to the same place that one has left behind. Hardly capable of containing her past within the perfective aspect of completed action, Iphigenie's interpretation of her family's curse can only generate a continuous series of open-ended questions.

> Mein eigen Schicksal macht mir bang und bänger.
> O soll ich nicht die stille Hoffnung retten
> Die in der Einsamkeit ich schön genährt?
> Soll dieser Fluch denn ewig walten? Soll
> Nie dies Geschlecht mit einem neuen Segen
> Sich wieder heben?
>
> vv. 1691–96

> My own fate alarms me more and more.
> Oh, should I not salvage that silent hope
> Which I nourished well in solitude?
> Ought this curse then prevail eternally? Ought
> This race with a new blessing never
> Rise again?

The ambiguity that calls for acts of interpretation also guarantees the active provisionality of every hermeneutic judgment—a provisionality, moreover, that Goethe employs as a principal component of the plot. Orest and Pylades have traveled to Tauris under instructions received from Apollo's oracle: As Pylades reminds his accursed friend:

> … Apoll
> Gab uns das Wort: im Heiligtum der Schwester
> Sei Trost und Hülf und Rückkehr dir bereitet.
>
> vv. 610–12

> … Apollo
> Gave us his word: in the sister's shrine
> Would consolation and help and return be brought to you.

Pylades does not hesitate to explicate the prophecy confidently and unequivocally: The "sister's shrine" is the temple to Diana; and the mission is to return the statue of the goddess back to Delphi, where she can be honored alongside her brother. Only then, will the infernal Furies cease to torment Orest (vv. 722–27). Yet Orest is already cured once he is reunited with Iphigenie, which ultimately leads Orest himself to revise the interpretation: the oracle does not refer to Apollo's sister but rather to his own sister (vv. 2113–17). Embedded in the dramatic action, Goethe demonstrates how shifting circumstances, unexpected encounters, and fresh discoveries prompt new and important receptions of divine prediction.

Open-ended provisionality can also encourage receptiveness to pressures that operate beyond the closed circuit of the poetic work. As many scholars have noted, in February 1779, when he began dictating his *Iphigenie*, Goethe was deeply troubled and frantically busy as the appointed head of the War Commission in Weimar, while Prussia was at war with Austria. His sympathy with his Thuringian neighbors, who were suffering from unemployment and financial straits, together with his assignment to recruit young men for Weimar's armed forces, overtaxed the energy he would have otherwise devoted to poetic composition. As he confessed to Charlotte von Stein: "Hier will das Drama gar nicht fort, es ist verflucht, der König von Tauris soll reden als wenn kein Strumpfwirker in Apolde hungerte" ("Here the drama does not want to go away, it is cursed, the king of Tauris is supposed to speak as if no hosier in Apolda was going hungry").[15] Like Iphigenie, Goethe too must endure a curse, one that threatens the harmony of his creative work with political and social dissonance. Goethe might have assured Duke Karl August that he could still find time to climb into his "old fortress of poetry" (*alte Burg der Poesie*),[16] yet the urgency of real-life concerns would continue to impinge on his poetic progress. As the editors of the Hamburg Edition of Goethe's works suggest, the formation of the *Iphigenie* seems to have emerged from "the tensional relationship between practical-political and poetic activity."[17] Whereas the neoclassical desire for harmonization and expiation strives towards completion in perfective aspect, accursed reality—be it the fate of the House of Atreus or the devastation of war in Central Europe—keeps the work open in imperfective aspect. Yet, must the drama, as well as the acts of reception that it reflects, always oscillate between these two aspects alone, either within the horizon of classicist containment or the horizon of actualism? Or is there perhaps a third aspect, one that might challenge the very requirement of a subjective horizon?

Rustle of Language

Theodor Adorno delivered his lecture *On the Classicism of Goethe's Iphigenie* on June 7, 1967, in Berlin—exactly four years after he gave his "Parataxis" lecture before the Hölderlin-Gesellschaft, but more importantly, a mere two months after Jauß

[15] Goethe 1962–1969: vol. 1, 264.

[16] Goethe to Herzog Carl August, March 8, 1779 (1962–1969: vol. 1, 265).

[17] Goethe 1981: vol. 5, 418. For further discussion on this issue, see Barry1996.

promoted reception as a provocation and nearly two months before Celan would meet Heidegger in Todtnauberg. From its inceptive broadcast, reception would be troubled by severe interference.

In the *Classicism* lecture, Adorno's primary aim aligns fairly well with Gadamer's redefinition of the classical away from fixed and normative tendencies. Specifically, Adorno criticizes the routine scholarship that presented Goethe's play as the noblest cultural achievement.[18] Especially targeted are the post-war interpretations that *used* the text to restore the virtues of the German spirit that had been tarnished by the perversions of the Nazi regime. Adorno always found such conciliatory gestures to be untenable. The human or humane quality that Adorno discerns in Goethe's work—its revered *Humanität*—is decidedly not a victory of civilization over savage passions; it is not the glorious result, presumably illustrated by Goethe's biography, of stabilizing the youthful outbursts of the *Sturm und Drang*. Rather, for Adorno, it denotes how civilization is locked in a battle with mythic elements that can never be perfectly reconciled. To the extent that it rests precisely on an idea of appeasement, the resplendent image of Weimar Classicism ignores the dialectical energy that recalls how every proclaimed victory over mythic violence continues to be menaced by that very violence. And it is precisely in this regard that Adorno departs from Gadamer's hermeneutic charity and hence from Jauß's particular ambitions.

As he formulates it in the concluding sentence of his lecture, Adorno hears a non-reconciliation in the murmuring of Goethe's language, *im Rauschen der Sprache*.

> Goethe continued the text of the *Magic Flute*. In the objectless and conceptless language of Mozart, a completely enlightened lucidity visibly coalesces with a completely secularized sacred element, which conceals itself in the murmuring [*Rauschen*] of the objective and conceptual language of Goethe.[19]

Throughout his late essays, Adorno repeatedly refers to *Rauschen* as signaling the subject's loss. One could say that *Rauschen* is the sound of the subject's surrender to objective form, which flows past and evades the writer's explicit design; yet, with this *Rauschen* the very conjecture of a subject, even one that is self-surrendering, is called into question. The sound can be heard but not used. The murmuring heard in Goethe's masterful drama correlates to the music that drives and undermines Mozart's opera of enlightened mastery, revealing a sacred or mythic element that troubles these rational

18 For a contemporary and rather lively account of the *Iphigenie* as an exemplary school-text, see Martin Walser, *Erfahrungen und Leseerfahrungen* (1965), as well as Wagner 1995:5–90.

19 "Goethe hat den Text der Zauberflöte fortgesetzt. In der gegenstands- und begriffslosen Sprache Mozarts verbindet sichtbar vollendet aufgeklärte Luzidität sich mit einem vollendet säkularisierten Sakralen, das sich im Rauschen der gegenständlichen und begrifflichen Sprache Goethes versteckt." Adorno 1998:514 (1992:170; translation modified).

mediations, including Adorno's own critical enterprise. Tellingly, the very last word of Adorno's lecture is the verb *versteckt*.

What would hardly have been concealed to the students hearing Adorno on that afternoon at the Freie Universität was the painful absence of one young man among their cohort—Benno Ohnesorg, the student of German and Romance Studies, who had been fatally shot, presumably by a plain-clothes police officer, only five days before. As we know, the incident occurred during a student demonstration protesting the state visit of the Shah of Iran, outside the Deutsche Oper, where the Shah happened to be enjoying nothing other than a performance of *The Magic Flute*. One did not have to wait for Adorno's closing allusion to this opera to sense the students' restlessness. It was the notorious lawyer, Horst Mahler, who pleaded with Adorno to address Fritz Teufel's indictment and Benno Ohnesorg's murder; yet once Adorno publicly announced that he preferred to speak on Goethe's classicism as planned, the SDS and *Kommune I* activists distributed leaflets condemning the Frankfurt School icon as morally complacent and politically irrelevant, as a thinker who chose to hide beneath the cover of aesthetic theories.[20]

On the afternoon of the lecture, after Peter Szondi introduced the speaker, Marxist banners were instantly unfurled from the balcony: *Ifigenisten aller Länder vereinigt euch!*—"Iphigenists of the world, unite!" In view of all the ensuing heckling and shouting, Adorno's closing reference to the *Magic Flute* would have only thrown fuel on the fire. Even if the radical left would have agreed with Adorno's stark critique of Weimar Classicism, they certainly could not support his vague wish for theoretical engagement, especially when it appeared to gloss over the brutal deaths of young men, not only on the fields of Vietnam but also on the side streets of Charlottenburg. Who could tolerate sophisticated analyses of the subject's surrender to language in the face of such concrete, tragic sacrifices? After that fatal evening of June 2, any attempt to attend to the subtle *Rauschen* discerned by Adorno's dialectical ear would be drowned out by the implacable *Geräusch* of the students' anger.

The protesters' explicit identification with Iphigenia ("Iphigenists of the world unite!"), this proclamation of solidarity with the defenseless Greek maiden who was marked for sacrifice by her own father for the sake of a profitable wind, is clearly an expression of alliance with Benno Ohnesorg and Fritz Teufel, whose violent treatment demanded violent responses against the military-industrial complex. Adorno was certainly sympathetic to the cause. Yet he dismissed the call to political activism as entirely futile, if not weakly naïve and narcissistic. Without question, one must dismantle unreflective assessments of the bright classicism of the *Iphigenie* plot. One must interrogate Euripides' miraculous story of Iphigenia's sudden rescue: How, at the moment of the fatal blow, Artemis placed a deer in the maiden's stead and whisked

20 For more on the historical context of Adorno's lecture, see Richter 2002 and Hohendahl 2011.

her off to the land of the Taurians. Transforming the sacrifice into a metaphorical sacrifice—substituting an animal for the human victim—should indeed be read as a clever ideological device: classicism as the triumph of symbolic exchange, which masks the oppression and fatal suffering of those who produce value within the system. Still, Adorno refused to condone revolutionary violence as a legitimate political strategy to contravene the system. Critique should participate in politics by remaining apart. In the days following that rowdy afternoon in Berlin, Adorno thus characterized the "happening" as an "Akt der Barbarei"—an "act of barbarism" that would have to be distinguished from the barbarism of the Taurians, who at least exhibited a large measure of hospitality. Of course, one would not have to dig too deeply into Adorno's damaged life to understand his allergy to crowds and popular uprisings. Counter-attacks, however justifiable, would only perpetuate a regressive barbarism and its renunciation of what Adorno demonstrates in the *Iphigenie* lecture as the play's fragile *Humanität.*

The *Humanität* is fragile because Goethe depicts his Greek characters—Iphigenie, Orest, and Pylades—as acting more barbarically than the barbarians. Adorno detects a frightening murmuring within the Greek portrayals of human freedom, self-determination, and universalism.[21] Whereas most readings demonstrate how the aesthetic form of Goethe's play harmoniously expresses a humane content, Adorno hears a dissonance, not only in the relation between form and content, but also within the content itself, which he splits in two, distinguishing the articulated content (*der Inhalt*) that is clearly formed by Goethe's subjective artistry and the substantive content (*der Gehalt*), which evades the poet's artistic plan. As Adorno states straightforwardly: "Humanity is the *Inhalt* of the play rather than its *Gehalt*" (157/499).[22] Here, we should return to Adorno's concluding sentence, which evokes the wishful combination of "a completely [*vollendet*] enlightened lucidity and a completely [*vollendet*] secularized sacred element." The emphatic repetition of the adverbial *vollendet* already demonstrates that the purported coalescence can never coalesce: the completedness of enlightened lucidity and the completedness of the secularized sacred prevent the amalgamation of the two poles from ever meeting. And it is precisely this failure that Adorno hears in the *Rauschen der Sprache*.

Horizons of Sense

Adorno's reading challenges two distinct approaches to the past—challenges that are discernible in Goethe's dramatic allegory. These approaches are best understood as

21 Reading Goethe's Iphigenie as an exemplification of autonomy persists in the scholarship. See, e.g., Rasch 1979 and Borchmeyer 1992.

22 The distinction between a work's *Inhalt* and its *Gehalt* was influentially promoted by Oskar Walzel, in *Gehalt und Gestalt im Kunstwerk des Dichters* (1923).

issues of verbal aspect, which qualify predication in accord with the subject's horizon. Regarding receptions of Goethe's *Iphigenie*, one finds, on the one hand, the perfective aspect that characterizes normative classicism, which takes Goethe's text as a storehouse of ageless and exemplary values, while on the other hand, there is the imperfective aspect that motivates the anti-traditional activism of the students—the "Iphigenists"—who attend to residues and resistances that evade the ambit of classicism and therefore continue to be operative in today's struggles. Here, the plight of Iphigenia is taken as a direct expression of current concerns. For Adorno, both the perfective aspect of conventional classicism and the continuous aspect of radical activism are only partially adequate insofar as they both constitute a fetishization of subjectivity, one that falsely constructs a symbolic conception of the past within definable horizonal borders that comprise the subject's position. Within the purview of these aspectual approaches, any dialectical energy dissipates into flat polemics.

In contrast to both dispositions, Adorno's aesthetic theory calls for relinquishing the horizonal control that spells subjective imposition and domination. By *localizing* the aesthetic object within a horizonal frame, both normative classicism and radical activism may render the work of art meaningful, they may allow the past to be eloquent, yet only by containing the artwork for the sake of their own contentment. Adorno resists the ideological allure of any such horizonal comprehensibility. Instead, he emphasizes the subjective surrender to the objective form of the aesthetic object, to the "primacy of the object," which forgoes the horizon altogether. The only aspect here would be the *simple* aspect of the aorist, which is in fact a non-aspectual aspect, an aspect without horizon (a-oriston), without totalizing definition vis-à-vis the subject. In Adorno's aoristic reading, a literary work like Goethe's *Iphigenie* eludes horizonal appropriation and integration, whether perfective or imperfective, timeless or current.

With aoristic, indefinable power, the work of art frustrates the subjective will to place it within the realm of the understandable and thus the usable. The aorist cannot be instrumentalized because it is fundamentally unplaceable. And in resisting subjective placement, it must remain unrestricted, discernible only in the unlocalizable *Rauschen* of the drama's language. Tellingly, in his earlier essay on Eichendorff, Adorno describes this poetic *Rauschen* as the sound that approaches the ego—an ego that can merely listen to it without being able to find a definitive place for it.[23] In this sense, the ego rehearses the predicament of Thoas, whose sovereignty is compromised: in the end, he can only listen to Iphigenie, without holding on to her.

Iphigenie's speech rushes past Thoas' designs, because for her, the present—the aspect of the here and now—is a site of pain and longing, with Greece posited as a distant and absent ideal, marked by temporal negations: by the No-Longer and the

23 Adorno, "Zum Gedächtnis Eichendorffs" [1957] (1998:79–84).

Not-Yet. Strikingly, in Goethe's setting, these displacing negations are but an audible muteness, resoundingly meaningless.

> Und an dem Ufer steh ich lange Tage,
> Das Land der Griechen mit der Seele suchend,
> Und gegen meine Seufzer bringt die Welle
> Nur dumpfe Töne brausend mir herüber.
>
> *Iphigenie auf Tauris*, vv. 11–14

> And long days I stand at the shore,
> Seeking with my soul the land of the Greeks,
> And in reply to my sighs the waves bring
> Only dull sounds rushing over.

The response of the roaring waves is no response at all. It frustrates comprehension and can offer no solace.

Marked by an alpha privative, the aoriston negates subjective horizons. Yet it is precisely the effort to discover a comprehensible horizon that characterizes two important engagements with Goethe's *Iphigenie* in the years following Adorno's lecture—namely, Rainer Werner Fassbinder's provocative revision of the drama in 1968 and Hans Robert Jauß's 1973 essay, which adduces historical readings of Racine's and Goethe's *Iphigenias* to illustrate his method of reception-aesthetics. Like Adorno's interpretation, both Fassbinder's antitheatrical staging and Jauß's theoretical interventions explicitly reject the perfective aspect of normative traditionalism, but in doing so they fall into the continuous aspect of current relevance or *Aktualismus*. In brief, the approaches of Fassbinder and Jauß, however different, rely upon a fusion of past and present horizons—a fusion that Adorno dismisses, specifically by putting all comprehending, subjectively rational horizons out of play.

Fassbinder's production of *Iphigenie auf Tauris* was first performed by his *antiteater* troupe on October 25, 1968, in the back room of the Witwe Bolte pub in Munich's Amalienstraße. Fassbinder's script is essentially a satirical parody that includes psychedelic music and slang, interspersing Goethe's poetry with quotations from Mao Zedong, Erika Runge, and pop lyrics, including Donovan's 1966 hit single, "Season of the Witch" is here sung, in English, as "Season of Fascists," with the chorus emphasizing in German *ists*. The entire performance is an explicit display of Actualism, all within the broader orbit of Brechtian didacticism. As the actors take to the stage, they sing "Deutschland, Deutschland über alles" to organ accompaniment. Iphigenie is a young woman, originally from East Prussia, who has been imprisoned for many years. Throughout the performance, she remains motionless within a large cage, the helpless victim of state oppression and violence, which is represented by the lecherous autocrat

Thoas. Orest and Pylades are homosexual lovers who together stand for the student counterculture. When he is not quoting Goethe's text, Orest speaks in Bavarian dialect; and when Thoas cross-examines Pylades, Fassbinder turns to the trial of Fritz Teufel, citing verbatim the way Teufel, the "jokester-guerilla" (*Spaßguerilla*), publicly embarrassed the judge by asking him about his sexual potency. Pylades, still impersonating Teufel, then declares his position:

> Just imagine if the people who have something against Vietnam will respond as firmly, then something would change considerably. The 2nd of June, which was a failure, has shown that it isn't working. That's why we're now trying to make the authorities look ridiculous, like you, for example. [24]

Fassbinder thus reworks Goethe's play to address issues of current relevance. Each position is fully locked within the horizon of the present—an aspect that is perhaps best demonstrated by the figure of Iphigenie trapped parenthetically in her cage. Moreover, Iphigenie's relative marginalization in the script could be read as a chief feature of Fassbinder's reception: Iphigenie is confined in a way that correlates to how Goethe's *Iphigenie*, the drama, is confined and marginalized by radical rewriting. Fixed in their roles, no character on stage undergoes a dramatic reversal. There is neither any true dialogue nor any dialectical progression. The activist uprising mounted by Orest and Pylades changes nothing; Thoas maintains his authoritarian power, unmoved by appeals to his humanity. Pylades runs off, Orest is arrested, and Iphigenie will continue to perish in isolation. Arkas, the epic narrator, played by Fassbinder in Munich, spells everything out with uncompromised clarity: "Die Geschichte ist einfach. Es geht um Macht, und einer hat sie. Natürlich. Und der gibt sie nicht her" ("The story is simple. It's about power, and one man has it. Naturally. And he's not giving it away").[25]

Fassbinder's rendition suggests that Goethe's *Iphigenie* will remain forever captive to authoritative control, forever in thrall to interpretations that aim to disguise their oppressive violence beneath the cover of humanism. The counterculture, like Fassbinder's *antiteater* troupe, might try to liberate this material from the quasi-fascist establishment, yet institutions of higher learning would appear to be in league with state power and therefore unwilling to let Goethe's drama serve any other purpose apart from being a shining exemplum of Weimar Classicism.

[24] "Stellen Sie sich mal vor, wenn die Leute, die gegen Vietnam was haben, so konsequent reagieren werden, dann würde sich erheblich was ändern. Der 2. Juni, der ein Mißerfolg war, hat bewiesen, daß es so nicht geht. Drum versuchen wir jetzt, die Autoritäten, wie zum Beispiel Sie, lächerlich zu machen." Rainer Werner Fassbinder, "Iphigenie auf Tauris von Johann Wolfgang von Goethe" [1968] (1986:23).

[25] Fassbinder 1986:27.

Nearly five years later, Hans Robert Jauß mounted yet another provocation designed to liberate Iphigenie and the *Iphigenie* from dogmatic control. Like Fassbinder, Jauß's hermeneutic endeavor insists on the constitutive role of current reading, yet rather than coerce the past material exclusively into the present horizon, Jauß turns to Gadamer's conception of *Horizontverschmelzung*, the fusion of the past and present horizons, resulting from a dialogic encounter between the interpreting subject and the interpreted text. Goethe's *Iphigenie* offers exemplary insights into the scope and promise of reception aesthetics, because this drama is itself constituted by a reception of prior material—that is, the tragedies by Euripides and Racine. According to Jauß, Goethe employed the Iphigenie plot to speak for his own interest in a humanist liberation from static schemes. In a similar way, readers today are invited to "apply" the text to their own life-situations. This task is achieved when the *Iphigenie* is saved from its foreclosed, classical form—a form that, in Jauß's view, "can no longer satisfy us today."[26] Yet Jauß's interest in "appropriation" (*Aneignung*) gives the lie to his appeal for a lateral, more egalitarian relationship between the text and its reader. Although Jauß appears to pull down the text's authority to a more level playing field, authority persists, not on the side of the text but rather on the side of the recipient. As a result, the synthesis of the two horizons simply rehearses the kind of positive dialectic that Adorno found non-viable.[27] Paradoxically, Jauß's fusion of horizons reconfirms the very symbolism of normative classicism that he attempted to defuse.

Whereas Jauß multiplies the number of horizons in any reading, Adorno removes the horizon altogether, insisting on an aoristic experience that calls for the subject's surrender to the non-localizable rustling of language. If Fassbinder's and Jauß's ideal reader is represented by Orestes—as the one who works to liberate *Iphigenie* from barbaric domination—Adorno's implied reader may be Iphigenie herself: the maiden once slated for sacrifice who now finds herself in a "second death," almost non-existent, lost in the sound of the rushing waves, incapable of discovering any place of her own, robbed of every horizon and thereby granted at least some portion of unlocalizable, ineloquent hope, however much it may evade actualization—the hope, perhaps, to hear what is here no longer.

Seminarium

As the twentieth century drew to a close, in *Mein Jahrhundert* (*My Century*, 1999), Günter Grass depicted the turbulent years around 1968 through the persona of an aging German Studies professor who thinks back on that time from his current perspective

26 Hans Robert Jauß, "Die Partialität des rezeptionsästhetishen Zugangs ("Racines und Goethes 'Iphigenie'" [1973], in Jauß 1982:734.

27 See Naumann-Bayer 2004.

in 1998. The unnamed professor is presently holding a seminar on the poetry of Paul Celan for a paltry gathering of three rather indifferent students, and as expected, his explication of "Todtnauberg" fails to capture interest, at least until one of the seminar participants, a young woman, also unnamed, asks a question regarding the parenthesis that Celan set in the poem's first version yet deleted from its final publication, the "line about a hope, today, for a thinking-man's coming (un-delayed coming) word"—*Zeile von einer Hoffnung, heute, auf eines Denkenden kommendes (un-gesäumt kommendes) Wort.*[28] The question exacerbates an existential crisis that the teacher has already been suffering. "Who was I then? Who am I today? What has become of the once oblivious-of-Being [*seinsvergessenen*] yet still radical sixty-eighter who only two years earlier just happened to be in Berlin when the first anti-Vietnam demonstrations took place?" (*MJ* 238/171) In other words, the seminar on Celan at the century's end has occasioned a moment of self-scrutiny concerning behavior from three decades before. After having enthusiastically participated in the first anti-war protests, why did he choose to address his forgetfulness of Being (*Seinsvergessenheit*) and abandon Berlin for Freiburg where he could think in the presence of the great thinker himself, Martin Heidegger? What motivated this renunciation of political activism, this decision to move apart rather than take part? As he underscores, the student's question regarding Celan's parenthetic hope for an "un-delayed [*un-gesäumt*]" word "in the heart" from Heidegger and the subsequent erasure of that hope itself demanded a response without delay. And although the professor does comply by explaining what Celan expected from the philosopher who had once sworn loyalty to the National Socialist regime, he nonetheless refrains from divulging his own choice to turn his back on the student movement (*MJ* 241/173).

Charged with "neglect" (*Versäumnis*), the teacher goes on to confess that, had he not fled to Berlin, he would have joined the demonstrators calling for the release of Iranian students, he would have attended the rally in front of the opera house, and that he, rather than Benno Ohnesorg, might well have been the victim of Karl-Heinz Kurras's murderous bullet; but instead, he ensconced himself in thinking in the relative tranquility of Freiburg and ended up being the one who drove Celan to Heidegger's cabin in the thick of the Black Forest. Still, he withholds the questions that plagued him.

> How often I imagined the conversation in the cottage, because between the rootless poet and the *Meister aus Deutschland*, between the Jew with the invisible yellow star and the former rector of Freiburg University with his perfectly round yet likewise invisible Party emblem, between the name-giver and the concealer, between the survivor constantly pronouncing himself dead

[28] Cited in Günter Grass, *Mein Jahrhundert* (1999a:240) [*My Century*, Michael Henry Heim, trans. (1999b:173). Subsequent citations are from these editions, marked *MJ*, with page numbers. Translations slightly modified.

> and the harbinger of Being and the coming of God, the Unutterable Words should have been found and were not, not a one.
>
> *MJ* 246–247/177–178

Here, Heidegger is blatantly identified as "Death," the "Meister aus Deutschland," from Celan's "Todesfuge"—a lethal presence that undermines any dialogue in Todtnauberg. The non-reception, rattled by the persistent visibility of the invisible, correlates moreover in many respects to the broken reception between Celan and Grass. As for the persona in *Mein Jahrhundert*, it was only after the assassination attempt on Rudi Dutschke in April 1968, that he reasserted his revolutionary zeal, exchanging the "jargon of authenticity" for Adorno's "jargon of dialectics" (*MJ* 248/178), until Adorno himself became the target of the students' humiliating and aggressive jeers. After recounting the notorious *Busenattentat*—when female students, in April 1969, removed their blouses and stormed Adorno at the lecture podium—after confirming that the attack drove the dialectician to his death four months afterwards, the professor informed his meager student audience of three that, in the following spring, while Heidegger persisted in never uttering the hoped-for word, "Paul Celan flung whatever remained of his life from a bridge into the Seine" (*MJ* 252/181). With that, two students left the seminar room while the young woman who asked about the deleted parenthesis stayed behind. A long period ensued as she stared at the professor in complete silence. When she finally rose from her seat, she simply said: "Gotta go now. […] You've got nothing more to give" (*MJ* 252/182).

The episode adumbrates the vehemence and confusion of the era—a parenthesis received but never fully integrated or comprehended, an anecdote from a book on a century that may reduce everyone to mere anecdotes, a sketchy reminiscence invented by an author who, soon after the book was published, would be regaled with the Nobel Prize for Literature, mainly for the verbal and moral achievement of *The Tin Drum*, and perhaps above all, an oblique epitaph for an erstwhile friend to whom he owed a massive debt, parting words never heard, pronounced years before Grass publicly spelled out the shame that would seem to have marred the friendship from the start.

Chapter 5
Florilegia

Submergence

According to his biographers, before succumbing to the dark waters of the Seine on or about April 20, 1970, Paul Celan left his copy of Wilhelm Michel's 1940 biography, *Das Leben Friedrich Hölderlins*, on his desk in his apartment at 6 avenue Émile Zola, close to the Pont Mirabeau.[1] Michel's volume was opened to the page where Celan had underlined a brief portion of a citation from Clemens Brentano:

> High contemplative grief has perhaps never been so gloriously expressed. *Sometimes this genius grows dark and sinks into the bitter well of his heart*; but mostly his apocalyptic star Wormwood shines wonderfully touchingly over the wide sea of his sentiment.[2]

The passage may be taken as a striking testament, as a final communication entrusted to posterity, one that would forever link Celan's ominous resolve to Hölderlin's tragic madness or *Umnachtung*. The presumed uniqueness of Hölderlin's case from the past ("perhaps never" [*vielleicht niemals*]), that "contemplative mourning has perhaps never been expressed so magnificently," is acknowledged and challenged by Celan's present mournful state, by a repetition that, all the same, hardly detracts from both poets' singularity. The *niemals* ("never") is asserted and qualified by an implicit *wieder einmal* ("once again"), which therefore relates to Jacques Derrida's conclusion concerning Celan's obsession with dates—namely, that "a date marks itself and becomes readable

1 See Schwerin 1981:81, Felstiner 2001:287, Thöming 2016:22.

2 "Niemals ist vielleicht hohe betrachtende Trauer so herrlich ausgesprochen worden. *Manchmal wird dieser Genius dunkel und versinkt in den bitteren Brunnen seines Herzens*; meistens aber glänzet sein apokalyptischer Stern Wermut wunderbar rührend über das weite Meer seiner Empfindung." The Brentano citation is found in Wilhelm Michel, *Das Leben Friedrich Hölderlins* (1940:516). Celan's personal copy of this biography was the 1967 edition published by the Insel Verlag, where the quote is found on p. 464.

only in freeing itself from the singularity that it nonetheless recalls."[3] Analogously, the tendency of Hölderlin's work, that it "sometimes [*manchmal*] becomes dark and sinks into the bitter wells of his heart"—this feature observed by Brentano, cited by Michel, and underscored by Celan—can be read only when it compromises the uniqueness that it nonetheless confirms. In each instance, one time as well as the other, we find the shared theme of fatal submergence: how the poet and therefore the poets, Hölderlin and Celan, sometimes sank into bitter depths, apart and yet together. The line that Celan inscribed on the printed page is thus seen as a caesura that unites him to Hölderlin yet does so only through separation, like every citation: a part of the latter work by remaining apart.

The condition held in common, this proclivity to immerse oneself in bitterness, does not, however, exhaust the profoundly personal significance of the citation. Rather, Brentano's lines touch upon a broader network of matters that manifests the intimacy that Celan discovered between Hölderlin's itinerary and his own. As Michel explicitly notes, the words are taken from Brentano's "Confessional Letter" (*Bekenntnisbrief*), written to the painter Philipp Otto Runge on January 21, 1810. The date would have been particularly resonant for Celan, insofar as it fell one day after the exemplary date that delineates a well-recognized meridian: from Hölderlin ("Tübingen, Jänner") through Büchner's Lenz ("who went through the mountains [*durch's Gebirg*] on the 20th of January"), to the notorious Wannsee Conference held on January 20, 1942. As Celan famously suggested in his Büchner-Prize speech: "Perhaps it is fair to say that every poem remains inscribed with its '20th of January.'"[4] The hypothesis is reiterated towards the end of the *Meridian* speech, when Celan alludes to his failed encounter, in July 1959, with Theodor Adorno in Nietzsche's Engadin: "I had come, both times, from a '20th of January,' from my '20th of January.' I have … encountered myself."[5] One time as well as the other. Ramifications continue to spread. Celan's prose account of the missed opportunity at Sils Maria, his *Gespräch im Gebirg* ("Conversation in the Mountains," 1959), itself hearkens back to yet another text, to Kafka's short piece, *Der Ausflug ins Gebirge* ("The Trip to the Mountains," 1912), in which a first-person narrative turns entirely on an encounter with a palpable no one: "When no one comes, then no one comes. […] No one at all."[6] An encounter with no one and therefore with oneself.

In citing Brentano's letter from January 21, Wilhelm Michel—himself a recipient of the Büchner Prize in 1925—unwittingly opened the floodgates, releasing the waters of multiple dates and cross-references that constituted Celan's idiosyncratic

3 Derrida 2005:35.

4 "Vielleicht darf man sagen, daß jedem Gedicht sein '20. Jänner' eingeschrieben bleibt" (Celan 2000: vol. 3, 196).

5 "Ich hatte mich, das eine wie das andere Mal, von einem '20. Jänner', von meinem '20. Jänner', hergeschrieben. Ich bin … mir selbst begegnet" (Celan 2000: vol. 3, 201).

6 "Wenn niemand kommt, dann kommt eben niemand. […] Lauter niemand." Franz Kafka, Der Ausflug ins Gebirge [1912] (Kafka 2002: vol. 1, 21).

immersion in the German poetic tradition. Celan presumably revisited Michel's biography upon returning from Stuttgart, where he had read some poems before the Hölderlin-Gesellschaft to commemorate the two-hundredth anniversary of the poet's birth on March 21, 1970. The occasion intensified a long-standing fascination with Hölderlin, which Celan, of course, shared with Heidegger. For Celan, however, the textual intersections traced by this meridional network evoke a persistent motif, the image of sinking and drowning. Hölderlin "sinks into the bitter well of his heart," just as Büchner's Lenz "plunged int the well,"[7] just as Kafka's Georg Bendemann was sentenced "to death by drowning."[8] Brentano, too, remains close by: In his novel *Godwi oder Das steinerne Bild der Mutter* ("Godwi or The Stone Image of the Mother," 1800/1801), the protagonist ultimately relates the traumatizing story of his infancy, how his desperate mother drowned while holding him in her arms.

As Jürgen Thöming points out, Celan anticipated death by drowning across his poetic career.[9] The evidence can be adduced to confirm a remark by Edith Silbermann, a friend from Celan's hometown of Czernowitz, regarding the poet's suicidal depression: "Water seems to have exerted a special attraction for him."[10] Celan's "Kenotaph," written in May 1954, immediately after he learned of Claire Goll's accusations of plagiarism, responds bitingly to Hans Egon Holthusen's early review of "Todesfuge," in which the literary critic characterized Celan as "a stranger [*Fremdling*] and outsider of poetic speech."[11] Hence, the opening lines of "Kenotaph" express both self-encouragement and self-surrender:

> Streu deine Blumen, Fremdling, streu sie getrost:
> du reichst sie den Tiefen hinunter,
> den Gärten.[12]
>
> Strew your flowers, stranger, strew them confidently:
> you hand them down to the depths,
> to the gardens.

The flowers, which represent Celan's poems—one recalls the "Arnika, Augentrost" in the opening line of "Todtnauberg," these words of flourishing yet futile hope —sink into the deep just like Hölderlin's poetry sometimes sinks into the bitter wells of his

7 Georg Büchner, *Lenz* [1839] (1997:139).
8 Kafka, *Das Urteil* [1913] (2002: vol. 1, 52).
9 Thöming 2016.
10 Edith Silbermann, *Begegnung mit Paul Celan: Erinnerung und Interpretation* [1987], cited in Thöming 2016:6.
11 See Barbara Wiedemann's commentary on "Kenotaph" in Celan 2005:639.
12 Celan 2005:84.

heart. The image, which rests on the traditional conceit of poetry as flowers, readily points to a passage from Hölderlin's *Hyperion* (1797):

> My tent stands by the Eurotas, and if I awake after midnight, the old river god rushes [*rauscht*] past me with a warning [*mahnend*], and smiling, I take the flowers from the shore and strew them in his shining wave and say to him: Take it as a sign, you lonely one! Soon the old life will bloom around you again.[13]

In Hölderlin's epistolary novel, the protagonist is expressing to Diotima the renewed promise of poetic flourishing in a restored connection to the past, symbolized by the stream that flows from antiquity. The river bears the flowers of the ancient poets into the present along the continuous current of history. Yet, whereas Hyperion's revitalizing petals float upon the watery surface, the flowers strewn in Celan's "Kenotaph" sink into an empty tomb, correlative to the "Grave in the air" (*Grab in den Lüften*) in "Todesfuge" which Holthusen thoughtlessly read as a mere sublimation "into the ether of pure poetry."[14] The abstracting purification implied by Holthusen's allusion to a Mallarméan poetics was untenable for Celan, insofar as it obliterated the concrete uniqueness of his poetic endeavor. Rather than ascend to the lofty heights of *la poésie pure*, Celan's flowers submerge into the depths, parenthetically disrupt the flow, and thus take root in thriving gardens at the sea's floor. Again, the unrepeatable singularity is repeatable, repeatable and therefore readable.

Figures of drowning, images of poetry plunging beneath the surface, inform the first half of Celan's "Tübingen, Jänner," by far his most direct and most well-known response to the Hölderlinian tradition.

> Zur Blindheit über-
> redete Augen.
> Ihre – « ein
> Rätsel ist Rein-
> Entsprungenes « – , ihre
> Erinnerung an
> schwimmende Hölderlintürme, möwen-
> umschwirrt.

13 "Am Eurotas stehet mein Zelt, und wenn ich nach Mitternacht erwache, rauscht der alte Flußgott mahnend mir vorüber, und lächelnd nehm' ich die Blumen des Ufers, und streue sie in seine glänzende Welle und sag' ihm: Nimm es zum Zeichen, du Einsamer! Bald umblüht das alte Leben dich wieder." Hölderlin, *Hyperion* [1797] (1953: vol. 2, 42).

14 Cited in Wiedemann's commentary to "Kenotaph" (Celan 2005:639).

Besuche ertrunkener Schreiner bei
diesen
tauchenden Worten[15]

Eyes per-
suaded to blindness.
Their — "a
riddle is purely-
arisen" —, their
memory of
swimming Hölderlin-towers, gull-
enswirled.

Visits of drowned joiners at
these
plunging words[16]

Given the titular confirmation of locale and date, the text evidently constitutes a poetized description of Celan's visit to the tower where Hölderlin resided for the latter half of his life.[17] In this regard, the participle *über-redet* ("per-suaded") denotes less a state of being "coaxed" or "convinced" and more a sense of being "overwhelmed," "dizzy" to the point of blindness, "taken in" by the flow of poetry that washes over and submerges the realities of present-day Tübingen.[18] Yet with the word doubly split by a hyphen and a line-break (*über- / redet*), an interruption is registered: perhaps a mark of hesitation, a tentative syncope, or confirmation of utter disorientation. Whatever the case may be, out of this formidable poetic current, a single verse emerges: a well-known line from Hölderlin's great hymn, "Der Rhein" (v. 46). In his 1942 seminar on Hölderlin's complementary ode, "Der Ister" (from the Greco-Roman name for the Danube), Martin Heidegger cites the passage from "Der Rhein" to demonstrate a poem's resistance to being instrumentalized: *Ein Räthsel ist Reinentsprungenes. Auch / Der Gesang kaum darf es enthüllen* ("A riddle is purely arisen. Also / The song may hardly divulge it"). As Heidegger comments, "The poetic word divulges the concealment [*Verborgenheit*] of the fluvial activity."[19] Celan appears to respect this divulged concealment, this without within, by bracketing the citation between two long dashes.

15 Celan 2005:133.

16 For the sake of literalness, I have slightly modified John Felstiner's translation in Celan 2001a:159.

17 See, e.g., Böschenstein 2007.

18 The dizzying effect lies at the center of Philippe Lacoue-Labarthe's reading of "Tübingen, Jänner" (1999:21–22).

19 Martin Heidegger, *Hölderlins Hymne "Der Ister"* (Summer Semester, 1942) [1984:21–22].

The concealment is palpably present and correlates to the swirling flight of gulls that encircle the multiple towers. Departed figures rush in to cloud the view further: the "drowned *Schreiner*"— the cabinetmaker, Ernst Zimmer, who sheltered the mad poet in his tower, and Johann Georg Schreiner, the lithographer who drew a portrait of Hölderlin during a visit to the tower in 1823, and also the poetry, like the verse from "Der Rhein," the sonically joined (*Rhein-rein-Schreiner*), "words" that "plunge" into the Neckar, like the flowers of "Kenotaph": Flowers grounded in the groundless depths.

Water and flowers. Flowers in water. It becomes ever clearer why Celan would have been attracted to the Brentano citation adduced in Michel's biography of Hölderlin: *Sometimes this genius grows dark and sinks into the bitter well of his heart*. Although, in his copy of the book, Celan did not underscore the remainder of the quote, Brentano's adversative qualification is still there to be read, even if it lies beneath the surface of the line that Celan drew: *But mostly his apocalyptic star Wormwood shines wonderfully touchingly over the wide sea of his sentiment.* Here, Brentano is alluding directly to Christian prophecy, conjuring the *Wermut* ("Wormwood") that names the falling star mentioned in the Book of Revelations. In Luther's translation:

> und es fiel ein großer Stern vom Himmel, der brannte wie eine Fackel und fiel auf den dritten Teil der Wasserströme und über die Wasserbrunnen. Und der Name des Sterns heißt Wermut. Und der dritte Teil der Wasser ward Wermut; und viele Menschen starben von den Wassern, weil sie waren so bitter geworden.
>
> Rev. 8:10–11

> and there fell a great star from heaven, burning as it were a lamp, and it fell upon the third part of the rivers, and upon the fountains of waters; And the name of the star is called Wormwood: and the third part of the waters became wormwood; and many men died of the waters, because they were made bitter. (KJV)

In Brentano's portrayal, then, Hölderlin's fiery star glistens (*glänzet*) apocalyptically, revealing or divulging divine truth like a bright torch whose light is reflected upon the watery surface of his poetic sentiment, at least until this brilliance plummets to the sea and poisons the waters with bitterness. "Wormwood" translates the Hebrew הנעל (*la'anah*, "curse"), and for Celan, it could be the curse of genial sentiment or *Empfindung*, which at any moment can fall from the celestial heights. *Wermut*, though, is not only a star but also an herbaceous plant, the *artemisia absinthium*, known for its bitterness, used moreover to produce absinthe, *la fée verte*, which is reputed to have driven many artists and poets into abysmal darkness, including Paul Verlaine.

Celan's life-long engagement with Hölderlin—this singular relationship between a recipient-poet and a designated forebearer—repeatedly evokes scenes of drowning. The verb *ertrinken* suggests drinking to fatal excess, drinking to a conclusive end. Again, one recalls the paternal sentence imposed in Kafka's "Judgment": "I sentence you to death by drowning" (*Ich verurteile dich zum Tode des Ertrinkens*). The penalty could arguably relate to immersing oneself in the poetic tradition, to imbibing the *tauchenden Worte* ("plunging words") and joining them in the depths, where poetry may continue to blossom in submerged gardens, possibly and therefore possibly impossibly. In any event, images of fluidity are persistently accompanied by images of flourishing, *fluere* and *florere*, words like flowers, strewn upon the watery surface then sinking deep below.

The Name Given to the Sea

Hölderlin, too, immersed himself in the poetry of the past. He, too, was a recipient who elected his model, as Celan notes in a late poem written down on November 29, 1969, following a visit to Israel:

> ICH TRINK WEIN aus zwei Gläsern
> und zackere an
> der Königszäsur
> wie Jener
> am Pindar,
>
> Gott gibt die Stimmgabel ab
> als einer der kleinen
> Gerechten,
>
> aus der Lostrommel fällt
> unser Deut.[20]
>
> I DRINK WINE from two glasses
> and plough at
> the King's caesura
> like that one
> ploughed at Pindar,
>
> God hands the tuning-fork over
> as one of the little

[20] Celan 2005:363.

righteous ones,

from the raffle drum falls
our jot.

Just as Celan toiled away at Hölderlin, so Hölderlin grappled with Pindar. The two glasses that contain the same wine may represent Pindar's fragments and the translations that Hölderlin worked on during his last years of lucidity;[21] or they may also evoke the two glasses set for the Seder feast, one for the father, the other for Elijah.[22] The point, however, is that the gesture of drinking is collective, not individual. Once again, the motif of fluidity is coupled with an image of cultivation and possible flourishing—specifically, by the motif of ploughing. The antiquated verb *zackern* is derived from *zacker gên*, "to go to the field [*zum Acker*]," a term that aptly describes the poet's labor insofar as turning over the soil can be expressed by the Latin *vertere*, *versus*: the turning of language into verse[23]—an apt agricultural metaphor of preparing the ground for the emergence of plant-life, including perhaps wormwood. Celan discovered the verb *zackern* from a letter that the privy councilor Johann Gerning wrote to Karl Ludwig von Knebel, a text that Celan also underlined in Michel's Hölderlin biography. In his letter, Gerning describes Hölderlin as a "poor fellow" (*ein armer Schlucker*), someone who "swallows" (*schluckt*) too much: *Hölderlin, der immer halbverrückt ist, zackert auch am Pindar* ("Hölderlin, who is always half-crazy, also ploughs at Pindar").[24] Together, the two verbs, *trinken* and *zackern*, reiterate and combine the tension between overwhelming fluidity and fertile ground, between *fluere* and *florere*.

Drinking from two glasses expresses an excess, perhaps one glass too much, just as King Oedipus "perhaps has one eye too many"—a conjecture that Wilhelm Waiblinger, a frequent visitor to the Tübingen Turm, ascribed to the benighted poet.[25] The figure of the king is conjured by Celan's *Königszäsur* ("king's caesura"), a term that clearly refers to the *Anmerkungen* that Hölderlin appended to his Sophocles translation, a reading of *Oedipus Tyrannus* that turns on an idiosyncratic theory of the caesura. The "king" also points to Hölderlin's reflections on Pindar Fragment 69 which he titled "Das Höchste" ("The Highest"), where νόμος ("das Gesetz") is portrayed as the "king,"

21 Cf. Glasova 2008:198–199.

22 Bambach 2014:254.

23 Böschenstein 1982–1983:148.

24 Gerning to Knebel, July 11, 1805; cited in Michel, *Das Leben Friedrich Hölderlins* (1940:483).

25 The text is from Waiblinger's novel, *Phaeton* [1823], subsequently titled "In lieblicher Bläue…" and printed in modern editions of Hölderlin's works, including Friedrich Beißner's edition (1953: vol. 2/1, 372–74).

who "leads […] the most righteous Right with the highest hand of all" (*führt* […] *das gerechteste Recht mit allerhöchster Hand*).[26]

> Νόμος ὁ πάντων βασιλεύς
> θνατῶν τε καὶ ἀθανάτων
> ἄγει δικαιῶν τὸ βιαιότατον
> ὑπερτάτᾳ χειρί.
>
> Pindar, Frag. 69[27]

> The law, king of all
> mortals and immortals,
> justly guides the utmost violence
> with sovereign hand.

As Celan was aware, the fragment served as key text for Carl Schmitt in outlining a theory of sovereignty that justifies the dictatorial exception, another parenthetical figure in that the sovereign sets the internal law by residing external to it.[28] within the frame of Celan's poem, the royal caesura functions as the limit or seam that joins two components together by keeping them apart. It is the line that distinguishes and unites the two glasses, the drinking and the ploughing, Hölderlin and Pindar, the lyrical *Ich* (Celan) and *Jener* ("that one," i.e., Hölderlin).

According to biographical accounts, Celan himself was clearly torn from within and from without, suffering multiple caesurae of division and union, as tersely expressed in a poem also inscribed in November 1969: "Die Pole sind in uns, unübersteigbar" ("The poles are in us, insurmountably").[29] An Eastern Jew exiled in the Catholic West, he was cut off from everything once familiar, persistently compelled to drink and plough from at least two glasses. The poles are indeed legion, characterized by varying species of negation: the no-longer and the not-yet, mortality and immortality, human instability and divine inscrutability. In addition, as scholars have pointed out, the *Königs-Zäsur* encodes the horror of the KZ, the *Konzentrationslager*, which initiated the schisms that forever severed the poet's life, an "insurmountable" abbreviation, further discernible through inversion in the verb *zackern*.[30] Thus, in the letter to Ilana Shmueli in which he enclosed the poem, "Ich trink Wein," Celan explains: "In the King's-Caesura, there we

26 Hölderlin 1975–2004: vol. 15, 354–355. Beginning with Martin Heidegger, this first piece of Hölderlin's Pindar-Fragmente project has been the subject of much scholarly interpretation and speculation. For a general review, see Bartel 2000.

27 Cited from Bruno Snell's edition (1959: vol. 2, Fr. 69).

28 For a critical discussion, see van den Berge 2019.

29 Celan 2005:362.

30 Cf. Felstiner 2001:277.

lie, there we now stand, you and I."[31] The central yet questionable position of God, who "provides" or "surrenders" the pitch to humankind ("Gott gibt die Stimmgabel ab"—"God provides the tuning fork"), may mark an evacuation of celestial guidance, like a star that falls to the sea. The sovereign law that Hölderlin, translating Pindar, associated with "the most righteous right" (*das gerechteste Recht*), yields now to Celan's diminution: "as one of the little righteous ones" (*als einer der kleinen Gerechten*). Consequently, what falls, falls from the "raffle drum" or "lottery wheel," subject to cadential chance: nothing but a "jot," a farthing or iota, but nonetheless, *our* jot (*unser Deut*), an interrupted "interpretation" (*Deutung*) or mutilated *Deutsch*, a mere drop in the "glorious-uninterpretable / flood that does not believe us" (*herrlich-undeutbare / Flut uns nicht glaubt*), which we have witnessed in "Vom Anblick der Amseln."[32]

I plow on the King's-Caesura like that one (ploughed) on Pindar—Tellingly, Pindar alone retains the privilege of being identified by a proper name, a named presence that contrasts with the merely pronominal appearance of the two modern poets who plough away at poetry of the past. Celan emerges in the poem only behind the lyric *Ich*, just as Hölderlin shows up only behind the demonstrative *Jener*. The import of these pronominal substitutions should not be underestimated; for the description of how latter-day poets are submerged by a powerful poetic current is the governing motif of the poem that long defined the nature of the Pindaric tradition, the second poem of Horace's fourth book of *Odes*, the so-called *Pindargedicht*:

Pindarum quisquis studet aemulari,
Iule, ceratis ope Daedalea
nititur pennis vitreo daturus
    nomina ponto.

monte decurrens velut amnis, imbres
quem super notas aluere ripas,
fervet immensusque ruit profundo
    Pindarus ore

laurea donandus Apollinari,
seu per audaces nova dithyrambos
verba devolvit numerisque fertur
    lege solutis

Horace *Odes* 4.2, 1–12

31 "In der Königszäsur, da liegen, da stehen wir jetzt, Du und Ich" (2004b:45).
32 Celan, *Atemwende* [1967] (2000: vol. 2, 94). See *supra*.

Pindar: whoever strives to emulate him,
Iullus, with the Deadalean strength of wax wings
he soars and is to give his name to the
glistening sea.

From the mount descending like a river, which
the rain has swollen over the usual banks,
he rages and boundless rushes with voice
profound, Pindarus,

who must be given the Apollonian laurel,
whether through bold dithyrambs new
words he rolls down, borne by numbers
free from the law

If the patriarchal traditions of Western literature can still be trusted as a sound basis for judgment, these opening strophes serve as a warning to writers who choose to rival their spiritual fathers. Horace's poem admonishes those poets who aim to usurp their precursors by appropriating their power, authority and legitimacy. Rather than take paternal directions as an inspirational resource, they treat their inheritance as an oppositional force to be overcome. They delude themselves into believing that they can outdo their progenitors, that they can ultimately beat them at their own game and thereby make a name for themselves. Time, after all, seems to be on the side of the younger; the future presumably belongs to those who live on, while the dead lie buried, sinking ever deeper into oblivion. This line of thinking, however, is typically shown to be foolhardy, and not only because epigones are just as mortal as their forebearers. Especially in the realm of the arts, the mortal condition has always been of little consequence. As Horace famously emphasized elsewhere, a poetic work constitutes a *monumentum*, a tomb but also and more importantly a warning memorial (< *monere*), a grave and also a garden, which guarantees that the worthy poet will survive in memory but only on the condition that he passes away (*Odes* 3.30). Thus, the name of the father can always overshadow and even eradicate the name of the son. In *Odes* 4.2, the persistent presence of Daedalus, the strength of the father (*ops Daedalea*) relegates the name Icarus to silence of the depths.

By collating Pindar's impact on subsequent Roman poetry with the horrible fate of Daedalus's son, Horace's ode characterizes poetic influence as a dangerous temptation. The term *influence* is particularly apt here, even if anachronistic. To be sure, the history of the word stems from astrological treatises dating from the early fourth century CE, more than three centuries after Horace published his ode. In the *Matheseos* of Julius Fimicus Maternus (ca. 335 CE)—incidentally, a possible forebear of Günter Grass's Walter Matern—*influentia* was coined to denote the "flow" (*fluxus*) of an ethereal fluid from the stars which acted as an occult force on the fate and character of humans. It is only in the twelfth century that the sense of *influentia* would be extended to describe the force that one person might exert upon another, again, as an invisible cause discernible only by its visible effects. Nonetheless, in portraying Pindar's poetry as a mighty river rushing down from a mountaintop, Horace well anticipates the post-classical definition of *influentia* as an arcane power that "flows or rushes in" (*influit*) on the poetry's recipients. The cataract of antiquity washes over the present, potentially tearing everything and everyone in its wake. By adducing the myth of Icarus, Horace simply exacerbates the threat. In his concise formulation, the streaming waters implicitly feed the sea into which the latecomer unwittingly plunges.

With an eye to the poem's original historical context, Horace's opening strophe appears to formulate a warning to Iullus Antonius, the son of Marc Antony and Fulvia, who, at least according to one scholiast, composed a long epic on Diomede.[33] One may presume that Iullus was encouraged to compose a Pindaric hymn for a public ceremony welcoming the Emperor Augustus back to Rome or perhaps Iullus was attempting to goad Horace himself into assuming such a task.[34] In any case, the influential power of Pindar's poetry, its potent fluency, is represented as fatally excessive, as a force that threatens to overwhelm lesser spirits, like the anonymous emulator conjured in the first line (*quisquis*).

This nameless, hypothetical figure—*quisquis*—around whom the brief cautionary tale is constructed, negatively draws attention to the prominence of proper names in the first strophe, all placed in emphatic initial position. Pindar's name first appears in the accusative case (*Pindarum*, v. 1) and thus may seem to be a viable object of study; yet, as the subsequent strophe underscores, it is Pindar alone who rushes on and retains his name, now in the nominative case (*Pindarus*, v. 8). Iullus heads the second verse, for now still in possession of his name, albeit in the vocative case (*Iule*, v. 2); yet if he wishes for his name to survive among future generations, he should refrain from the temptation of transcendent boldness. Otherwise, he and, by extension, other poets, including Horace himself, will be as nameless as the unnamed son of Daedalus. The word for "name" (*nomen*), here in the accusative (*nomina*, v. 4), provides the first three syllables of the pentasyllabic Adonean only to be lost to the sea: *nomina ponto*. The *nomen* plunges into the depths and is literally reversed into *nemo* ("no one"). The emulator, motivated by the influence of greatness, ends up being a no one, a nothing—*ein Niemand, ein Nichts*—having drowned in the paternal source. Whoever strives to rival Pindar should take heed of such a foreboding *omen*.

Rather than brave the menacing current from Greek antiquity, Horace's lyrical ego opts for a more modest approach, likening himself to a tiny bee from Apulia which

33 Pseudo-Acron on Horace *Odes* 4.2, in Otto Keller's edition (1902–1904: vol. 1, 332).

34 For more on the historical context, see Fraenkel 1957:432–34 and Putnam 1986:51.

flits along the still waters of the Tiber, culling from the attractive purple flowers that bloom along the banks.

ego apis Matinae
more modoque
grata carpentis thyma per laborem
plurimum circa nemus uvidique
Tiburis ripas operosa parvus
carmina fingo.

Horace *Odes* 4.2, 27–32

I, in the Matine bee's
manner and mode,
culling pleasing thyme by hard work
around the many groves and banks
of the moist Tiber – I, a little man, form
songs full of labor.

Composed in regular Sapphic meter, Horace's poem has already distinguished itself from Pindar's wild dithyrambs. His verses are not "free from law" (*lege solutis*, v. 12), but rather bound by prosodic limitations. For this reason, as the opening warning already implies, his ode counts as a *recusatio*, as a refusal that resists the fatal attraction of Pindaric dominance.[35] The ominous power of domineering *influence* is replaced by the more feasible and more promising process of *cross-pollination* and *mellification.* In culling the nectar from the flourishing poems bequeathed to present generations, the poet not only creates new, honeyed verses, but also bears the pollen that will allow the cumulative tradition to reproduce and live on. Instead of drowning in the rushing waters, poetry blooms along the dampened banks.

In Horace's representation, the paradigm of influence seems to reduce latter-day poets to being passive recipients of an inundating power that upholds only the name of the source and thereby consigns epigones to unproductive namelessness. Antiquity is thus parenthetic, located within the received text by virtue of remaining powerfully to the side. In response to this parenthetic nature, the paradigm of pollination and mellification offers a method that is selective and astute, creative and lasting. Horace's poem may appear to be marking a contrast between a Pindaric and a non-Pindaric mode, yet the distinction rests more on the side of reception—that is, between a viable and

[35] On *Horace's Odes* 4.2 and the significance of the *recusatio*, see Wimmel1965 and Syndikus 1972–1973: vol. 2, 296–97.

non-viable approach to one's poetic inheritance. Rather than conceive the ancient tradition as a possession, the apian manner respects it as a without within.

Horace's contrast evidently alludes to Callimachus's *Hymn to Apollo*, in which a personification of Envy (Φθόνος) rebukes the singer for his restraint when praising a god who deserves a hymn "as great as the sea" (ὅσα πόντος, v. 106). Suddenly, however, Apollo himself, whose presence has been summoned by this very hymn, reproaches Envy's complaint:

τὸν Φθόνον ὡπόλλων ποδί τ᾽ ἤλασεν ὧδέ τ᾽ ἔειπεν·
Ἀσσυρίου ποταμοῖο μέγας ῥόος, ἀλλὰ τὰ πολλὰ
λύματα γῆς καὶ πολλὸν ἐφ᾽ ὕδατι συρφετὸν ἕλκει.
Δηοῖ δ᾽οὐκ ἀπὸ παντὸς ὕδωρ φορέουσι μέλισσαι,
ἀλλ᾽ ἥτις καθαρή τε καὶ ἀχράντος ἀνέρπει
πίδακος ἐξ ἱερῆς ὀλίγη λιβὰς ἄκρον ἄωτον.

Callimachus *Hymn to Apollo* 107–112

Apollo struck Envy with his foot and said:
"The Assyrian river's current is great, but much
of the earth's dirt and much filth it drags upon its waters.
Not of every water do the bees bear to Deo,
rather the slight stream, pure and undefiled, that trickles
from the holy fount, the choicest blossom."

Accordingly, although Horace may portray Pindar's effect as a mighty river, it would be a mistake to understand the more discerning approach as somehow anti-Pindaric. For Pindar's epinicia are just as committed to desultory discernment so that the praise may produce the "choicest blossom."

The Callimachean-Horatian metaphor derives from ancient sources. In *Pythian* 10, for example, Pindar asserts that "the blossom of celebration hymns flit from one theme to another like a bee" (ἐγκωμίων γὰρ ἄωτος ὕμνων / ἐπ᾽ ἄλλοτ᾽ ἄλλον ὥτε μέλισσα θύνει λόγον, vv. 54–55). As Pindar likewise asserts in *Isthmian* 7, it is this flowering, this — "choicest blossom" (ἄκρον ἄωτον), that renders the poetic stream glorious:

ἀμνάμονες δὲ βροτοί
ὅ τι μὴ σοφίας ἄωτον ἄκρον
κλυταῖς ἐπέων ῥοαῖσιν ἐξίκηται ζυγέν.

Pindar *Isthmian* 7.17–19

but mortals forget
whatever does not attain the choicest blossom of skill
yoked to the glorious currents of words.

Hence, in adopting "the manner and mode of the Matine bee," Horace's poet stands to rise to Pindar's level of accomplishment. In other words, he can be *nominated* to the Pindaric tradition by decidedly resisting the temptation to Pindarize.

On this basis, Horace's Pindar-ode articulates an antithesis of mutually implicated components. Unlike the flood that washes "over well-known banks" (*super notas* [...] *ripas*, v. 6), the finer, more deliberate method of the bee works precisely within the traditional "banks of the Tiber" (*Tiburis ripas*, v. 31), gleaning miniscule pieces of inherited efforts. Still, the flourishing depends on the rising waters, just as the "wax" that held together the Daedalian wings (*ceratis* [...] *pennis*, vv. 2–3) depends on the bee's industry. On the most literal level, Horace's bee (*apis*) seems to be composed of the very elements that make up the banks (*ripas*). Consequently, although as anonymous as the unnamed poet who foolishly apes Pindar, the apian poet retains subjective agency, as an *ego*, however "slight" (*parvus*, v. 31), a nominative *Niemand* or no one, who is not silenced by the intimidating waves of the past but rather is able to take in what blossoms in the flood's wake and thus produce "songs full of labor" (*operosa* [...] *carmina*, vv. 31–32). One can perhaps already hear the "rose" in this careful crafting (*ope-rosa*), the blossoming of fresh poetry, offered by no one who is nonetheless someone, a flower for others to pluck in turn—a "no one's rose," a *Niemandsrose*.

Despite the explicit warning, Horace's opening portrayal of Pindaric influence would come to be valued as an exemplary description of divine or quasi-divine enthusiasm, a vatic impetuosity that should drive poetic genius to innovate language (*nova verba*, v. 11) and thereby renovate culture. In the German Pindaric tradition, from Friedrich Gottlieb Klopstock on, the innovation primarily involved deeply moving, almost uncontrollable passion proclaimed in free verse, unfettered by metrical rules and rhyme (*lege solutis*, 12), which promised to fuel a rejuvenating expansion of poetry's expressive capacities. As Immanuel Kant famously formulated it, genius is a natural, original talent that, in following no rules, gives art its rules.[36] Thus, although the Pindaric flood might have been acknowledged as perilous, the danger was ultimately worthwhile inasmuch as it could wash over the well-marked banks of convention, exceeding the limits of the familiar and the comfortable. In this respect, Jochen

[36] Immanuel Kant, *Kritik der Urteilskraft*, § 46 (1900ff: vol. 5, 307).

Schmidt assesses the effect of Horace's *Pindargedicht* on German poets of the 1770s as a striking paradox, as a text that stood "for the tradition of breaking tradition."[37]

As a *Stürmer und Dränger*, Johann Wolfgang Goethe certainly made a name for himself by cultivating a Pindaric persona, which was readily discerned by those who met him. In a letter to Johann Gleim and Klamer Schmidt (1774), Wilhelm Heinse resorted to Horace's characterization to describe the young poet. "Goethe was at our home, a beautiful boy of 25, who is genius and power and strength from spine to toe; a heart full of feeling, a spirit full of fire with eagle-wings, *qui ruit immensus ore profundo*."[38] Undaunted by the Icarian fate, Goethe himself repeatedly evokes the Horatian image in his early lyrics, for example at the conclusion of *Wandrers Sturmlied* (ca. 1772):

> Wie vom Gebürg herab
> Kieselwetter ins Tal,
> Glühte deine Seel' Gefahren, Pindar
>
> Goethe, "Wandrers Sturmlied," vv. 107–09[39]

> As down from the mountains
> Gravel-weather rushes into the valley,
> Your soul glowed against dangers, Pindar

Again, one recalls Celan's "Vom Anblick der Amseln," the "line written long ago by a sharp, flat pebble," which the speaker aims to hurl into the flood. In a related key, in *Mahomets Gesang*, another hymn in free verse from roughly the same period, Goethe celebrates the revolutionary potential of poetry that surges forth from a sublime source (*Felsenquell*). Like the spread of a new religion, the tumultuous river-poetry creates a vertical link to the heavens:

> Jünglingfrisch
> Tanzt er aus der Wolke
> Auf die Marmorfelsen nieder,
> Jauchzet wieder
> Nach dem Himmel.
>
> Goethe, "Mahomets Gesang," vv. 8–12[40]

> Youth-fresh
> He dances out from the cloud
> Down onto the marble cliffs,

[37] Schmidt 1984:72. See also Henkel 1981.

[38] Heinse to Gleim and Klamer Schmidt, September 13, 1774, cited in Henkel 1981:174.

[39] Goethe 1988:36.

[40] Goethe 1988:42–43.

Rejoices again
Toward heaven.[41]

In Goethe's poetics, the genial flood does not end in a watery tomb, in which the poet surrenders his name. On the contrary, with relentless momentum, the New saturates the valley and thereby prepares the ground for fresh flowers to blossom in its wake—*Drunten werden in dem Tal / Unter seinem Fußtritt Blumen* ("Below in the valley grow / Flowers beneath his footstep," vv. 18–19).

Decades later, following the cataclysm of 1789, Hölderlin adopted Horace's figure to evoke the violence of fate:

so stürzt
Der Strom hinab, er suchet die Ruh, es reißt,
Es ziehet wider Willen ihn, von
Klippe zu Klippe, den Steuerlosen
Das wundebare Sehnen dem Abgrund zu

Hölderlin, "Stimme des Volkes," vv. 13–17[42]

thus rushes
The stream downwards, it seeks rest, it tears,
It pulls him against his will, from
Cliff to cliff, him the rudderless one,
The wondrous longing towards the abyss

As in Goethe, the fluvial surging signals a welcomed renewal, notwithstanding its vehemence—*Rauschen die Ströme doch auch, und dennoch, / Wer liebt sie nicht?* ("The streams are also rushing, and yet, / Who does not love them?" "Stimme des Volkes," vv. 4–5)—a dithyrambic celebration, a Dionysian *Rausch* ("intoxication") that fertilizes the land. Most of Hölderlin's river poems—"Der Main," "Der Neckar," "Der Ister," "Der gefesselte Strom," "Am Quell der Donau," "Der Rhein"—all derive in some way from Horace's simile and its restorative, animating potential. Accordingly, in the prose commentary to the Pindar fragment that he titled "Das Belebende" ("The Enlivening Essence"), Hölderlin describes the mythic Centaurs with the image taken "from the "spirit of a river" (*vom Geiste eines Stromes*):

41 Translation, slightly modified, by David Wellbery (1986:133). See Wellbery's magisterial reading in the chapter, "Genius and the Wounded Subject" (1986:121–185).

42 Hölderlin 1953: vol. 2, 49.

> His image is therefore to be found in places of nature where the shore is rich in rocks and caves, especially in places where the river originally had to leave the chain of mountains and cross their direction. Centaurs are therefore also originally teachers of natural science.[43]

Similarly, the opening of Hölderlin's "Stuttgart" depicts how the swollen streams irrigate the cultural desert:

> Wieder ein Glück ist erlebt. Die gefährliche Dürre geneset,
> Und die Schärfe des Lichts senget die Blüte nicht mehr.
> Offen steht jetzt wieder ein Saal, und gesund ist der Garten,
> Und von Regen erfrischt rauschet das glänzende Tal,
> Hoch von Gewächsen, es schwellen die Bäch' und alle gebundnen
> Fittige wagen sich wieder ins Reich des Gesangs.
>
> Hölderlin, "Stuttgart," 1–6 (GSA 2:89)

> Another stroke of luck has been experienced. The dangerous drought
> recovers,
> And the sharpness of the light no longer scorches the blossom.
> A hall now stands open again, and healthy is the garden,
> And the glistening vale rushes, refreshed by the rain
> High with plants, the brooks swell and all the bounded
> Wings venture again into the realm of song.

After the deluge, flowers blossom from the moistened fields as a sign of peace, as a remedied accord with nature. The latter-day poet's wings are now "bound" but still audacious, remaining in flight and avoiding a cataclysmic, Icarian fall.

The colorful efflorescence can be regarded as a gift that genius bestows to culture, the *flores poetarum*, long after the poets are gone. Yet, for Hölderlin, the flowers may also represent nature's own language, a language that cannot be assigned to any human subject, words that belong to no one. In Hölderlin's *Empedokles* tragedy, the poet-philosopher offers the people consolation before he leaves Akragas:

> Es sprechen, wenn ich ferne bin, statt meiner
> Des Himmels Blumen, blühendes Gestirn

43 "Sein Bild ist deswegen an Stellen der Natur, wo das Gestade reich an Felsen und Grotten ist, besonders an Orten, wo ursprünglich der Strom die Kette der Gebirge verlassen und ihre Richtung quer durchreißen mußte. Centauren sind deswegen auch ursprünglich Lehrer der Naturwissenschaft." Hölderlin 1975–2004: vol. 15, 363. For fuller discussion, see Böschenstein1995.

Und die der Erde tausendfach entkeimen,
Die göttlichgegenwärtige Natur
Bedarf der Rede nicht.

Hölderlin, *Empedokles* (1953: vol. 4, 68)

They speak, when I am far away, instead of me
The flowers of heaven, blossoming stars
And they germinate the earth a thousandfold,
The divinely present nature
Has no need of speech.

After Empedokles has spoken to the population of Akragas, flowers "germinate" (*entkeimen*) and "speak" (*sprechen*) in his place, yet they speak beyond human speech—"Divinely-present nature has no need of speech." Reaching heavenwards toward the stars that shine down upon the earth, the flowers re-establish the vertical axis that connects the transitory with the eternal. Human speech (*Rede*) has been supplanted—anagrammatically—by the verdant Earth (*Erde*), Ascribing the gift of speech to flowers may appear to be a metaphorical gesture, one that transfers a human capacity to a non-human entity, however, as Anke Bennholdt-Thomsen has convincingly argued, for Hölderlin, whereas Empedokles' words function as a verbal *medium* that communicates divine nature, the flowers and stars speak more directly, more naturally and thus *im-mediately*. In predicating the capacity of speech to flowers, therefore, Hölderlin is hardly engaging in a metaphorical transfer but rather in a vital "restitution."[44] Both the blossoms below and the constellations above communicate without passing through the detour of verbal language.

The ideal is most memorably expressed by the line that concludes the fifth strophe of Hölderlin's *Brod und Wein—Nun, nun müssen dafür Worte, wie Blumen, entstehn* ("Now, now words for it must arise, like flowers," GSA 2, 93–99). In Hölderlin's elegy, the imperative, that words must emerge or originate like flowers, responds to the restored presence of the gods among mortals. Specifically, such words must bloom forth in order for nameless humankind to name what is "most loved"—*nun aber nennt er sein Liebstes* ("But now he names his most loved," *ibid.*). The simile, *Worte, wie Blumen*, as in all similes, does not express an identity: The words must not *be* flowers, but rather be *like* flowers in their emergence; just as Pindar's poetry is not a river, but rather like a river in its rushing power. Indeed, the natural language of flowers, freshly blooming, shows itself to be quite distinct from mere verbiage, which typically cannot employ the brand new and the unique. The *nova verba* do not rest on conventional

44 Bennholdt-Thomsen 1967:15.

usage. As Paul de Man elaborates: "In everyday use words are exchanges and put to a variety of tasks, but they are not supposed to originate anew; on the contrary, one wants them to be as well known, as 'common' as possible, to make certain that they will obtain for us what we want to obtain."[45] For this reason, "in poetic language, words are not used as signs, not even as names, but in order to name" (67). Finally, de Man emphasizes that, when words originate like flowers, they are free from imitation. Such words "do not follow a model other than themselves which they copy or from which they derive the pattern of their growth. By calling them natural objects, we mean that their origin is determined by nothing but their own being" (67).

With an eye to Horace's Pindar-Ode, when words imitate a prototype, they risk giving their name to the sea. Yet, when words blossom like flowers, they retain the power to name, to be what they are, usable by no one, like the rose evoked by Angelus Silesius (Johannes Scheffler), the rose that is "ohne Warum":

> Die Ros' ist ohn warumb, sie blühet weil sie blühet
> Sie achtt nicht jhrer selbst, fragt nicht ob man sie sihet.[46]
>
> The rose is without why, it blooms because it blooms
> It does not regard itself, asks not whether one sees it.

The rose is grounded only in itself and therefore unusable as a sign or a name, insofar as every sign or name is always steered heteronomously, grounded in what it signifies or names. In contrast to a sign or a name, the rose is groundless, "without why"—grounded, that is, in its own self-grounding, which renders it useless for any purpose apart from its own. This groundless self-grounding comes into paradoxical view with the second line of the distich, which provides the reason (*Grund*) for the rose's lack of "reason" (*Grund*): The second verse announces why the rose is without why.[47] And thus, the rose names what is brand new, precisely by functioning not as a name, by referring to no one; again, by being a rose for no one, a *Niemandsrose*.

Anemone Nemorosa

Having bloomed from the water-saturated soil, flowers are there for plucking—by Horace's Matine bee which collects poetic nectar, by Hölderlin's Hyperion as a gift to the river-god, by Celan's lyrical *Ich* as a contribution to the gardens that flourish

[45] Paul de Man, "Intentional Structure of the Romantic Image" (1970:66).

[46] Angelus Silesius, *Cherubinischer Wandersmann Buch I*, No. 289; cited in Heidegger, *Der Satz vom Grund*, (1997:58).

[47] For a brilliant, far-reaching meditation on this point, see Thomas Schestag's essay, "Worte, wie Blumen" in his edition of Francis Ponge, *L'Opinion changée quant aux fleurs* (2005:267–323).

beneath the waves. Some uncharitable critics, however, like Hans Egon Holthusen, at least as he is depicted in Celan's "Kenotaph," may pluck too much, assume the tradition to be a possession, and thereby be associated with those who are blind:

> Er aber hielts, da er manches erblickt,
> mit den Blinden:
> er ging und pflückte zuviel:
> er pflückte den Duft —
> und die's sahn, verziehn es ihm nicht.
>
> Celan, "Kenotaph," vv. 8–12[48]

> But he holds it, because he sees many things,
> with the blind:
> he went and plucked too much:
> he plucked the fragrance —
> and those who saw it did not forgive him.

Some, like past and present visitors to the Hölderlin Turm, may drink in too many of the *tauchenden Worte* and become dizzy with blindness ("Tübingen, Jänner"), while others may become so inflated by poetic influence that they risk giving their name to the sea. Still, there are those who somehow survived the flood, even if only provisionally. They may flit along the banks and absorb the nectar to create songs full of labor—*operosa carmina.*

Without question, the flowers may be bitter, like the *Buschwindröschen* ("wood anemone," *anemone nemorosa*), which flourishes in shady groves (*nemorosa*), a rose whose name also evokes "no one" (*nemo*), a blossom that is known, like wormwood, for its bitter, poisonous properties. In April 1943, while suffering in the work camp at Tabaresti, Celan inscribed a poem entitled "Windröschen" on a postcard sent to his close friend Ruth Kraft. The poem focuses on the *anemone nemorosa*—Celan's initial title for this poem—and describes the clumpy flowers, which "tremble from evening, / bloom shimmeringly ahead of our darkness" (*von Abend zittern, / blühn schimmernd unsrer Dunkelheit voraus*).[49] The flower is a species of the *Ranunculacae*, which in German is called *Hahnenfußgewächse*, an allusion to the "cock" (*Hahn*) that crowed after Jesus's arrest. Writing in April, Celan is drawn to these plants, which are commonly referred to as *Osterblumen* ("Easter flowers"). As the poem continues: "The Easter flowers hang with life / and with my mouth on my face dreaming of you" (*Die Osterblumen hängen mit dem Leben / und meinem Mund dir träumend am Gesicht*)—deathly flowers that

[48] Celan 2005:84.
[49] Celan 2005:413.

thrive from the spring rain and promise a resurrection in which the workcamp inmate cannot believe: a rose fatefully for no one.

Flowers are there for plucking, almost like the strings of a lyre or a harp. In Greek, the verb for plucking the strings—different, however, from the verb for plucking flowers—is ψάλλειν, from which the noun *psalm* is derived, as in the *Psalm* that Celan included in his *Niemandsrose* collection (1963). The poem addresses an evacuated heaven, in praise of no one, yet a substantial No one, against whom or towards whom an equally nameless "we" blossoms:

> Gelobt seist du, Niemand.
> Dir zulieb wollen
> wir blühn.
> Dir
> entgegen.
>
> Ein Nichts
> waren wir, sind wir, werden
> wir bleiben, blühend:
> die Nichts —, die
> Niemandsrose.

Celan, "Psalm," vv. 3–12[50]

> Blessed art thou, No One.
> For your sake we will
> bloom.
> Towards
> you.
>
> A Nothing
> we were, we are, we shall
> remain, blooming:
> the Nothing —, the
> No-One's-Rose.

The blossoms that we are arise again, now of their own accord and not as the creation of a higher being, which Celan emphasizes in the opening strophe: "No one kneads us again from earth and clay" (*Niemand knetet uns wieder aus Erde und Lehm*). We are

[50] Celan 2005:132.

like flowers, like words.[51] Even when drowned beneath the most bitter flood of history, the submerged gardens continue to thrive. Anthologies for no one and therefore for everyone.

Praesentia in Absentia

Reception always implies a return.

In the fifth episode of *Ulysses*, which Joyce both confirmed and disclaimed as "Lotus-Eaters," Henry Flower a.k.a. Leopold Bloom receives an intimate letter with flattened yellow petals pinned to the page. The note was signed by a woman named Martha, which, given Bloom's own subterfuge, is likely an alias, devised to shield a romantic dalliance on the side, an affair that the cautious paramours have restricted to clandestine correspondence. Exercising prudence, the fictitious Bloom impersonates a fictitious Flower and conceals the private missive within the folds of his newspaper. He waits until he is at some distance from the post office in Dublin's Westland Row before reading the message not once but twice. First, he goes through the simple prose straightforwardly and readily gets the gist of the communication. Then, a slight pause to catch his breath. Something off to the side has impinged on his thoughts. "He tore the flower gravely from its pinhold smelt its almost no smell and placed it in his heart pocket. Language of flowers. They like it because no-one can hear. Or a poison bouquet to strike him down." (*U* 5, 64).

The scene of reading is saturated with signs: in addition to the typescript message, there are the yellow petals which, like words, also lie flatly on the paper, all surrounded by the columns in the newspaper, a journalistic parergon that Bloom may or may not regard. A personal letter, florally decorated, rests within a public frame. Both by means of a typed note and yellow petals, Martha aimed to make her absence secretly present. Yet the blooms, quite expectedly, also distract, not only because the intended reader is named Flower or Bloom, but also because they function as a supplementary or competing language, explicitly the "language of flowers" or a "poison bouquet," a non-verbal discourse that diverts in a fashion both titillating and troubling, given that the yellow rose is conventionally understood as a sign of adultery.

Bloom's ambivalence towards the affair at a distance, both as a tantalizing flirtation and as a potentially damaging adventure that may poison his marriage, will unfold and grow in complexity as the novel continues. For now, however, tucking the silently loud petals away close to his chest should have allowed him to re-read the letter undistractedly, and yet, as he goes through the text a second time, the language of flowers

[51] The interpretive literature on Celan's "Psalm" is extensive and complex. For an excellent reading, with bibliography, see Procopan 2004.

which no-one can hear sprout through the cracks of the syntactic path and parenthetically disrupt the sense.

> Angry *tulips* with you darling *manflower* punish your *cactus* if you don't please poor *forgetmenot* how I long *violets* to dear *roses* when we soon *anemone* meet all naughty *nightstalk* wife Martha's perfume. (*U* 5, 64; my italics).

Full comprehension of what the letter entails is useless. And so, Bloom decides to dismiss it entirely. "Having read it all he took it from the newspaper and put it back in his sidepocket."

The episode has programmatic import insofar as Bloom the protagonist is depicted as a reader, a reader, of course, who is being read. Yet Bloom is, according to certain standards, a failed reader: He holds on to the distracting petals, keeps them close by "in his heart pocket," while dismissing the straightforward text, consigning it to his "sidepocket." Whereas the figurative language of flowers or *flores rhetoricae*, which typically enhance and potentially obscure the message, are generally subordinated, relegated to the side of the principal sense, Bloom accords the petals which "no-one can hear" a central place near the heart—for no-one, then, but himself—and banishes the clear and primary text off to the side. What is presumably para is en, and what is presumably en is para. Correlatively, when we read Leopold Bloom a.k.a. Henry Flower, a question is imposed: Ought we to stay within the bounds of the main, realist plot and track Bloom's movements simply as the ordinary activities on a most ordinary day, or should we attend to the inserted asides in search of a modern-day Odysseus?

To the extent that it implies a return, reception must grapple with a fundamental problem. As Jean François Lyotard formulates it: "How can one be sure that what returns is what disappeared, that its appearance is also a re-appearance? The first reaction hinges on the notion of reality. What has gone by is not there, what is there is present."[52] The problem is as old as Homer. After twenty years abroad, Odysseus returns to Ithaca, yet the substantial amount of time has not changed him at all, which is why Athena must magically camouflage him as a decrepit stranger. Signs, of course, are provided. The old dog has his trusty sense of smell, the nurse finds the telltale wound, and Penelope can revert to the secret of the marital bed. Telemachus the son is the only one who takes the disguised figure at his word. And like Telemachus, the charitable reader takes Joyce at his word: "Through its title and its itinerary the *Odyssey* will return to us by means of *Ulysses*, claims the writer."[53] Yet words, although claiming to be credible vehicles of meaning, are still only signs. Hence the conclusion that motivates Lyotard's reading:

52 Jean François Lyotard, "Going Back to the Return" [1988] (1992:193).

53 Lyotard 1992:193.

"If the *Odyssey* re-appears in *Ulysses*, it is by its absence."[54] Woe betide those who take what is off to the side as central or what is absent as present.

That said, one may want to consider the fatherly wisdom that Joyce once imparted to his daughter Lucia: "Absence is the highest form of presence."[55] The oft-repeated adage was in fact a citation from long before, a line that Joyce appropriated from a review of his address at University College Dublin, presented in 1902 when the artist was a young man of twenty. The review, printed in *St Stephen's*, the university's paper, mocked Joyce's talk on the Irish poet James Clarence Mangan by claiming that the arrogant speaker dubiously hoped to persuade everyone that "absence is the highest form of presence."[56] In his fragmentary *Autobiography*, published posthumously, Mangan—Joyce's boyhood hero—provides a single anecdote from his own schooldays to "illustrate the peculiar condition of [his] moral and intellectual being":

> I had been sent to Mr. Courtney's Academy in Derby-square. It was the first evening of my entrance (in 1820), when I had completed my eleventh year. Twenty boys were arranged in a class; and to me, as the latest comer, was allotted the lowest place—a place with which I was perfectly contented. The question propounded by the schoolmaster was, "What is a parenthesis?"[57]

After the other pupils struggled to articulate a satisfactory reply, Mangan spoke up:

> "Sir," said I, "I have only come into the school to-day, and have not had time to look into the grammar; but I should suppose a parenthesis to be something included in a sentence, but which might be omitted from the sentence, without injury to the meaning of the sentence." (679)

The answer earned Mangan a spot at the head of the class, which he quickly assumed with "boyish pride," before resuming his original place, bracketed in the back row. The lad's astuteness, coupled with his unwillingness to be the center of attention—and despite calling attention to this indifference—attracted the praise of the faculty: "You'll be a rattling fellow, my boy; but see and take care of yourself" (680).

A care, perhaps, that can only be accomplished by playing the part apart, by remaining without within.

54 Lyotard 1992:195.

55 Joyce to Lucia Joyce, May 29, 1935 (1957: vol. 3, 357).

56 Cited in Ellmann 1982:96.

57 James Clarence Mangan, "Fragment of an Unpublished Autobiography," *The Irish Monthly*, vol. 10, No. 113 (November 1882:679).

Bibliography

Adorno, Theodor W. 1955. Prismen: Kulturkritik und Gesellschaft. Berlin: Suhrkamp.

———. 1973. *The Jargon of Authenticity*. Knut Tarnowski and Frederic Will, trans. Evanston: Northwestern University Press.

———. 1990. "Punctuation Marks," Shierry Weber Nicholsen, trans. *The Antioch Review* 48:300–305.

———. 1992. *Notes to Literature*, vol. 2., Shierry Weber Nicholsen, trans. New York: Columbia University Press.

———. 1998. *Noten zur Literatur*, Rolf Tiedemann, ed. Frankfurt am Main: Suhrkamp.

Albrecht, Michael von. 1964. *Die Parenthese in Ovids Metamorphosen und ihre dichterische Funktion*. Hildesheim: Georg Olms.

Ash, John. 1810. *Grammatical Institutes: or, An Easy Introduction to Dr. Lowth's English Grammar*. Banbury: Rusher. Orig. pub. 1761.

Augstein, Rudolf and Wolff, Georg. 1976. "Nur noch ein Gott kann uns retten." Interview with Martin Heidegger. In *Der Spiegel*, No. 23, May 31, 1976:193–219.

Bambach, Charles. 2014. *Thinking the Poetic Measure of Justice: Hölderlin-Heidegger-Celan*. Albany: SUNY Press.

Barry, David. 1996. "'Ist uns nichts übrig?': The Residue of Resistance in Goethe's *Iphigenie auf Tauris*," *German Life and Letters* 49:283–296.

Bartel, Heike. 2000. *Centaurengesänge: Friedrich Hölderlins Pindarfragmente*. Würzburg: Königshausen & Neumann.

Baumann, Gerhart. 1986. *Erinnerungen an Paul Celan*. Frankfurt am Main: Suhrkamp.

Beja, Morris. 1971. *The Epiphany in the Modern Novel*. Seattle: University of Washington Press.

Bennholdt-Thomsen, Anke. 1967. *Stern und Blume: Untersuchungen zur Sprachfassung Hölderlins*. Bonn: Bouvier.

Borchmeyer, Dieter. 1992. "Iphigenie auf Tauris." In *Goethes Dramen: Interpretationen*, Walter Hinderer, ed. Stuttgart: Reclam, 117–157.

Böschenstein, Bernhard. 1982–1983. "Hölderlin und Celan." *Hölderlin-Jahrbuch* 23:147–155.

———. 1995. "Le Renversement du texte: Hölderlin interprète Pindare,“ *Littérature* 99:53–61.

———. 2007. "Celan und Hölderlin—Gespräch als Gegenwort," *Hölderlin: Sprache und Raum. Turm-Vorträge* 6. Valérie Lawitschka, ed. Tübingen: Hölderlin-Gesellschaft: 292–306.

Büchner, Georg. 1997. *Werke und Briefe*, Karl Pörnbacher, Gerhard Schaub, Hans-Joachim Simm, and Edda Ziegler, eds. Munich: Deutscher Taschenbuch Verlag.

Celan, Paul. 1958. *Ansprache bei Verleihung des Bremer Literaturpreises an Paul Celan.* Stuttgart: Deutsche-Verlags-Anstalt.

———. 1978. "Todtnauberg," Michael Hamburger, trans. *Chicago Review* 29:58–59.

———. 1997. *Gedichte aus dem Nachlass.* Bertrand Badiou, Jean-Claude Rambach, and Barbara Weidemann, eds. Frankfurt am Main: Suhrkamp.

———. 2000. *Gesammelte Werke*, 7 vols., Beda Allemann and Stefan Reichert, eds. Frankfurt am Main: Suhrkamp.

———. 2001a. *Selected Poems and Prose.* John Felstiner, trans. New York: Norton.

———. 2001b. *Paul Celan–Gisèle Lestrange: Correspondence I*, Bertrand Badiou, ed. Paris: Seuil.

———. 2004a. *Paul Celan – Rudolf Hirsch: Briefwechsel*, Joachim Seng, ed. Frankfurt am Main: Suhrkamp.

———. 2004b. *Paul Celan—Ilana Shmueli: Briefwechsel*, Ilana Shmueli and Thomas Sparr, eds. Frankfurt am Main: Suhrkamp.

———. 2005. *Die Gedichte. Kommentierte Gesamtausgabe.* Barbara Wiedemann, ed. Frankfurt am Main: Suhrkamp.

———. 2020. *Lichtzwang: Vorstufen–Textgenese–Endfassung.* Tübinger Ausgabe. Jürgen Wertheimer, ed. Frankfurt am Main: Suhrkamp.

Chambers, Ross. 1999. *Loiterature.* Lincoln: University of Nebraska Press.

Childress, Lynn. 1989. "'Les Phéniciens et L'Odyssée': A Source for 'Lestrygonians,'" *James Joyce Quarterly* 26:259–269.

Cohen, S. Marc and Michaels, Gareth B., trans. 1991. *Ammonius. On Aristotle's Categories.* Ithaca: Cornell University Press.

Connor, Steven. 2015. "Parables of the Para-: The Peregrinations of a Prefix." https://stevenconnor.com/para.html.

Conte, Gian Biagio. 1986. *The Rhetoric of Imitation: Genre and Poetic Memory in Virgil and Other Latin Poets.* Charles Segal, ed. Ithaca: Cornell University Press.

Croessman, H. K. 1959. *Joyce, Gorman and the Schema of Ulysses: An exchange of letters—Paul Leon, Herbert Gorman, Bennett Cerf.* Carbondale: Southern Illinois University Press.

de Certeau, Michel. 1984. *The Practice of Everyday Life.* Steven Rendall, trans. Berkeley: University of California Press.

de Man, Paul. 1970. "Intentional Structure of the Romantic Image." In *Romanticism and Consciousness*, Harold Bloom, ed. New York: Norton: 65–77.

Derrida, Jacques. 2005. *Sovereignties in Question: The Poetics of Paul Celan*, Thomas Dutoit and Outi Pasanen, eds. New York: Fordham University Press.

Detienne, Marcel and Vernant, Jean-Pierre. 1991. *Cunning Intelligence in Greek Culture and Society*. Janet Lloyd, trans. Chicago: The University of Chicago Press.

Dettmar, Kevin J. H. 1993. "Selling *Ulysses*," *James Joyce Quarterly* 31:795–811.

Diggle, J., ed. 1981. *Euripides. Fabulae*. Oxford: Oxford University Press.

Donne, John. 1959. *Devotions upon Emergent Occasions*. Ann Arbor: University of Michigan Press. Orig. pub. 1624.

Düttmann, Alexander García. 1991. *Das Gedächtnis des Denkens*. Frankfurt am Main: Suhrkamp.

Eco, Umberto. 1989. *The Aesthetics of Chaosmos: The Middle Ages of James Joyce*, Ellen Esrock, trans. Cambridge: Harvard University Press.

Elbay, Caroline. 2016. *Joyce, Weininger, Sex and Character: A comparative study*. PhD diss., Queen's University, Belfast.

Ellmann, Richard. 1982. *James Joyce*. Oxford: Oxford University Press. Orig. pub. 1959.

———. 1972. *Ulysses on the Liffey*. New York: Oxford University Press.

Espinal, M. Teresa. 1991. "The Representation of Disjunctive Constituents," *Language* 67:726–762.

Espinet, David, Figal, Günter, Keiling, Tobias and Miković, Nikola, eds. 2018. *Heideggers 'Schwarze Hefte' im Kontext: Geschichte, Politik, Ideologie*. Tübingen: Mohr Siebeck.

Fassbinder, Rainer Werner. 1986. "Iphigenie auf Tauris von Johann Wolfgang von Goethe." *Antiteater: Fünf Stücke nach Stücken*. Frankfurt am Main: Verlag der Autoren.

Felstiner, John. 2001. *Paul Celan: Poet, Survivor, Jew*. New Haven: Yale University Press.

Fonatnier, Pierre. 1977. *Les figures du discours*. Paris: Flammarion. Orig. pub. 1821–1830.

Fóti, Véronique. 1992. *Heidegger and the Poets: Poiēsis, Sophia, Technē*. Atlantic Highlands: Humanities Press.

Fournier, Jean-Baptiste. 2018. "Intentionality and Epiphany: Husserl, Joyce, and the Problem of Access." In *Cognitive Joyce*. Sylvain Belluc and Valérie Bénéjam, eds. London: Palgrave.

Fowler, Frank. 1982. "'Doch mir verzeih Diane…': Thoas and the Disputed Ending of Goethe's *Iphigenie*," *New German Studies* 10:135–150.

Fraenkel, Eduard. 1957. *Horace*. Oxford: Clarendon Press.

Freedman, Ariela. 2009. "The Metamorphoses of *Ulysses*," *Joyce Studies Annual*: 67–88.

Frizen, Werner. 2024. “Paul Celan und Günter Grass: ‘kommunizierende Gefäße,’” *Deutsche Vierteljahrsschrift für Literaturwissenschaft und Geistesgeschichte* 98:105–152.

Gadamer, Hans-Georg. 1990. *Wahrheit und Methode: Grundzüge einer philosophischen Hermeneutik*. Tübingen: Mohr Siebeck. Orig. pub. 1960.

———. 2004. *Truth and Method*, Joel Weinsheimer and Donald G. Marshall, trans. New York: Continuum.

Garber, Marjorie. 2009. *Academic Instincts*. Princeton: Princeton University Press.

Genette, Gérard. 2018. *Palimpsests: Literature in the Second Degree* (1982), Channa Newman and Claude Doubinsky, trans. Lincoln: University of Nebraska Press.

Gifford, Don and Seidman, Robert J. 1989. *Ulysses Annotated: Notes for James Joyce's* Ulysses, Revised and expanded edition. Berkeley: University of California Press.

Gilbert, Stuart. 1955. *James Joyce's* Ulysses*: A Study*. New York: Vintage. Orig. pub. 1930.

Glasova, Anna. 2008. *Counter-Quotation: The Defiance of Poetic Tradition in Paul Celan and Osip Mandelstam*. PhD diss., Northwestern University.

Goethe, Johann Wolfgang. 1962–1969. *Briefe*. 4 vols. K. R. Mandelkow and B. Morawe, eds. Hamburg: Wegner.

———. 1981. *Werke*. Hamburger Ausgabe (HA), vol. 5. Lieselotte Blumenthal and Eberhard Haufe, eds. Munich: Beck.

———. 1988. *Gedichte*. Erich Trunz, ed. Munich: Beck.

———. 1989. *Sämtliche Werke, Briefe, Tagebücher und Gespräche*. Frankfurter Ausgabe. Vol. 29, Dieter Borchmayer, ed. Frankfurt am Main.: Deutscher Klassiker Verlag.

Goldhill, Simon. 2017. “The Limits of the Case Study: Exemplarity and the Reception of Classical Literature,” *New Literary History* 48:415–435.

Gosetti-Ferencei, Jennifer. 2014. “Death and Authenticity: Reflections on Heidegger, Rilke, Blanchot,” *Existenz* 9:16–25.

Grass, Günter. 1963. *Hundejahre*. Berlin: Luchterhand.

———. 1990. *Schreiben nach Auschwitz*. Frankfurter Poetik-Vorlesung. Munich: Luchterhand.

———. 1997. *Werkausgabe*, 16 vols., Volker Neuhaus and Daniela Hermes, eds. Göttingen: Steidl.

———. 1999a. *Mein Jahrhundert*. Göttingen: Steidl.

———. 1999b. *My Century*, Michael Henry Heim, trans. New York: Harcourt.

———. 2010. *The Tin Drum*, Breon Mitchell, trans. Boston: Mariner Books.

———. *Die Blechtrommel*. Munich: dtv, 2011. Orig. pub. 1959.

———. 2020. *Werke*. Neue Göttinger Ausgabe (NGA), 24 vols., Dieter Stolz und Walter Frizen, eds. Göttingen: Steidl.

Grethlein, Jonas. 2011. "*Historia magistra vitae* in Herodotus and Thucydides? The exemplary use of the past and ancient and modern temporalities," in *The Western Time of Ancient History: Historiographical Encounters with the Greek and Roman Pasts*, Alexandra Lianeri, ed. Cambridge: Cambridge University Press: 247–263.

———. 2021. "Author and Characters: Ancient, Narratological, and Cognitive Views on a Tricky Relationship," *Classical Philology* 116:208–230.

Groden, Michael. 1977. *Ulysses in Progress*. Princeton: Princeton University Press.

Güthenke, Constanze. 2020. "'For Time is / nothing if not amenable': exemplarity, time, reception," *Classical Receptions Journal* 12:46–61.

Hall, Anthony. 2004. *Operation Overlord: D-Day, Day by Day*. Philippines: Zenith.

Halliwell, Stephen. 2002. *The Aesthetics of Mimesis: Ancient Texts and Modern Problems*. Princeton: Princeton University Press.

Hamacher, Werner. 2011. "Wasen: On Celan's 'Todtnauberg,'" Heidi Hart, trans., *The Yearbook of Comparative Literature* 57:15–54.

———. 2019. *Keinmaleins: Texte zu Celan*. Frankfurt am Main: Klostermann.

Hegel, G. W. F. 1975. *Aesthetics: Lectures on Fine Art*, vol 2. T. M. Knox, trans. Oxford: Clarendon Press.

Heidegger, Martin. 1953. *Einführung in die Metaphysik*. Tübingen: Max Niemeyer.

———. 1959. *Unterwegs zur Sprache*. Friedrich-Wilhelm von Hermann, ed. Frankfurt am Main: Klostermann.

———. 1962. *Being and Time*, John Macquarrie and Edward Robinson, trans. New York: Harper & Row.

———. 1968. *What is called Thinking?* Fred D. Wieck and J. Glenn Gray, trans. New York: Harper & Row.

———. 1971. *Poetry, Language, Thought*, Albert Hofstadter, trans. New York: Harper Collins.

———. 1974. *An Introduction to Metaphysics*, Ralph Mannheim, trans. New Haven: Yale University Press.

———. 1975. *Einführung in die Metaphysik*, Petra Jaeger, ed. Frankfurt am Main: Klostermann.

———. 1977. *Holzwege*. Frankfurt am Main: Klostermann.

———. 1982. *Parmenides*. Manfred S. Frings, ed. Frankfurt am Main: Klostermann.

———. 1984a. *Was heißt Denken?* Tübingen: Niemeyer. Orig. pub. 1961.

———. 1984b. *Hölderlins Hymne "Der Ister."* Walter Biemel, ed. Frankfurt am Main: Klostermann.

———. 1991. *Die Metaphysik des deutschen Idealismus*, Günter Seubold, ed. Frankfurt am Main: Klostermann.

———. 1993. *Sein und Zeit*. 17th ed. Tübingen: Max Niemeyer. Orig. pub. 1927.

———. 1997. *Der Satz vom Grund*. Petra Jaeger, ed. Frankfurt am Main: Klostermann. Orig. pub. 1971.

———. 2002. *Grundbegriffe der aristotelischen Philosophie*, Mark Michalski, ed. Frankfurt am Main: Klostermann.

———. 2009. *Basic Concepts of Aristotelian Philosophy*, Robert D. Metcalf and Mark B. Tanzer, trans. Bloomington: University of Indiana Press.

———. 2014. *Überlegungen II–VI. Schwarze Hefte 1931–1938*. Peter Tawny, ed. Frankfurt am Main: Klostermann.

Hellingrath, Norbert von. 1911. *Pindarübertragungen von Hölderlin: Prolegomena zu einer Erstausgabe*. Jena: Diederichs.

Henkel, Arthur. 1981. "Der deutsche Pindar—Zur Nachahmungsproblematik im 18. Jahrhundert." In *Geschichte des Textverständnisses am Beispiel von Pindar und Horaz*, Walther Killy, ed. *Wolfenbüttler Forschungen* 12. Munich: Kraus: 173–194.

Herwig, Wolfgang. 1969. *Goethes Gespräche: Eine Sammlung zeitgenössischer Berichte aus seinem Umgang*, vol. 2. Stuttgart: Artemis.

Hillard, Derek. 2007. "Birdsongs: Celan and Kafka," *Colloquia Germanica* 40:297–314.

Hiscock, Matthew. 2020. "Reception Theory, New Humanism, and T. S. Eliot," *Classical Receptions Journal* 12:323–329.

Hogrebe, Wolfram. 2020. *Das Zwischenreich—Tò μεταξύ*. Frankfurt am Main: Klostermann.

Hohendahl, Peter Uwe. 2011. "A Precaious Balance: Adorno and German Classicism," *New Literary History* 42:31–52.

Hölderlin, Friedrich. 1953. *Sämtliche Werke*, 6 vols. Großer Stuttgarter Ausgabe. Friedrich Beißner, ed. Stuttgart.

———. 1975–2004. *Sämtliche Werke*. Frankfurter Ausgabe, 20 vols. D. E. Sattler, ed. Frankfurt am Main: Roter Stern.

Holub, Robert. 1995. "Reception Theory: School of Constance," in *The Cambridge History of Literary Criticism*, vol. 8: *From Formalism to Poststructuralism*, Robert Selden, ed. Cambridge: Cambridge University Press: 319–346.

Hopkins, David. 2010. *Conversing with Antiquity: English poets and the classics, from Shakespeare to Pope*. Oxford: Oxford University Press.

Husserl, Edmund. 1962. *Die Krisis der europäischen Wissenschaften und die transzendentale Phänomenologie*. Walter Biemel, ed. The Hague: Martinus Nijhoff. Orig. pub. 1954.

———. 1970. *The Crisis of European Sciences and Transcendental Philosophy*, David Carr, trans. Evanston: Northwestern University Press.

Inwood, Brad. 1985. *Ethics and Human Action in Early Stoicism*. Oxford: Clarendon Press.

Jakobson, Roman. 1964. *Style in Language*. Thomas A. Sebeok, ed. Cambridge: The M.I.T. Press.

Jauß, Hans Robert. 1967. *Literaturgeschichte als Provokation der Literaturwissenschaft*. Konstanz: Universitätsverlag.

———. 1970. "Literary History as a Challenge to Literary Theory," Elizabeth Benzinger, trans. *New Literary History* 2:7–37.

———. 1982. *Ästhetische Erfahrung und literarische Hermeneutik*. Frankfurt am Main: Suhrkamp.

Joyce, James. 1939. *Finnegans Wake*. New York: Viking.

———. 1957. *Letters*, 3 vols., Stuart Gilbert, ed. New York: Viking Press.

———. 1963. *Stephen Hero*. Theodore Spencer, ed., rev. by John J. Slocum and Herbert Cahoon. New York: New Directions.

———. 1973. *A Portrait of the Artist as a Young Man*. New York: Viking. Orig. pub. 1916.

———. 1974. *Lettere*, Giorgio Melchiori, ed. Milan: Mondadori.

———. 2022. *Ulysses*. Hans Walter Gabler, ed. New York: Vintage.

Kafka, Franz. 1990. *Tagebücher*, Hans-Gerd Koch, Michael Müller and Malcom Pasley, ed. Frankfurt am Main: Fischer.

———. 2002. *Gesammelte Werke* (KGW), 12 vols. Hans-Gerd Koch, ed. Frankfurt am Main: Fischer.

Kain, Richard. 1972. "The Significance of Stephen's Meeting Bloom: A Survey of Interpretations," *James Joyce Quarterly* 10:147–160.

Kant, Immanuel. 1900ff. *Werke*, 23 vols. Akademie Ausgabe. Berlin: Berlin: Reimer/de Gruyter.

Keller, Otto, ed. 1902–1904. *Pseudoacronis Scholia in Horatium Vetustiora*, 2 vols. Leipzig: Teubner.

Kenner, Hugh. 1980. *Ulysses*. Boston: G. Allen & Unwin.

Kent, Roland, trans. 1938. *Varro. On the Latin Language*, vol. 1. Cambridge, Mass.: Harvard University Press.

Ker, James. 2004. "Nocturnal Writers in Imperial Rome: The Culture of *Lucubratio*," *Classical Philology* 99:209–242.

Kiefer, Sascha. 2002. "Frühe Polemik und späte Differenzierung: Das Heidegger-Bild von Günter Grass in *Hundejahre* (1963) und *Mein Jahrhundert* (1999)," *Weimarer Beiträge* 48:242–259.

Kierkegaard, Søren. 1967. *Journals and Papers*, 7 vols. Howard V. and Edna H. Hong, eds. Bloomington: Indiana University Press.

Kisiel, Theodore. 1993. *The Genesis of Heidegger's* Being & Time. Berkeley: University of California Press.

Krimmer, Elisabeth. 2008. "'Ein Volk von Opfern?' Germans as Victims in Günter Grass's *Die Blechtrommel* and *Im Krebsgang*," *Seminar* 44:272–290.

Kristeva, Julia. 1986. *The Kristeva Reader*. Toril Moi, ed. New York: Columbia University Press.

———. 1988. "Towards a Semiology of Paragrams." In *The Tel Quel Reader*, Patrick Ffrench and Roland-François Lack, eds. New York: Routledge: 25–49.

Lacoue-Labarthe, Philippe. 1999. *Poetry as Experience*, Andrea Tarnowski, trans. Stanford: Stanford University Press.

Lamb, Jonathan. 2017. *Shakespeare in the marketplace of words*. Cambridge: Cambridge University Press.

Lennard, John. 1991. *But I Digress: The Exploitation of Parentheses in English Printed Verse*. Oxford: Clarendon Press.

Lyon, James. 2006. *Paul Celan and Martin Heidegger: An Unresolved Conversation, 1951–1970*. Baltimore: Johns Hopkins University Press.

Lyotard, Jean François. 1992. "Going Back to the Return." Madeleine Burt Merlini, trans. *The Languages of Joyce: Selected Papers from the 11th International James Joyce Symposium*. Philadelphia: J. Benjamins: 193–210.

MacDuff, Sangam, McFadzean, Angus, and Beja, Morris, eds. 2024. *Collected Epiphanies of James Joyce*. Tallahassee: University Press of Florida.

Mangan, James Clarence. 1882. "Fragment of an Unpublished Autobiography," *The Irish Monthly*, vol. 10, No. 113:675–689.

Martin, Elaine. 2011. "Intertextuality: An Introduction," *The Comparatist* 35:148–151.

Martindale, Charles. 1993. *Redeeming the Text: Latin poetry and the hermeneutics of reception*. Cambridge: Cambridge University Press.

———. 2013. "Reception—a new humanism? Receptivity, pedagogy, the transhistorical," *Classical Receptions Journal* 5:169–183.

Marx, Karl and Engels, Friedrich. 1975–2004. *Collected Works*, 50 vols. Richard Dixon et al., trans. New York: International Publishers.

McClelland, John. 1973. "Sonnet ou Quatorzain?: Marot et le choix d'une forme poétique." *Revue d'histoire littéraire de la France* 73:591–607.

McMorran, Ciaran. 2020. *Joyce and Geometry*. Gainesville: University Press of Florida.

Melchiori, Giorgio. 2004–2005. "Joyce and Eternity: From Dante to Vico," *Papers on Joyce* 10/11:171–185.

Michalski, Mark. 2005. "Hermeneutic Phenomenology as Philology," Jamey Findling, trans. In *Heidegger and Rhetoric*, Daniel M. Gross and Ansgar Kemmann, eds. Albany: SUNY Press: 65–80.

Michel, Wilhelm. 1940. *Das Leben Friedrich Hölderlins*. Bremen: Schünemann.

Minden, Michael. 2013. "'Grass auseinander-geschrieben': Günter Grass's *Hundejahre* and Mimesis," *German Quarterly* 86:25–42.

Mitchell, Andrew J. 2016. "Heidegger's Breakdown: Health and Healing under the Care of Dr. V.E. von Gebsattel," *Research in Phenomenology* 46:70–97.

Mörchen, Hermann. 1983. *Adorno und Heidegger: Untersuchung einer philosophischen Kommunikationsverweigerung*. Stuttgart: Klett-Cotta.

Nabokov, Vladimir. 1970. *Lolita. Annotated edition*. Alfred Appel, Jr., ed. New York: Vintage.

Naumann-Bayer, Waltaud. 2004. "Negative versus positive Dialektik: Goethe's *Iphigenie*, gelesen von Adorno und Hans Robert Jauß." In *Adorno im Widerstreit: Zur Präsenz seines Denkens*, Wolfram Ette, ed. Freiburg: Kalr Alber: 439–451.

Neuhaus, Volker. 1992. *Günter Grass*. Stuttgart: Metzler.

Nietzsche, Friedrich. 1997. *Untimely Meditations*, R. J. Hollingdale, trans. Cambridge: Cambridge University Press.

———. 1999. *Sämtliche Werke: Kritische Studienausgabe* (KSA), 15 vols. Giorgio Colli and Mazzino Montinari, eds. Munich: dtv.

Norris, Margot. 2010. "Stephen Dedalus's Anti-Semitic Ballad: A Sabotaged Climax in Joyce's *Ulysses*," *European Joyce Studies* 18:54–75.

Ott, Hugo. 1988. "Martin Heidegger und der Nationalsozialismus." In *Heidegger und die praktische Philosophie*, Annemarie Gethmann-Siefert and Otto Pöggeler, eds. Frankfurt am Main: Suhrkamp: 64–77.

Owen, S. G. 1915. *P. Ovidi Nasonis: Tristium libri quinque; Ibis; Ex Ponto libri quattuor; Halieutica Fragmenta*. Oxford: Oxford University Press.

Parkes, M. B. 2008. *Pause and Effect: An Introduction to the History of Punctuation in the West*. London: Taylor & Francis.

Peacham, Henry. 1593. *The Garden of Eloquence*. 2nd ed., London.

Peradotto, John. 1990. *Man in the Middle Voice*. Princeton University Press.

Plard, Henri. 1984. "Une source du chapître Niobe dans *Die Blechtrommel* de Grass," *Etudes Germaniques* 39:284–287.

Pöggeler, Otto. 1986. *Spur des Worts: Zur Lyrik Paul Celans*. Freiburg: K. Alber.

———. 1988. "Heideggers politisches Selbstverständnis." In *Heidegger und die praktische Philosophie*. A. Gethmann-Siefert und O. Pöggeler, eds. Frankfurt am Main: Suhrkamp: 17–63.

———. 1989. "'Praktische Philosophie' als Antwort an Heidegger." In *Martin Heidegger und das "Dritte Reich": Ein Kompendium*, Bernd Martin, ed. Darmstadt: Wissenschaftliche Buchgesellschaft: 62–92.

Procopan, Norina. 2004. "Paul Celans Gedicht Psalm: Von der Wirklichkeit hervorbringenden Kraft der dichterischen Sprache," *Caietele Echinox*: 269–276.

Putnam, Michael. 1986. *Artifices of Eternity: Horace's Fourth Book of Odes*. Ithaca: Cornell University Press.

Puttenham, George. 1589. *The Arte of English Poesie*. London: Richard Field.

Rasch, Wolfdietrich. 1979. *Goethes 'Iphigenie auf Tauris' als Drama der Autonomie*. Munich: Beck.

Richter, Gerhard. 2002. "Introduction: Who's Afraid of the Ivory Tower? A Conversation with Theodor W. Adorno," *Monatshefte* 94:10–23.

Rickard, John. 1999. *Joyce's Book of Memory: The Mnemotechnic of* Ulysses. Durham: Duke University Press.

Rilke, Rainer Maria. 1930. *Die Aufzeichnungen des Malte Laurids Brigge. Schriften in Prosa*, vol. 2. Leipzig: Insel. Orig. pub. 1910.

———. 1990. *The Notebooks of Malte Laurids Brigge*. Stephen Mitchell, trans. New York: Vintage.

Rudolph, Enno. 2015. "Review. Heideggers Schwarze Hefte im Echo." *Philosophische Rundschau* 62:141–154.

Saussure, Ferdinand de. 1959. *Course in General Linguistics*. Wade Baskin, ed. New York: Philosophical Library.

Savage, Robert. 2005. "Adorno's Philopolemology: The 'Parataxis' Speech as Example," *European Journal of Social History* 8:281–295.

Scheible, Jeff. 2013. "Within, Aside, and Too Much: On Parentheticality across Media," *American Literature* 85:689–717.

Schenk, Klaus. 2016. "*Treffen in Paris*: Intertextuelle Lektüre zum Kontakt von Paul Celan und Günter Grass." *Celan-Referenzen: Prozesse eine Traditionsbildung in der Moderne*, Natalia Blum-Barth and Christine Waldschmidt, eds. Göttingen: Vanderhoeck & Ruprecht: 101–120.

Schestag, Thomas. 2005. "Worte, wie Blumen." In *Francis Ponge. L'Opinion changée quant aux fleurs*, Thomas Schestag, ed. Basel/Vienna: Urs Engeler: 267–323.

Schmidt, Jochen. 1984. "Pindar als Genie-Paradigma im 18. Jahrhundert," *Goethe-Jahrbuch* 101:63–73.

Schneider, Stefan. 2015. "Parenthesis: Modern features, meanings, discourse functions and ellipsis." In *Parenthesis and Ellipsis: Cross-Linguistic and Theoretical Perspectives*, Marlies Kluck, Dennis Ott, and Mark de Vries, eds. Berlin: de Gruyter: 277–300.

Schwerin, Christoph. 1981. "Bittere Brunnen des Herzens: Erinnerungen an Paul Celan," *Der Monat* 2:73–81.

Schwyzer, Eduard. 1939. *Die Parenthese im engern und im weiteren Sinne*. Abhandlungen der Preußischen Akademie der Wissenschaften, Philosophische-historische Klasse 6.

Semsch, Klaus. 2005. "Rezeptionsästhetik," *Historisches Wörterbuch der Rhetorik*, Gert Ueding, ed. Tübingen: Niemeyer: vol. 7, 1363–1374.

Sengoopta, Chandak. 2000. *Otto Weininger: Sex, Science and Self in Imperial Vienna*. Chicago: The University of Chicago Press.

Senn, Fritz. 2014. "Errant Commas and Stray Parentheses," *European Joyce Studies* 23:11–32.

———. 2022. *Ulysses polytropos: Essays on James Joyce's* Ulysses. Leiden: Brill.

Serres, Michel. 2007. *The Parasite*. Lawrence R. Schehr, trans. Minneapolis: University of Minnesota Press.

Sloane, Thomas, ed. 2001. *Encyclopedia of Rhetoric*. Oxford: Oxford University Press.

Snell, Bruno. 1959. *Pindar. Pindari Carmina cum fragmentis*, 2 vols. Bruno Snell, ed. Leipzig: Teubner.

Syndikus, Hans Peter. 1972–1973. *Die Lyrik des Horaz: Eine Interpretation der Oden*, 2 vols. Darmstadt: Wissenschaftliche Buchgesellschaft.

Thöming, Jürgen. 2016. "'Die Blume Heute schmilzt hinweg': Paul Celans Signale zum Ertrinkenstod," *Studia austriaca* 24:5–27.

Twain, Mark. 1880. *A Tramp Abroad*. Hartford: American Publishing Company.

van den Berge, Lukas. 2019. "Law, king of all: Schmitt, Agamben, Pindar," *Law and Humanities* 13:198–222.

Wagner, Irmgard. 1995. *Critical Approaches to Goethe's Classical Dramas*. Columbia: Camden House.

Waldanger, Geoffrey. 2018. "Inheriting Hölderlin: Adorno, Parataxis," *Modern Language Notes* 133:585–603.

Walser, Martin. 1965. *Erfahrungen und Leseerfahrungen*. Frankfurt am Main: Suhrkamp.

Walzel, Oskar. 1923. *Gehalt und Gestalt im Kunstwerk des Dichters*. Berlin: Athenaion.

Weininger, Otto. 1920. *Geschlecht und Charakter: Eine prinzipielle Untersuchung*. Vienna: Wilhelm Braumüller. Orig. pub. 1903.

Wellbery, David. 1996. *The Specular Moment: Goethe's Early Lyric and the Beginnings of Romanticism*. Stanford: Stanford University Press.

Weninger, Robert. 2012. *The German Joyce*. Tallahassee: University of Florida Press.

Williams, Robert Grant. 1993. "Reading the Parenthesis," *SubStance* 70:53–66.

Wimmel, Walter. 1965. "Recusatio-Form und Pindarode," *Philologus* 109:83–103.

Zahavi, Dan. 2003. *Husserl's Phenomenology*. Stanford: Stanford University Press.

Zilcosky, John. 2005. "Poetry after Auschwitz? Celan and Adorno Revisited," *Deutsche Vierteljahrsschrift für Literaturwissenchaft und Geistesgeschichte* 79:670–691.

Ziolkowski, Theodore. 1961. "James Joyces Epiphanie und die Überwindung der empirischen Welt in der modernen deutschen Prosa." *Deutsche Vierteljahrsschrift für Literaturwissenschaft und Geistesgeschichte* 35:594–616.

Index